Cambridge
Collections

Victorian literature

a collection of fiction and non-fiction

Edited by Linda Marland
Series editor: Michael Marland

CAMBRIDGE
UNIVERSITY PRESS

CAMBRIDGE UNIVERSITY PRESS
Cambridge, New York, Melbourne, Madrid, Cape Town, Singapore,
São Paulo, Delhi

Cambridge University Press
The Edinburgh Building, Cambridge CB2 8RU, UK

www.cambridge.org
Information on this title: www.cambridge.org/9780521703178

First published 2007

Printed in the United Kingdom at the University Press, Cambridge

A catalogue record for this publication is available from the British Library

ISBN 978-0-521-70317-8 paperback

Cover image: Halfpenny Ices, plate 4 from 'Street Incidents', c. 1876
(woodbury type photo), Thomson, John (1837–1921)/ ©Museum of
London, UK/The Bridgeman Art Library

Cover design by Smith

Picture research by Sandie Huskinson-Rolfe of PHOTOSEEKERS

Contents

Acknowledgements

The volume editor and publishers acknowledge the following sources of copyright material and are grateful for the permissions granted. While every effort has been made, it has not always been possible to identify the sources of all the material used, or to trace all copyright holders. If any omissions are brought to our notice, we will be happy to include the appropriate acknowledgements on reprinting.

p. 31 'How to reach the pole', from *The Graphic*, 6 October 1877, as reprinted in *History as Hot News 1865–1897*, compiled by Leonard de Vires, published by John Murray, 1973; p. 33 'Messages Without Wires' from *The Faber Book of Reportage* by John Carey, 1987; p. 39 from *The War of the Worlds* by H. G. Wells, print rights reproduced by permission of A. P. Watt Ltd, on behalf of the author, electronic rights reproduced with permission of Ollie Record Productions, copyright © Ollie Record Productions, all rights reserved. www.thewaroftheworlds.com; p. 95 from *A London Child of the Seventies* from *A London Family 1870–1900*, published 1934 by M. V. Hughes.

The publishers would like to thank the following for permission to reproduce illustrations: 12, 71, 93, 144, 209 MEPL; 40, © Central Saint Martin's College of Art and Design, London / The Bridgeman Art Library; 63, © Linley Sambourne House, London / The Bridgeman Art Library; 94, Getty Images; 114, The Art Archive / Bibliothèque des Arts Décoratifs, Paris / Dagli Orti; 139, © Private Collection / Ken Walsh / The Bridgeman Art Library; 147, The Royal Collection © 2006 Her Majesty Queen Elizabeth II; 157, © Guildhall Library, City of London / The Bridgeman Art Library; 179, Illustration from 'The Humour of Dickens' by R. J. Cruikshank, News Chronicle Publications Dept (OOC); 205, Illustrated London News Picture Library; 214, illustration from 'The Small House at Allington' by Anthony Trollope, with kind permission of The Trollope Society.

General introduction

Silently the lamplighter appears at dusk to light the streets with his long taper. Children in grand houses know their bedtime is approaching. The fall of the lamp's light reveals ladies and gentlemen stepping out to their horse-drawn carriages, but it also flickers and hisses over the wretched children of the poor, huddled together under archways and in squalid alleys. For this is the Victorian age, a time of contrasts greater than you might imagine.

Changes that happened during the 64 years of Queen Victoria's reign seemed like miracles to many people. Science and technology lengthened lives, helped with pain and prevented diseases. Lord Macaulay wrote: 'They spanned great rivers and estuaries with bridges unknown to the people who came before; they enabled men to descend to the depths of the sea, to soar into the air in balloons, to cross the land in railways and travel in steamships which run ten knots an hour against the wind'.

If you were educated, if you were rich, if you were male, you could run with these changes. If you were poor, if you were female, you might fall under those running feet.

All through this time, books, journals and newspapers told and interpreted the stories of the age. It was a golden age of writing, and it was a golden age of reading. You might even have the luck to hear Charles Dickens read his own stories aloud, if he came to your town on one of his glorious reading tours. Even in far-away America, you might have been one of those story-hungry people who gathered on the quayside for the ship to come in with the latest instalment of *The Old Curiosity Shop*. 'What happened to Little Nell?' was the cry as it came in sight.

W. H. Smith opened bookshops on railway stations in the railway boom when trains first brought people into Euston Station in London in 1838. The Smith family even tried to make the train timetables start after the morning publication of *The Times*. Their 'yellow back' novels of science fiction, romance and adventure, sold for reading on the journey, were like our 'airport novels' of today. Books and newspapers were sold at W. H. Smith shops on stations all along the London and

Western Railway. Cliff-hanger weekly chapters of stories and articles in learned journals about new ideas in science, technology and education were available to the literate public as never before.

The four sections of this anthology – Adventures, Childhood, Urbanisation and Relationships – tell you about the lives of Victorians in fiction and non-fiction.

Within these four sections, the texts are arranged so that the more difficult ones are placed at the end of the section. To support your reading, certain words (these are numbered) in the text are explained in the footnotes. Ideas for further reading accompany each text. Each section concludes with a range of reading, writing, speaking, listening and drama activities to help you explore and enjoy the authors' ideas, opinions, style and language. Through this exploration you will, I hope, gain an insight into what makes a good text work, in terms of its structure and content, and think about what we can learn from the situations the characters find themselves in. The text-specific activities pages are divided into the following activity types: *Before you read* (pre-reading stimulation activities), *What's it about?* (comprehension-style questions) and *Thinking about the text* (activities which move beyond the text itself). At the very end of each section, a series of *Compare-and-contrast* activities provide opportunities to compare two or more texts.

In this volume, you'll be able to read about the writers and chroniclers, the dreamers and inventors; and while you study, you could be thinking about your own family. Who were *your* Victorians?

Linda Marland

1 Adventures

When Queen Victoria first came to the throne it was an adventure to travel a short distance from your home. Mrs Gaskell in her novel *Cranford* (published in 1853 but set much earlier) describes two sisters, Miss Matty and Miss Deborah, as they sit by candlelight each night to think over the day's events in their little town. The outside world is beyond their imaginations.

By the time Queen Victoria died, more people had travelled by balloon, train and steamship across the world than Miss Matty could ever have dreamed of. Men plotted routes to the Poles. The novelist H. G. Wells wrote of wars between worlds and conjured up Martians on Earth. Even intrepid lady explorers, very brave in a time when women were meant to be like Miss Matty and look after their homes, had ventured to places without maps. Alexandra David-Neel (1868–1969) disguised herself as a beggar and crossed the Himalayas on foot. 'To the one who knows how to look and feel, every movement of this free life is an enchantment,' she said firmly in the face of male criticism. *The Spectator* wrote of Isabella Bird, whose encounter with bears you can read about here: 'There never was anybody who had adventures as well as Miss Bird'.

In this section you can read about the adventures that the Victorians set off to have over land, across sea and in the air. You can also read about the adventure that Charles Kingsley (1819–1875) gives Tom, a little chimney sweep boy, in the story *The Water Babies*. When he shakes his soot-covered body onto the hearthrug of a room in the grand house he has come to clean, he has certainly travelled from one world to another. From poverty and dirt, he has arrived in the clean, grand world of the rich – a distance you could not measure with miles and a direction beyond the scope of a compass.

Activities

1   You will find real and fantastical adventures in this section. Talk to a partner about the best trip *you* ever made and also the one you would go on if you could time-travel back to the Victorian age.

2   Have you ever had the feeling that you've travelled from one world to another just by seeing how someone else lived – someone richer, poorer or simply different in some distinctive way? You can get that feeling sometimes by looking at pictures in a magazine, but it can happen in real life too. Describe such a time.

3   Plan an adventure for your class with limitless funds. Choose a handful of different countries with spectacular things to see and do in each one and make up a speedy itinerary as Phileas Fogg does on page 25, moving from one place to another by different means of transport. You have to be back home in two weeks.

The Water Babies

by Charles Kingsley

What's the best way to sweep a chimney? Send a child up it! That's what some people thought in Victorian times. Getting filthy, getting stuck, getting burnt, even dying: it didn't really matter. It would only be a poor working boy, and there were lots more available out there. The writer of this story, however, thought it did matter: it mattered a lot.

In this opening chapter we meet Tom, who takes his horrible life for granted. And then something astonishing happens to him . . .

Once upon a time there was a little chimney-sweep, and his name was Tom. That is a short name, and you have heard it before, so you will not have much trouble in remembering it. He lived in a great town in the North Country, where there were plenty of chimneys to sweep, and plenty of money for Tom to earn and his master to spend. He could not read nor write, and did not care to do either; and he never washed himself, for there was no water up the court where he lived. He had never been taught to say his prayers. He never had heard of God, or of Christ, except in words which you never have heard, and which it would have been well if he had never heard. He cried half his time, and laughed the other half. He cried when he had to climb the dark flues,[1] rubbing his poor knees and elbows raw; and when the soot got into his eyes, which it did every day in the week; and when his master beat him, which he did every day in the week; and when he had not enough to eat, which happened every day in the week likewise. And he laughed the other half of the day, when he was tossing halfpennies with the other boys, or playing leapfrog over the posts, or bowling stones at the horses' legs as they trotted by, which last was excellent fun, when there was a wall at hand behind which to hide. As for chimney-sweeping, and being hungry, and being beaten, he

---

[1] **flues**   insides of chimneys

took all that for the way of the world, like the rain and snow and thunder, and stood manfully with his back to it till it was over, as his old donkey did to a hailstorm; and then shook his ears and was as jolly as ever; and thought of the fine times coming, when he would be a man, and a master sweep, and sit in the public-house with a quart of beer and a long pipe, and play cards for silver money, and wear velveteens² and ankle-jacks³ and keep a white bulldog with one grey ear, and carry her puppies in his pocket, just like a man. And he would have apprentices, one, two, three, if he could. How he would bully them, and knock them about, just as his master did to him; and make them carry home the soot sacks, while he rode before them on his donkey, with a pipe in his mouth and a flower in his buttonhole, like a king at the head of his army. Yes, there were good times coming; and, when his master let him have a pull at the leavings of his beer, Tom was the jolliest boy in the whole town.

One day a smart little groom rode into the court where Tom lived. Tom was just hiding behind a wall, to heave half a brick at his horse's legs, as is the custom of that country when they welcome strangers; but the groom saw him, and halloed to him to know where Mr Grimes, the chimney-sweep, lived. Now, Mr Grimes was Tom's own master, and Tom was a good man of business, and always civil to customers, so he put the half-brick down quietly behind the wall, and proceeded to take orders.

Mr Grimes was to come up next morning to Sir John Harthover's, at the Place, for his old chimney-sweep was gone to prison, and the chimneys wanted sweeping. And so he rode away, not giving Tom time to ask what the sweep had gone to prison for, which was a matter of interest to Tom, as he had been in prison once or twice himself. Moreover, the groom looked so very neat and clean, with his drab⁴ gaiters,⁵ drab breeches,⁶ drab jacket,

---

²**velveteens**   trousers made of velvet
³**ankle-jacks**   boots that come above the ankle
⁴**drab**   dull brown or grey
⁵**gaiters**   a cloth or leather covering your legs
⁶**breeches**   riding trousers

snow-white tie with a smart pin in it, and clean round ruddy face, that Tom was offended and disgusted at his appearance, and considered him a stuck-up fellow, who gave himself airs because he wore smart clothes, and other people paid for them; and went behind the wall to fetch the half-brick after all; but did not, remembering that he had come in the way of business, and was, as it were, under a flag of truce.

His master was so delighted at his new customer that he knocked Tom down out of hand, and drank more beer that night than he usually did in two, in order to be sure of getting up in time next morning; for the more a man's head aches when he wakes, the more glad he is to turn out, and have a breath of fresh air. And, when he did get up at four the next morning, he knocked Tom down again, in order to teach him (as young gentlemen used to be taught at public schools) that he must be an extra good boy that day, as they were going to a very great house, and might make a very good thing of it, if they could but give satisfaction.

And Tom thought so likewise, and, indeed, would have done and behaved his best, even without being knocked down. For, of all places upon earth, Harthover Place (which he had never seen) was the most wonderful, and, of all men on earth, Sir John (whom he had seen, having been sent to gaol by him twice) was the most awful.

Now, I dare say, you never got up at three o'clock on a midsummer morning. Some people get up then because they want to catch salmon; and some because they want to climb Alps; and a great many more because they must, like Tom. But, I assure you, that three o'clock on a midsummer morning is the pleasantest time of all the twenty-four hours, and all the three hundred and sixty-five days; and why everyone does not get up then, I never could tell, save that they are all determined to spoil their nerves and their complexions by doing all night what they might just as well do all day. But Tom, instead of going out to dinner at half-past eight at night, and to a ball at ten, and finishing off somewhere between twelve and four, went to bed at

seven, when his master went to the public-house, and slept like
a dead pig; for which reason he was as pert as a gamecock[7] (who
always gets up early to wake the maids) and just ready to get up
when the fine gentlemen and ladies were just ready to go to bed.

So he and his master set out; Grimes rode the donkey in front,
and Tom and the brushes walked behind; out of the court, and up
the street, past the closed window-shutters, and the winking weary
policemen, and the roofs all shining grey in the grey dawn.

They passed through the pitmen's village, all shut up and
silent now, and through the turnpike;[8] and then they were out
in the real country, and plodding along the black dusty road,
between black slag[9] walls, with no sound but the groaning and
thumping of the pit-engine in the next field. But soon the road
grew white, and the walls likewise; and at the wall's foot grew
long grass and gay flowers, all drenched with dew; and instead
of the groaning of the pit-engine, they heard the skylark saying
his matins[10] high up in the air, and the pitbird warbling in the
sedges, as he had warbled all night long.

All else was silent. For old Mrs Earth was still fast asleep;
and, like many pretty people, she looked still prettier asleep
than awake. The great elm-trees in the gold-green meadows
were fast asleep above, and the cows fast asleep beneath them;
nay, the few clouds which were about were fast asleep likewise,
and so tired that they had lain down on the earth to rest, in long
white flakes and bars, among the stems of the elm-trees, and
along the tops of the alders by the stream, waiting for the sun
to bid them rise and go about their day's business in the clear
blue overhead.

On they went; and Tom looked, and looked, for he never
had been so far into the country before; and longed to get over
a gate, and pick buttercups, and look for birds' nests in the

---

[7]**gamecock**   a bird bred for fighting
[8]**turnpike**   a gate across the road that you must pay to go through
[9]**slag**   a mixture of clay and coal-dust produced during coal-mining
[10]**matins**   morning prayers

hedge; but Mr Grimes was a man of business, and would not have heard of that.

Soon they came up with a poor Irishwoman, trudging along with a bundle at her back. She had a grey shawl over her head, and a crimson madder[11] petticoat; so you may be sure she came from Galway. She had neither shoes nor stockings, and limped along as if she were tired and footsore; but she was a very tall handsome woman, with bright grey eyes, and heavy black hair hanging about her cheeks. And she took Mr Grimes' fancy so much, that when he came alongside he called out to her: 'This is a hard road for a gradely[12] foot like that. Will ye up, lass, and ride behind me?'

But, perhaps, she did not admire Mr Grimes' look and voice; for she answered quietly: 'No, thank you; I'd sooner walk with your little lad here.'

'You may please yourself,' growled Grimes, and went on smoking.

So she walked beside Tom, and talked to him, and asked him where he lived, and what he knew, and all about himself, till Tom thought he had never met such a pleasant-spoken woman. And she asked him, at last, whether he said his prayers, and seemed sad when he told her that he knew no prayers to say.

Then he asked her where she lived, and she said far away by the sea. And Tom asked her about the sea; and she told him how it rolled and roared over the rocks in winter nights, and lay still in the bright summer days, for the children to bathe and play in it; and many a story more, till Tom longed to go and see the sea, and bathe in it likewise.

At last, at the bottom of a hill, they came to a spring. Out of a low cave of rock, at the foot of a limestone crag, the great fountain rose, quelling, and bubbling, and gurgling, so clear that you could not tell where the water ended and the air began,

---

[11]**madder**   a dye that turns material a reddish-purple colour: popular in
    Galway in the Connemara region of Ireland
[12]**gradely**   fine

and ran away under the road, a stream large enough to turn a mill; among blue geranium, and golden globe-flower, and wild raspberry, and the birdcherry with its tassels of snow.

And there Grimes stopped, and looked; and Tom looked too. Tom was wondering whether anything lived in that dark cave, and came out at night to fly in the meadows. But Grimes was not wondering at all. Without a word, he got off his donkey, and clambered over the low road wall, and knelt down, and began dipping his ugly head into the spring – and very dirty he made it.

Tom was picking the flowers as fast as he could. The Irishwoman helped him, and showed him how to tie them up; and a very pretty nosegay[13] they had made between them. But when he saw Grimes actually wash, he stopped, quite astonished; and when Grimes had finished, and began shaking his ears to dry them, he said: 'Why, master, I never saw you do that before.'

'Nor will again, most likely.' T'wasn't for cleanliness I did it, but for coolness. I'd be ashamed to want washing every week or so, like any smutty collier[14] lad.'

'I wish I might go and dip my head in,' said poor little Tom. 'It must be as good as putting it under the town-pump; and there is no beadle[15] here to drive a chap away.'

'Thou come along,' said Grimes; 'what dost want with washing thyself? Thou did not drink half a gallon of beer last night, like me.'

'I don't care for you,' said naughty Tom, and ran down to the stream, and began washing his face.

Grimes was very sulky, because the woman preferred Tom's company to his; so he dashed at him with horrid words, and tore him up from his knees, and began beating him. But Tom was accustomed to that, and got his head safe between Mr Grimes' legs, and kicked his shins with all his might.

'Are you not ashamed of yourself, Thomas Grimes?' cried the Irishwoman over the wall.

---

[13]**nosegay**   a small bunch of flowers
[14]**collier**   a coal-miner
[15]**beadle**   an official person in a parish whose job it was to keep order

Grimes looked up, startled at her knowing his name; but all he answered was, 'No, nor never was yet,' and went on beating Tom.

'True for you. If you ever had been ashamed of yourself, you would have gone over into Vendale long ago.'

'What do you know about Vendale?' shouted Grimes; but he left off beating Tom.

'I know about Vendale, and about you, too. I know, for instance, what happened in Aldermire Copse, by night, two years ago come Martinmas.'

'You do?' shouted Grimes; and leaving Tom, he climbed up over the wall, and faced the woman. Tom thought he was going to strike her; but she looked him too full and fierce in the face for that.

'Yes; I was there,' said the Irishwoman quietly.

'You are no Irishwoman, by your speech,' said Grimes, after many bad words.

'Never mind who I am. I saw what I saw; and if you strike that boy again, I can tell what I know.'

Grimes seemed quite cowed,[16] and got on his donkey without another word.

'Stop!' said the Irishwoman. 'I have one more word for you both; for you will both see me again before all is over. Those that wish to be clean, clean they will be; and those that wish to be foul, foul they will be. Remember.'

And she turned away, and through a gate into the meadow. Grimes stood still a moment, like a man who had been stunned. Then he rushed after her, shouting, 'You come back.' But when he got into the meadow, the woman was not there.

Had she hidden away? There was no place to hide in. But Grimes looked about, and Tom also, for he was as puzzled as Grimes himself at her disappearing so suddenly; but look where they would, she was not there.

---

[16]**cowed**   frightened by threats

Grimes came back again, as silent as a post, for he was a little frightened; and, getting on his donkey, filled a fresh pipe, and smoked away, leaving Tom in peace.

And now they had gone three miles and more, and came to Sir John's lodge-gates.

But Tom and his master did not go in through the great iron gates, as if they had been dukes or bishops, but round the back way, and a very long way round it was; and into a little back-door, where the ash-boy let them in, yawning horribly; and then in a passage the housekeeper met them, in such a flowered chintz dressing-gown, that Tom mistook her for My Lady herself, and she gave Grimes solemn orders about, 'You will take care of this, and take care of that,' as if he was going up the chimneys, and not Tom. And Grimes listened, and said every now and then, under his voice, 'You'll mind that, you little beggar?' and Tom did mind, all at least that he could. And then the housekeeper turned them into a grand room, all covered up in sheets of brown paper, and bade them begin, in a lofty and tremendous voice; and so after a whimper or two, and a kick from his master, into the grate Tom went, and up the chimney, while a housemaid stayed in the room to watch the furniture; to whom Mr Grimes paid many playful and chivalrous[17] compliments, but met with very slight encouragement in return.

How many chimneys Tom swept I cannot say; but he swept so many that he got quite tired, and puzzled too, for they were not like the town flues to which he was accustomed, but such as you would find – if you would only get up them and look, which perhaps you would not like to do – in old country-houses, large and crooked chimneys, which had been altered again and again, till they ran one into another. So Tom fairly lost his way in them; not that he cared much for that, though he was in pitchy darkness, for he was as much at home in a chimney as a mole is underground; but at last, coming down as he thought the right chimney, he came down the wrong one,

---

[17]**chivalrous** gallant, courteous

and found himself standing on the hearthrug in a room the like of which he had never seen before.

He had never been in gentlefolks' rooms but when the carpets were all up, and the curtains down, and the furniture huddled together under a cloth, and the pictures covered with aprons and dusters; and he had often enough wondered what the rooms were like when they were all ready for the quality[18] to sit in. And now he saw, and he thought the sight very pretty.

The room was all dressed in white – white window-curtains, white bed-curtains, white furniture, and white walls, with just a few lines of pink here and there. The carpet was all over gay little flowers; and the walls were hung with pictures in gilt frames, which amused Tom very much. There were pictures of ladies and gentlemen, and pictures of horses and dogs. The horses he liked; but the dogs he did not care for much, for there were no bulldogs among them, not even a terrier. But of the two pictures which took his fancy most, one was of a man in long garments, with little children and their mothers round him, who was laying his hand upon the children's heads. That was a very pretty picture, Tom thought, to hang in a lady's room. For he could see that it was a lady's room by the dresses which lay about.

The other picture was that of a man nailed to a cross, which surprised Tom much. He fancied that he had seen something like it in a shop window. But why was it there? 'Poor man,' thought Tom, 'and he looks so kind and quiet. But why should the lady have such a sad picture as that in her room? Perhaps it was some kinsman[19] of hers, who had been murdered by the savages in foreign parts, and she kept it there for a remembrance.' And Tom felt sad, and awed, and turned to look at something else.

The next thing he saw, and that too puzzled him, was a washing-stand, with ewers[20] and basins, and soap and brushes,

---

[18]**quality** rich people
[19]**kinsman** a relative
[20]**ewer** a jug holding water for washing

and towels, and a large bath full of clean water – what a heap of things all for washing! 'She must be a very dirty lady,' thought Tom, 'by my master's rule, to want as much scrubbing as all that. But she must be very cunning to put the dirt out of the way so well afterwards, for I don't see a speck about the room, not even on the very towels.'

And then, looking toward the bed, he saw that dirty lady, and held his breath with astonishment.

Under the snow-white coverlet, upon the snow-white pillow, lay the most beautiful little girl that Tom had ever seen. Her cheeks were almost as white as the pillow, and her hair was like threads of gold spread all about over the bed. She might have been as old as Tom, or maybe a year or two older; but Tom did not think of that. He thought only of her delicate skin and golden hair, and wondered whether she was a real live person, or one of the wax dolls he had seen in the shops. But when he saw her breathe, he made up his mind that she was alive, and stood staring at her, as if she had been an angel out of heaven.

No. She cannot be dirty. She never could have been dirty, thought Tom to himself. And then he thought, 'And are all people like that when they are washed?' And he looked at his own wrist, and tried to rub the soot off, and wondered whether it ever would come off. 'Certainly I should look much prettier then, if I grew at all like her.'

And looking round, he suddenly saw, standing close to him, a little ugly, black, ragged figure, with bleared eyes and grinning white teeth. He turned on it angrily. What did such an ugly little creature want in that sweet young lady's room? And behold, it was himself, reflected in a great mirror, the like of which Tom had never seen before.

And Tom, for the first time in his life, found out that he was dirty; and burst into tears with shame and anger; and turned to sneak up the chimney again and hide; and upset the fender[21] and threw the fire-irons down, with a noise as of ten thousand tin kettles tied to ten thousand mad dogs' tails.

Up jumped the little white lady in her bed, and, seeing Tom, screamed as shrill as any peacock. In rushed a stout old nurse from the next room, and seeing Tom likewise, made up her mind that he had come to rob, plunder, destroy, and burn; and dashed at him, as he lay over the fender, so fast that she caught him by the jacket.

But she did not hold him. Tom had been in a policeman's hands many a time, and out of them too, what is more; and he would have been ashamed to face his friends for ever if he had been stupid enough to be caught by an old woman; so he doubled under the good lady's arm, across the room, and out of the window in a moment.

He did not need to drop out, though he would have done so bravely enough. Nor even to let himself down a spout,[22] which would have been an old game to him; for once he got up by a spout to the church roof, he said to take jackdaws' eggs,

---

[21]**fender**   rail going round a fireplace to stop the coal falling out
[22]**spout**   a drainpipe

but the policeman said to steal lead; and, when he was seen on high, sat there till the sun got too hot, and came down by another spout, leaving the policemen to go back to the station-house and eat their dinners.

But all under the window spread a tree, with great leaves and sweet white flowers, almost as big as his head. It was magnolia, I suppose; but Tom knew nothing about that, and cared less; for down the tree he went, like a cat, and across the garden lawn, and over the iron railings, and up the park towards the wood, leaving the old nurse to scream murder and fire at the window.

The under-gardener, mowing, saw Tom, and threw down his scythe; caught his leg in it, and cut his shin open, whereby he kept his bed for a week; but in his hurry he never knew it, and gave chase to poor Tom. The dairymaid heard the noise, got the churn between her knees, and tumbled over it, spilling all the cream; and yet she jumped up, and gave chase to Tom. A groom cleaning Sir John's hack at the stables let him go loose, whereby he kicked himself lame in five minutes; but he ran out and gave chase to Tom. Grimes upset the soot-sack in the new-gravelled yard, and spoilt it all utterly; but he ran out and gave chase to Tom. The old steward opened the park-gate in such a hurry, that he hung up his pony's chin upon the spikes, and, for aught I know, it hangs there still; but he jumped off, and gave chase to Tom. The ploughman left his horses at the headland, and one jumped over the fence, and pulled the other into the ditch, plough and all; but he ran on, and gave chase to Tom. The keeper, who was taking a stoat out of a trap, let the stoat go, and caught his own finger; but he jumped up, and ran after Tom; and considering what he said, and how he looked, I should have been sorry for Tom if he had caught him. Sir John looked out of his study window (for he was an early old gentle-man) and up at the nurse, and a marten[23] dropped mud in his eye, so that he had at last to send for the doctor; and yet he ran out, and gave chase to Tom. The Irishwoman, too, was walking

---

[23]**marten**   a little furry mammal

up to the house to beg – she must have got round by some byway – but she threw away her bundle, and gave chase to Tom likewise. Only My Lady did not give chase; for when she had put her head out of the window, her nightwig fell into the garden, and she had to ring up her lady's-maid, and send her down for it privately, which quite put her out of the running, so that she came in nowhere, and is consequently not placed.

In a word, never was there heard at Harthover Place – not even when the fox was killed in the conservatory, among acres of broken glass, and tons of smashed flower-pots – such a noise, row, hubbub, babel, shindy, hullabaloo, stramash, charivari and total contempt of dignity, repose and order, as that day, when Grimes, the gardener, the groom, the dairymaid, Sir John, the steward, the ploughman, the keeper and the Irishwoman, all ran up the park, shouting 'Stop thief', in the belief that Tom had at least a thousand pounds' worth of jewels in his empty pockets; and the very magpies and jays followed Tom up, screaking and screaming, as if he were a hunted fox, beginning to droop his brush.

And all the while poor Tom paddled up the park with his little bare feet, like a small black gorilla fleeing to the forest. Alas for him! there was no big father gorilla therein to take his part – to scratch out the gardener's inside with one paw, toss the dairymaid into a tree with another, and wrench off Sir John's head with a third, while he cracked the keeper's skull with his teeth as easily as if it had been a coconut or a pavingstone.

However, Tom did not remember ever having had a father; so he did not look for one, and expected to have to take care of himself; while as for running, he could keep up for a couple of miles with any stagecoach, if there was the chance of a copper[24] or a cigar-end, and turn coach-wheels[25] on his hands and feet ten times following, which is more than you can do. Wherefore his pursuers found it very difficult to catch him; and we will hope that they did not catch him at all.

---

[24]**copper**   a penny
[25]**coach-wheel**   cart-wheel

But the Irishwoman, alone of them all, had seen which way Tom went. She had kept ahead of everyone the whole time; and yet she neither walked nor ran. She went along quite smoothly and gracefully, while her feet twinkled past each other so fast that you could not see which was foremost; till every one asked each other who the strange woman was; and all agreed, for want of anything better to say, that she must be in league with Tom.

But when she came to the plantation, they lost sight of her; and they could do no less. For she went quietly over the wall after Tom, and followed him wherever he went. Sir John and the rest saw no more of her; and out of sight was out of mind.

Further reading

Read on in chapter 2 of *The Water Babies* if you would like to know what happens to Tom next and find out about the mysterious Irishwoman. Chapter 3 of *Oliver Twist* by Charles Dickens has another cruel chimney sweep on the lookout for a 'climbing boy': 'Mr Gamfield did happen to labour under the slight imputation of having bruised three or four boys to death already'.

The main character in George MacDonald's book *At the Back of the North Wind* (1871) is a poor stable boy living in Victorian London who goes on a curious journey away from his hard and horrible working life.

Lisa Tetzer's 1941 historical novel *The Black Brothers* about child chimney sweeps (written in Switzerland, where she had fled from the Nazis) was translated in 2004 for English readers.

Around the World in Eighty Days
by Jules Verne

Phileas Fogg takes on a new servant: the home-loving Jean Passepartout. What happens next is completely unexpected. Passepartout could never have imagined that the orderly household of his exacting new master is about to be left behind for an extraordinary adventure. In 24 hours his life is turned around. Here, Passepartout meets Phileas Fogg for the first time.

Although not palatial,[1] the house on Savile Row was remarkable for its level of comfort. Because of the regular habits of its occupant, the service was far from onerous.[2] Nevertheless, Phileas Fogg demanded an extraordinary punctuality and reliability from his one servant. That very day, 2 October, he had given notice to James Forster: the fellow had made the mistake of bringing in his shaving-water at a temperature of 84°F, rather than the statutory 86. Mr Fogg was even now expecting his successor, due to report between eleven and half past.

Phileas Fogg sat squarely in his armchair, both feet together like a soldier on parade, hands firmly on knees, body erect, and head held high. He was watching the hand moving on the clock: a complicated apparatus that showed the hours, minutes, seconds, days, dates, and years. In keeping with his daily habit, Mr Fogg was due to go to the Reform Club[3] on the stroke of 11.30.

A knock came on the door of the morning-room where Phileas Fogg was waiting. James Forster, the sacked servant, appeared.

'The new valet,'[4] he announced.

A man of about thirty came in and bowed.

'You are French and called John?'

---

[1] **palatial**   like a palace
[2] **onerous**   heavy, burdensome
[3] **Reform Club**   a famous gentleman's club
[4] **valet**   a manservant

'Jean, if sir pleases – Jean Passepartout,[5] a nickname that has stuck with me and was first applied due to my natural ability to get out of scrapes. I consider myself an honest fellow, sir, but if truth be told I have had several occupations. I used to be a wandering singer and a circus rider; I was a trapeze artist like Léotard and a tightrope walker like Blondin; then I became a gymnastics instructor in order to make greater use of my skills; and lastly I was a sergeant in the Paris Fire Brigade. I have some remarkable fires in my c.v.[6] But I left France five years ago: wishing to try family life, I became a personal manservant in England. Then, finding myself without a job, I heard that Mr Phileas Fogg was the most particular and stay-at-home man in the whole of the United Kingdom. I presented myself at sir's house in the hope of being able to live in peace and quiet and forget the very name of Passepartout . . . '

'Passepartout suits me very well. You have been recommended to me – I have excellent references on your account. Are you aware of my terms?'

'Yes, sir.'

'Very well, then. What time do you make it?'

'Eleven twenty-two,' replied Passepartout, pulling an enormous silver watch from the depths of his waistcoat pocket.

'Your watch is slow.'

'Pardon me, sir, but that's impossible.'

'You're four minutes slow. It is of no consequence. What matters is to note the difference. So, starting from this moment, 11.29 a.m. on Wednesday, 2 October 1872, you are in my employ.'

Whereupon Phileas Fogg got up, took his hat in his left hand, placed it on his head with the action of an automaton, and vanished without uttering another word.

---

[5]**Passepartout**   a French word: someone who passes/travels everywhere
[6]**c.v.**   curriculum vitae: a document giving details of your education and achievements, with dates

Passepartout heard the front door shut once: that was his new master going out; then a second time: his predecessor James Forster leaving in turn.

He stood alone in the house on Savile Row.

He immediately began an inspection, systematically working his way up from the cellar to the attic. The house was clean, well-ordered, austere,[7] puritanical,[8] in sum designed for service; and it pleased him. The impression it made was of a fine snail's shell, but a shell lit and heated by gas, since carburetted hydrogen proved quite sufficient for all its needs. Passepartout found his bedroom on the second floor without difficulty. It met with his satisfaction. An electric bell and speaking-tubes communicated with the mezzanine[9] and first-floor apartments. On the mantelpiece an electric clock kept perfect time with the clock in Phileas Fogg's bedroom, the two devices striking the second simultaneously.

'This is a piece of alright, suits me down to the ground, down to the ground!' he said to himself.

He spotted a card displayed above the clock in his room. It was the schedule of his daily duties. From eight in the morning, the regulation time when Phileas Fogg got up, till half-past eleven, when he left for his lunch at the Reform Club, it specified all the details of the service he was to provide: the tea and toast at 8.23, the water for shaving at 9.37, the hairdressing at twenty to ten, etc. Then from 11.30 a.m. until twelve midnight, when the methodical gentleman went to bed, everything was noted, planned, regulated. Passepartout took great pleasure in contemplating this schedule and committing its various entries to memory.

As for *Monsieur*'s wardrobe, it was well organized and perfectly comprehensive. Each pair of trousers, waistcoat, or jacket bore an order number. This number was marked on a register

---

[7]**austere**   very plain, with few comforts
[8]**puritanical**   strict and plain-looking
[9]**mezzanine**   a floor between the ground and the first floor

of incoming and outgoing items, showing the date on which each garment was to be worn, depending on the time of the year. Likewise for the shoes.

In sum, the house on Savile Row – surely a temple to disorder in the days of the illustrious but dissipated[10] Sheridan[11] – constituted a well-appointed abode showing that its inhabitant was very comfortably off. There was no library and no books – of no use to Mr Fogg as the Reform Club put two libraries at his disposal, one devoted to literature, and the other to law and politics. In the bedroom stood a safe of average size, built to withstand both fire and theft. No arms were to be found in the house, neither hunting gear nor weapons of war. Everything pointed to the most pacific[12] of habits.

Having examined the residence in detail, Passepartout rubbed his hands together. His broad face beamed, and he exclaimed cheerfully:

'To the ground. Just what I need. We'll get on famously, Mr Fogg and me. A home-loving and regular man. A genuine piece of machinery. Well, I shan't mind serving a machine!'

Phileas Fogg had left his house on Savile Row at half-past eleven and placed his right foot 575 times in front of his left and his left foot 576 times in front of his right. He had thus reached the Reform Club, a vast edifice in Pall Mall that cost no less than £120,000 to build.

Mr Fogg immediately made his way to the dining-room, whose nine windows opened out on to a fine garden with trees already turned to gold by the autumn. There he sat at his usual table with the service laid out ready for him. Lunch consisted of an *hors d'oeuvre*[13] of steamed fish in a Reading Sauce of the highest quality, scarlet roast beef with mushrooms, rhubarb-and-gooseberry tart, and some Cheshire cheese – all washed down

---

[10]**dissipated**   loose in morals, falling apart
[11]**Sheridan**   a famous playwright (1751–1816)
[12]**pacific**   peaceful
[13]*hors d'oeuvre*   a dish before a main meal

with a few cups of that excellent tea specially grown for the Reform Club.

At 12.47, the gentleman got up and moved into the vast drawing-room, a sumptuous area adorned with paintings in elaborate frames. There a servant gave him an uncut copy of *The Times*, which Phileas Fogg managed to unfold and cut with a proficiency indicating great experience of that exacting operation. Reading this newspaper occupied Phileas Fogg until 3.45, and the *Standard* – which came next – until dinner. This meal took place in the same way as luncheon, but with the addition of Royal British Sauce.

At twenty minutes to six the gentleman returned to the huge drawing-room and absorbed himself in the *Morning Chronicle*.

Half an hour later, various members of the Reform Club made their entrance and headed for the hearth, where a good coal fire was burning. These were the usual partners of Mr Phileas Fogg, like him fanatical whist[14] players: the engineer Andrew Stuart, the bankers John Sullivan and Samuel Fallentin, the brewer Thomas Flanagan, and Gauthier Ralph, one of the governors of the Bank of England – figures of considerable wealth and respectability, even in this club composed of the leading lights of industry and finance.

'Well, Ralph,' asked Thomas Flanagan, 'what's the latest news on this theft business?'

'Well,' answered Andrew Stuart, 'the Bank won't see its money again.'

'I am confident, on the contrary,' intervened Gauthier Ralph, 'that we will soon be able to lay our hands on the thief. Very smart police inspectors have been sent to America, the Continent, and all the main ports of entry and exit, so that this gentleman will have quite a job escaping them.'

'But do we have the thief's description?' asked Andrew Stuart.

---

[14]**whist**   a card game for four players

'First of all, he's not a thief,' Ralph replied quite seriously.

'What, not a thief, this individual who's made off with £55,000 worth of banknotes?'

'No,' answered Gauthier Ralph.

'So he's a manufacturer, is he?' enquired John Sullivan.

'The *Morning Chronicle* assures us that he is a gentleman.'

The person making this remark was none other than Phileas Fogg, whose head now emerged from the sea of paper piled up around him. At the same time Mr Fogg greeted his colleagues, who returned the compliment.

The case in question – which the various newspapers were heatedly discussing – had taken place three days previously, on 29 September. A wad of notes amounting to the enormous sum of £55,000 had been taken from the desk of the Chief Cashier of the Bank of England.

To those surprised that such a theft could be carried out so easily, Assistant Governor Gauthier Ralph merely replied that the Cashier was at that time occupied recording a receipt of 3s. 6d., and that one cannot keep one's eyes on everything.

It is important to note – and this makes the matter slightly easier to fathom – that that remarkable establishment, the Bank of England, seems to possess the utmost regard for the public's dignity. No guards, no retired soldiers, no grills. The gold, the silver, and the notes are left lying about, at the mercy, as it were, of the first passer-by. It would be unthinkable to cast doubt on the honesty of a member of the public. One of the acutest observers of British society even recounts the following incident: he was in a room in the Bank one day, and felt the wish to examine more closely a gold bar weighing about seven or eight pounds, lying on the cashier's desk. He took the ingot, examined it, then passed it on to his neighbour, who handed it on to someone else, with the result that it went from hand to hand to the end of a dark corridor, then half an hour later returned to its normal place – without the cashier even looking up.

But on 29 September, things didn't happen quite like that. The wad of banknotes never came back, and when the magnificent clock dominating the 'drawing-office' announced that it was five o'clock and that the offices were closing, the Bank of England had no choice but to pass £55,000 through its account of profits and losses.

Once the theft had been properly recorded, 'detectives' chosen from among the best policemen were sent to the main ports of Liverpool, Glasgow, Le Havre, Suez, Brindisi, New York, etc. They had been promised a reward of £2,000 plus 5 per cent of the sum recovered. While waiting for the information that the promptly initiated enquiries would clearly produce, the job of the inspectors was to carefully observe everyone entering and leaving the country.

Now, as the *Morning Chronicle* had pointed out, there was in fact very good reason to believe that the thief did not belong to any of the known criminal gangs of England. During that same day of 29 September, a well-dressed gentleman with good manners and a distinguished bearing had been noticed walking to and fro in the cash room where the theft took place. The enquiries had allowed a relatively accurate description of the gentleman to be produced, and it had been immediately sent to every detective in the United Kingdom and Europe. Some optimistic souls, Gauthier Ralph amongst them, believed consequently that the thief would find it difficult to escape.

As one can imagine, this case was in the news in London and everywhere else. People discussed it and took impassioned positions for or against the Metropolitan Police being successful. The reader will not therefore be surprised to learn that the members of the Reform Club also debated the question, all the more so since one of the Bank's Assistant Governors was amongst their number.

The esteemed Gauthier Ralph did not doubt the success of the enquiries, believing that the reward on offer would ensure that the police showed due zeal and intelligence.

But his colleague Andrew Stuart was far from sharing his confidence. Accordingly the discussion continued at the whist table, with Stuart partnering Flanagan, and Fallentin, Phileas Fogg. During the game the players did not speak, but between the rubbers the conversation carried on all the more heatedly.

'I maintain,' said Stuart, 'that the odds are in favour of the thief, who is clearly an experienced operator.'

'Come on!' answered Ralph. 'There's not a single country left he can hide in.'

'Really?'

'And where do you think he might go, then?'

'I can't say,' replied Stuart. 'But after all, the world is big enough.'

'It used to be,' Fogg said quietly. 'Will you cut?' he added, presenting the cards to Flanagan.

The discussion was interrupted by the play. But soon Andrew Stuart said:

'What d'you mean, "used to be"? Has the Earth suddenly got smaller by some chance?'

'Unquestionably it has,' responded Ralph. 'I share Mr Fogg's view. The Earth has shrunk because it can be covered ten times as quickly now as a hundred years ago. And in the case we are discussing, this will make the search faster.'

'And the thief's escape easier!'

'Your turn to play, Mr Stuart,' observed Fogg.

But the doubting Stuart was not convinced, and once the game was over:

'You must admit, Ralph, that you have a funny way of saying the Earth has shrunk! Because you can now go round it in three months . . . '

'Eighty days,' interjected Fogg.

'Yes indeed, good sirs,' confirmed Sullivan. 'Eighty days, now they've opened the section of the Great Indian Peninsular Railway from Rothal to Allahabad. This is the calculation done by the *Morning Chronicle*:

London to Suez via the Mont Cenis Tunnel and Brindisi, by railway and steamship	7 days
Suez to Bombay, by steamship	13 days
Bombay to Calcutta, by railway	3 days
Calcutta to Hong Kong (China), by steamship	13 days
Hong Kong to Yokohama, by steamship	6 days
Yokohama to San Francisco, by steamship	22 days
San Francisco to New York, by railroad	7 days
New York to London, by steamship and railway	9 days
Total	80 days

'Possibly 80 days!' exclaimed Stuart, trumping a winner in his excitement. 'But not allowing for unfavourable weather, headwinds, shipwrecks, derailments, etc.'

'All included,' said Fogg, continuing to play – for the discussion was no longer respecting the whist.

'Even if the Indians and Red Indians tear up the rails?' cried Stuart. 'Even if they stop the trains, plunder the carriages, and scalp the passengers?'

'All included,' repeated Phileas Fogg, laying down his hand. 'Two winning trumps.'

Andrew Stuart picked up the hands and started shuffling. 'In theory you may be right, but in practice . . . '

'In practice too, Mr Stuart.'

'Well I should like to see you do it.'

'Your choice. Let's go together.'

'Heaven forbid!' exclaimed Stuart. 'But I would gladly wager £4,000 that such a journey, carried out under the conditions specified, is simply not possible.'

'On the contrary, perfectly possible,' replied Fogg.

'Well do it, then!'

'Go round the world in 80 days?'

'Yes!'

'All right then.'

'Starting when?'

'Starting now.'

'It's pure madness!' cried Andrew Stuart, beginning to get annoyed by his partner's obstinacy. 'Let's get on with the game!'

'Please reshuffle, then,' said Phileas Fogg, 'because there's been a misdeal.'

Andrew Stuart picked up the cards with a shaking hand; then, suddenly laying them back down again:

'Very well, Mr Fogg. I'll bet you £4,000.'

'My dear Stuart,' said Fallentin, 'steady on. You can't be serious.'

'When I say I'll bet,' answered Stuart, 'it is always serious.'

'Very well!' said Mr Fogg, and turned to his colleagues:

'I have £20,000 in my account at Baring Brothers. I'll be glad to venture this sum.'

'Twenty thousand!' cried Sullivan. 'Twenty thousand pounds that you could lose through an unforeseen mishap!'

'The unforeseen does not exist.'

'But, Mr Fogg, this period of 80 days is merely the minimum it can be done in!'

'A properly used minimum is enough for anything.'

'But in order to do it, you'll have to mathematically jump from trains into steamships and from steamships on to trains!'

'I'll jump mathematically.'

'You must be joking!'

'An Englishman never jokes about anything as important as a bet. I hereby wager £20,000 with anyone who wishes that I will carry out the tour of the world in 80 days or less, i.e. in 1,920 hours or 115,200 minutes. Will you accept?'

'We accept,' replied Messrs Stuart, Fallentin, Sullivan, Flanagan and Ralph after a brief discussion.

'Good. The boat-train leaves at 8.45. I'll be on it.'

'This very evening?' enquired Stuart.

'This very evening,' answered Phileas Fogg. Then, consulting a pocket diary, 'Since today is Wednesday, 2 October, I must be back in London, in this drawing-room of the Reform Club, at 8.45 p.m. on Saturday, 21 December, failing which the £20,000 presently deposited in my account at Baring Brothers will belong to you *de facto* and *de jure*.[15] Here is a cheque for that amount, gentlemen.'

The wager was witnessed, and signed there and then by all six interested parties. Phileas Fogg had remained cool. He had certainly not bet in order to win, and he had pledged only £20,000 – half his fortune – because he planned to spend the other half on this difficult, not to say impossible, undertaking. As for his adversaries, they seemed a little upset, not because of the amount at stake, but because they felt unhappy at fighting with such one-sided odds.

Seven o'clock struck. Mr Fogg was asked if he wanted to stop playing so as to make preparations for his departure.

'I'm always ready,' replied the impassive gentleman as he dealt.

'Diamonds are trumps,' he said. 'Your lead, I believe, Mr Stuart.'

At 7.25 Phileas Fogg, having won a good twenty guineas, said goodbye to his honourable colleagues and left the Reform Club. At 7.50 he opened his front door and went in.

Passepartout, who had meticulously studied the schedule, was a little surprised to see Mr Fogg displaying irregularity, by appearing at this most unusual time. According to the card, the tenant of Savile Row was not due back until the stroke of midnight.

Phileas Fogg first went up to his room, and then called:
'Passepartout.'

The manservant didn't reply. The call couldn't possibly be addressed to him. It wasn't the right time.

'Passepartout,' repeated Mr Fogg, not raising his voice.

The manservant appeared.

'I had to call you twice.'

'But it's not midnight yet,' answered Passepartout, watch in hand.

---

[15] *de facto* **and** *de jure*   in fact and in law

'I know,' said Phileas Fogg, 'and I'm not finding fault. We're leaving for Calais in ten minutes.'

An experimental sort of grimace appeared on the Frenchman's round face. He couldn't have heard properly.

'Is sir travelling?'

'He is,' replied Phileas Fogg. 'We're going around the world.'

Passepartout, his eyes wide-staring, his eyebrows completely raised, his arms hanging loose, his whole body sagging, showed all the signs of an astonishment verging on stupefaction.

'Around the world?' he murmured.

'In 80 days,' was Mr Fogg's rejoinder. 'There is not a moment to lose.'

'But what about the trunks?'[16] said Passepartout, unconsciously rocking his head from side to side.

'No trunks. Just an overnight bag. Two woollen shirts and three pairs of stockings. The same for you. We'll buy things on the way. You will bring down my mackintosh and travelling rug. Wear stout shoes. Although we'll be doing little or no walking. Off you go now.'

Passepartout tried to reply. He couldn't. He left Mr Fogg's room, went up to his own, collapsed on to a chair, and uttered a slightly colloquial[17] phrase from his native land:

'Well,' he said, 'I'll be blowed. And me who was looking for the quiet life!'

And, mechanically, he got ready to leave. Around the world in 80 days! Was he dealing with a madman? Unlikely . . . Was it possibly a joke? They were going to Dover, okay. Calais: won't say no. After all, that had to be nice, as he hadn't set foot on his native soil for five years. Perhaps they would even go to Paris: he would certainly be glad to see the great capital again. But a gentleman so careful with his movements would clearly stop there . . . Yes, that had to be it. But he was going to travel all the same, this gentleman, so stay-at-home until now!

---

[16]**trunks**   large travelling boxes or cases
[17]**colloquial**   conversational or informal

By eight o'clock, Passepartout had prepared a modest bag containing his own and his master's wardrobes. Then, his mind still troubled, he left the room, carefully closed the door, and went to find Mr Fogg.

Mr Fogg was ready. He was carrying under his arm Bradshaw's *Continental Railway, Steam Transit and General Guide*, which would provide him with all the information he needed for his travels. He took the bag from Passepartout, opened it, and dropped in a thick wad of those fine banknotes that are tender in all countries.

'You haven't forgotten anything?'

'No, sir.'

'My mackintosh and rug?'

'They're here.'

'Good, take this.'

Mr Fogg handed over the bag.

'And take care; there's £20,000 inside.'

The bag almost fell from Passepartout's hands, as if the £20,000 had been in solid gold.

Master and servant went downstairs and double-locked the front door.

There was a cab-stand at the end of Savile Row. Phileas Fogg and his servant got into a cab which headed quickly for Charing Cross Station, one of the termini of the South-Eastern Railway.

At 8.20 the cab drew up at the station entrance. Passepartout got out. His master followed and paid the driver.

At this moment, a poor beggar-woman holding a child by the hand, barefoot in the mud, a shawl in rags over her torn clothing, and wearing a ragged hat from which drooped a single bedraggled plume, came up to Mr Fogg and asked for charity.

Mr Fogg got out the twenty guineas he had just won at the whist table and gave them to the beggar.

'Take this, my good woman,' he said. 'I'm glad I met you.'

And then he continued on his way.

Passepartout felt a damp sensation in his eyes. His master had taken a step forward in his heart.

The two men entered the concourse. Phileas Fogg instructed Passepartout to buy two first-class tickets for Paris. Then, turning round, he noticed his five colleagues from the Reform Club.

'Gentlemen,' he said, 'I am leaving. The various visas stamped on the passport I am taking for this express purpose will allow you to verify my journey when I come back.'

'Oh, Mr Fogg!' replied Gauthier Ralph politely. 'There is no need. We shall count on your word as a gentleman.'

'Better all the same.'

'You haven't forgotten when you need to be back?' enquired Andrew Stuart.

'In 80 days,' answered Mr Fogg. 'On Saturday, 21 December 1872, at 8.45 p.m. Till we meet again, gentlemen.'

At 8.40 Phileas Fogg and his servant sat down in the same compartment. At 8.45 a whistle sounded and the train pulled off.

It was a dark night, with a drizzle falling. Phileas Fogg, sitting back in his corner, did not speak. Passepartout, still in a state of shock, was mechanically hugging the bag containing the banknotes.

But the train had not got past Sydenham, before Passepartout produced a real cry of despair!

'What's the matter?' asked Mr Fogg.

'The matter . . . in my hurry . . . thinking about other things . . . I forgot . . . '

'What?'

' . . . to turn off the gas in my bedroom!'

'Well, my boy,' said Mr Fogg coldly, 'it's burning at your expense!'

Further reading

If you liked this, you'll like other adventure stories by Jules Verne such as *Journey to the Centre of the Earth* and *20,000 Leagues under the Sea*. When you think that Victorian readers were only just beginning to feel that these journeys might actually be possible, it makes them even more exciting.

How to Reach the Pole

from *The Graphic*, 6 October 1877

'All attempts to reach the North Pole have, up to the present time, resulted in failure . . . ' So what might succeed?

A sense of adventure, some knowledge of balloons – Royal Navy Commander Cheyne certainly had a plan . . .

All attempts to reach the North Pole have, up to the present time, resulted in failure, but a novel plan has been suggested by Commander Cheyne, R.N., to employ balloons. Three balloons, connected in the manner shown, would carry six men, besides three tons weight of gear, boat-cars, stores, provisions, tents, sledges, dogs, compressed gas, and ballast. The triangular framework, connecting the balloons, would be fitted with foot-ropes, so that the occupants could go from one balloon to another in the same manner as sailors lie out upon the yards of a ship, and the balloon would be equi-poised[1] by means of bags of ballast suspended from this framework, and hauled to the required positions by ropes. Trail ropes would be attached to the balloons, so as to prevent their ascent above a certain height (about 500 feet), at which elevation they would be balanced in the air, the spare ends of the ropes trailing over the ice . . . Commander Cheyne proposes that the balloons should start about the end of May, on the curve of a wind circle, of known diameter, ascertained approximately by meteorological obser-vations. It is estimated that, with a knowledge of the diameter of the wind circle, and the known distance from the Pole, the balloons could be landed within at least twenty miles of the long-wished-for goal . . .

---

[1]**equi-poised**   balanced evenly

Further reading

Panorama and *History as Hot News* are both books edited by Leonard de Vries which contain articles from two popular magazines of the time: *The Graphic* and *The Illustrated London News*. *Panorama* shows the world of the early Victorians from 1842 to 1865, and *History* from 1865 to 1897. The magazines presented 'news in pictures', covering dreams of flying machines as well as reports of battles. You can get a real flavour of the age by reading the news as the Victorians themselves did.

Victorian Inventions – also edited by Leonard de Vries – is 'an account of discoveries in Transport, Electricity, Optics, Aeronautics, Telephone, and a wealth of oddities with 192 contemporary illustrations'.

Messages Without Wires

by Guglielmo Marconi

Imagine making a scientific breakthrough and testing it out while the world held its breath . . . Imagine sitting down at a simple table in a little hut at the top of a cliff, getting ready to be proved right or wrong . . .

Perhaps of all the discoveries of the day, nothing was more momentous than this.

First-hand account of Guglielmo MARCONI as he awaited the signal from Poldhu, Cornwall, in a hut on the cliffs at St John's, Newfoundland.

'Shortly before mid-day I placed the single earphone to my ear and started listening. The receiver on the table before me was very crude – a few coils and condensers and a coherer – no valves, no amplifiers, not even a crystal. But I was at last on the point of putting the correctness of all my beliefs to test. The answer came at 12.30 when I heard, faintly but distinctly, "pip-pip-pip." I handed the phone to KEMP. "Can you hear anything?" I asked. "Yes," he said, "the letter S" – he could hear it. I knew then that all my anticipations had been justified. The electric waves sent out into space from Poldhu had traversed the Atlantic – the distance, enormous as it seemed then, of 1,700 miles – unimpeded by the curvature of the earth. The result meant much more to me than the mere successful realization of an experiment. As Sir Oliver LODGE had stated, it was an epoch in history. I now felt for the first time absolutely certain that the day would come when mankind would be able to send messages without wires not only across the Atlantic but between the farthermost ends of the earth.'

Further reading

If you'd like to look at more Victorian non-fiction *Panorama* and *History as Hot News* are both books edited by Leonard de Vries which contain articles from two popular magazines of the time: *The Graphic* and *The Illustrated London News*. *Panorama* shows the world of the early Victorians from 1842 to 1865, and *History* from 1865 to 1897. The magazines presented 'news in pictures', covering dreams of flying machines as well as reports of battles. You can get a real flavour of the age by reading the news as the Victorians themselves did.

Victorian Inventions – also edited by Leonard de Vries – is 'an account of discoveries in Transport, Electricity, Optics, Aeronautics, Telephone, and a wealth of oddities with 192 contemporary illustrations'.

A Lady's Life in the Rocky Mountains
by Isabella Bird

Isabella Bird was alone on horseback, riding through the mountains. She knew people would want to know what she looked like, so she wrote this note at the front of the book:

> 'For the benefit of other lady travellers,' she explains, she's 'wearing the "American Lady's Mountain Dress", a half-fitting jacket, a skirt reaching to the ankles, and full Turkish trousers gathered into frills which fall over the boots – a thoroughly serviceable and feminine costume for mountaineering and other rough travelling in any part of the world.'

But was she ready for grizzly bears?

After I had ridden about ten miles the road went up a steep hill in the forest, turned abruptly, and through the blue gloom of the great pines which rose from the ravine in which the river was then hid, came glimpses of two mountains, about 11,000 feet in height, whose bald grey summits were crowned with pure snow. It was one of those glorious surprises in scenery which make one feel as if one must bow down and worship. The forest was thick, and had an undergrowth of dwarf spruce and brambles, but as the horse had become fidgety and 'scary' on the track, I turned off in the idea of taking a short cut, and was sitting carelessly, shortening my stirrup, when a great, dark, hairy beast rose, crashing and snorting, out of the tangle just in front of me. I had only a glimpse of him, and thought that my imagination had magnified a wild boar, but it was a bear. The horse snorted and plunged violently, as if he would go down to the river, and then turned, still plunging, up a steep bank, when, finding that I must come off, I threw myself off on the right side, where the ground rose considerably, so that I had not far to fall. I got up covered with dust, but neither shaken nor bruised. It was truly grotesque and humiliating. The bear ran in one direction, and the horse in another. I hurried after the latter, and twice he stopped till I was close to him, then turned round and cantered away. After walking about a mile in deep dust, I picked up first the saddle-blanket and next my bag, and soon came upon the horse, standing facing me, and shaking all over. I thought I should catch him then, but when I went up to him he turned round, threw up his heels several times, rushed off the track, galloped in circles, bucking, kicking, and plunging for some time, and then throwing up his heels as an act of final defiance, went off at full speed in the direction of Truckee, with the saddle over his shoulders and the great wooden stirrups thumping his sides, while I trudged ignominiously[1] along in the dust, laboriously[2] carrying the bag and saddle-blanket.

I walked for nearly an hour, heated and hungry, when to my joy I saw the ox-team halted across the top of a gorge, and one of the teamsters leading the horse towards me. The young man said that, seeing the horse coming, they had drawn the team across the road to stop him, and remembering that he had passed them with a lady on him, they feared that there had been an accident, and had just saddled one of their own horses to go in search of me. He brought me some water to wash the dust from my face, and re-saddled the horse, but the animal snorted and plunged for some time before he would let me mount, and then sidled along in such a nervous and scared way, that the teamster walked for some distance by me to see that I was 'all right.' He said that the woods in the neighbourhood of Tahoe had been full of brown and grizzly bears for some days, but that no one was in any danger from them. I took a long gallop beyond the scene of my tumble to quiet the horse, who was most restless and troublesome.

I dreamt of bears so vividly that I woke with a furry death-hug at my throat, but feeling quite refreshed. When I mounted my horse after breakfast the sun was high and the air so keen

---

[1]**ignominiously** shamefully
[2]**laboriously** with hard work

and intoxicating that, giving the animal his head, I galloped up and down hill, feeling completely tireless. Truly, that air is the elixir[3] of life. I had a glorious ride back to Truckee. The road was not as solitary as the day before. In a deep part of the forest the horse snorted and reared, and I saw a cinnamon-coloured bear with two cubs cross the track ahead of me. I tried to keep the horse quiet that the mother might acquit me of any designs upon her lolloping children, but I was glad when the ungainly, longhaired party crossed the river. Then I met a team, the driver of which stopped and said he was glad that I had not gone to Cornelian Bay, it was such a bad trail, and hoped I had enjoyed Tahoe. The driver of another team stopped and asked if I had seen any bears. Then a man heavily armed, a hunter probably, asked me if I were the English tourist who had 'happened on' a 'grizzlie' yesterday. Then I saw a lumberer taking his dinner on a rock in the river, who 'touched his hat' and brought me a draught of ice-cold water, which I could hardly drink owing to the fractiousness of the horse, and gathered me some mountain pinks, which I admired. I mention these little incidents to indicate the habit of respectful courtesy to women which prevails in that region. These men might have been excused for speaking in a somewhat free-and-easy tone to a lady riding alone, and in an unwonted fashion. Womanly dignity and manly respect for women are the salt of society in this wild West.

My horse was so excitable that I avoided the centre of Truckee, and skulked through a collection of Chinamen's shanties to the stable, where a prodigious[4] roan horse, standing seventeen hands high, was produced for my ride to the Donner Lake. I asked the owner if there were not ruffians about who might make an evening ride dangerous. A story was current of a man having ridden through Truckee two evenings before with a chopped-up human body in a sack behind the saddle, and

---

[3]**elixir**   a drug or essence capable of prolonging life
[4]**prodigious**   wonderful, marvellous or powerful

hosts of stories of ruffianism are located there, rightly or wrongly. This man said, "There's a bad breed of ruffians, but the ugliest among them all won't touch you. There's nothing Western folk admire so much as pluck in a woman." I had to get on a barrel before I could reach the stirrup, and when I was mounted my feet only came half-way down the horse's sides. I felt like a fly on him. The road at first lay through a valley without a river, but some swampishness nourished some rank swamp-grass, the first *green* grass I have seen in America; and the pines, with their red stems, looked beautiful rising out of it. I hurried along, and came upon the Donner Lake quite suddenly, to be completely smitten by its beauty. It is only about three miles long by one and a half broad, and lies hidden away among mountains, with no dwellings on its shores but some deserted lumberers' cabins. Its loneliness pleased me well. I did not see man, beast, or bird from the time I left Truckee till I returned.

Further reading

Isabella Bird kept travelling! If you'd like to read other books by her, try *Unbeaten Tracks in Japan* (1880), *Journeys in Persia and Kurdistan* (1891), *Among the Tibetans* (1894), *Korea and Her Neighbours* (1898) and *The Yangtze Valley and Beyond* (1899). You could also try two other wonderful books: *The Blessings of a Good Thick Skirt* by Mary Russell (Collins, 1986) about the lives of several Victorian women travellers, and *Wayward Women: A Guide to Women Travellers* by Jane Robinson (Oxford University Press, 1990), which contains travelling-tales spanning 16 centuries, each roughly a page long.

The War of the Worlds
by H. G. Wells

Martians have attacked England!

One man tells this story of maddened fear and panic. We learn too of his brother's desperate attempt to leave London, along with thousands of others milling and jostling through the streets in motor-cars, hansom cabs and carriages, on cycles and on horse-back, on the railways and on buses. The terrible Heat-Ray belches black vapour as people struggle like ants to escape.

The Exodus[1] from London

So you understand the roaring wave of fear that swept through the greatest city in the world just as Monday was dawning – the stream of flight rising swiftly to a torrent, lashing in a foaming tumult round the railway-stations, banked up into a horrible struggle about the shipping in the Thames, and hurrying by every available channel northward and eastward. By ten o'clock the police organization, and by mid-day even the railway organizations, were losing coherency, losing shape and efficiency, guttering, softening, running at last in that swift liquefaction of the social body.[2]

All the railway lines north of the Thames and the South-Eastern people at Cannon Street had been warned by midnight on Sunday, and trains were being filled, people were fighting savagely for standing-room in the carriages, even at two o'clock. By three, people were being trampled and crushed even in Bishopsgate Street; a couple of hundred yards or more from Liverpool Street Station revolvers were fired, people stabbed, and the policemen who had been sent to direct the traffic, exhausted and infuriated, were breaking the heads of the people they were called out to protect.

[1]**Exodus**   mass departure
[2]**swift liquefaction of the social body**   rapid breaking-down of society

And as the day advanced and the engine-drivers and stokers refused to return to London, the pressure of the flight drove the people in an ever-thickening multitude away from the stations and along the northward-running roads. By midday a Martian had been seen at Barnes, and a cloud of slowly sinking black vapour drove along the Thames and across the flats of Lambeth, cutting off all escape over the bridges in its sluggish advance. Another bank drove over Ealing, and surrounded a little island of survivors on Castle Hill, alive, but unable to escape.

After a fruitless struggle to get aboard a North-Western train at Chalk Farm – the engines of the trains that had loaded in the goods yard there *ploughed* through shrieking people, and a dozen stalwart men fought to keep the crowd from crushing the driver against his furnace – my brother emerged upon the Chalk Farm Road, dodged across through a hurrying swarm of vehicles, and had the luck to be foremost in the sack[3] of a cycle shop. The front tyre of the machine he got was punctured in dragging it through the window, but he got up and off, notwithstanding, with no further injury than a cut wrist. The steep foot of Haverstock Hill was impassable owing to several overturned horses, and my brother struck into Belsize Road.

So he got out of the fury of the panic, and, skirting the Edgware Road, reached Edgware about seven, fasting[4] and wearied, but well ahead of the crowd. Along the road people were standing in the roadway curious, wondering. He was passed by a number of cyclists, some horsemen, and two motor-cars. A mile from Edgware the rim of the wheel broke, and the machine became unrideable. He left it by the roadside and trudged through the village. There were shops half opened in the main street of the place, and people crowded on the pavement and in the doorways and windows, staring astonished at this extraordinary procession of fugitives that was beginning. He succeeded in getting some food at an inn.

For a time he remained in Edgware, not knowing what next to do. The flying people increased in number. Many of them, like my brother, seemed inclined to stop in the place. There was no fresh news of the invaders from Mars.

At that time the road was crowded, but as yet far from congested. Most of the fugitives at that hour were mounted on cycles, but there were soon motor-cars, hansom cabs,[5] and carriages hurrying along, and the dust hung in heavy clouds along the road to St Albans.

It was perhaps a vague idea of making his way to Chelmsford, where some friends of his lived, that at last induced my brother to strike into a quiet lane running eastward. Presently he came upon a stile, and, crossing it, followed a footpath north-eastward. He passed near several farm-houses and some little places whose names he did not learn. He saw few

---

[3]**sack**   violent robbery by a mob of people
[4]**fasting**   hungry; abstaining from food
[5]**hansom cabs**   two-wheeled carriages pulled by one horse

fugitives until, in a grass lane towards High Barnet, he happened upon the two ladies who became his fellow-travellers. He came upon them just in time to save them.

He heard their screams, and, hurrying round the corner, saw a couple of men struggling to drag them out of the little pony-chaise[6] in which they had been driving, while a third with difficulty held the frightened pony's head. One of the ladies, a short woman dressed in white, was simply screaming; the other, a dark, slender figure, slashed at the man who gripped her arm, with a whip she held in her disengaged hand.

My brother immediately grasped the situation, shouted, and hurried towards the struggle. One of the men desisted and turned towards him, and my brother, realizing from his antagonist's face that a fight was unavoidable, and being an expert boxer, went into him forthwith, and sent him down against the wheel of the chaise.

It was no time for pugilistic[7] chivalry, and my brother laid him quiet with a kick, and gripped the collar of the man who pulled at the slender lady's arm. He heard the clatter of hoofs, the whip stung across his face, a third antagonist struck him between the eyes, and the man he held wrenched himself free and made off down the lane in the direction from which he had come.

Partly stunned, he found himself facing the man who had held the horse's head, and became aware of the chaise receding from him down the lane, swaying from side to side and with the women in it looking back. The man before him, a burly rough,[8] tried to close, and he stopped him with a blow in the face. Then, realizing that he was deserted, he dodged round and made off down the lane after the chaise, with the sturdy man close behind him, and the fugitive, who had turned now, following remotely.

Suddenly he stumbled and fell: his immediate pursuer went headlong, and he rose to his feet to find himself with a couple of

---

[6]**pony-chaise**   a light, open cart
[7]**pugilistic**   fighting with fists
[8]**rough**   a rough-looking person

antagonists again. He would have had little chance against them had not the slender lady very pluckily pulled up and returned to his help. It seems she had had a revolver all this time, but it had been under the seat when she and her companion were attacked. She fired at six yards' distance, narrowly missing my brother. The less courageous of the robbers made off, and his companion followed him, cursing his cowardice. They both stopped in sight down the lane, where the third man lay insensible.

'Take this!' said the slender lady, and gave my brother her revolver.

'Go back to the chaise,' said my brother, wiping the blood from his split lip.

She turned without a word – they were both panting – and they went back to where the lady in white struggled to hold back the frightened pony. The robbers had evidently had enough of it. When my brother looked again they were retreating.

'I'll sit here,' said my brother, 'if I may,' and he got up on the empty front seat. The lady looked over her shoulder.

'Give me the reins,' she said, and laid the whip along the pony's side. In another moment a bend in the road hid the three men from my brother's eyes.

So, quite unexpectedly, my brother found himself, panting, with a cut mouth, a bruised jaw and bloodstained knuckles, driving along an unknown lane with these two women.

He learnt they were the wife and the younger sister of a surgeon living at Stanmore, who had come in the small hours from a dangerous case at Pinner, and heard at some railway-station on his way of the Martian advance. He had hurried home, roused the women – their servant had left them two days before – packed some provisions, put his revolver under the seat – luckily for my brother – and told them to drive on to Edgware, with the idea of getting a train there. He stopped behind to tell the neighbours. He would overtake them, he said, at about half past four in the morning, and now it was nearly nine and they had seen nothing of him since. They could not stop in Edgware because of the growing traffic through the place, and so they had come into this side-lane.

That was the story they told my brother in fragments when presently they stopped again, nearer to New Barnet. He promised to stay with them at least until they could determine what to do, or until the missing man arrived, and professed to be an expert shot with the revolver – a weapon strange to him – in order to give them confidence.

They made a sort of encampment by the wayside, and the pony became happy in the hedge. He told them of his own escape out of London, and all that he knew of these Martians and their ways. The sun crept higher in the sky, and after a time their talk died out and gave place to an uneasy state of anticipation. Several wayfarers came along the lane, and of these my brother gathered such news as he could. Every broken answer he had deepened his impression of the great disaster that had come on humanity, deepened his persuasion of the immediate necessity for prosecuting this flight. He urged the matter upon them.

'We have money,' said the slender woman, and hesitated.

Her eyes met my brother's and her hesitation ended.

'So have I,' said my brother.

She explained that they had as much as thirty pounds in gold besides a five-pound note, and suggested that with that they might get upon a train at St Albans or New Barnet. My brother thought that was hopeless, seeing the fury of the Londoners to crowd upon the trains, and broached his own idea of striking across Essex towards Harwich and thence escaping from the country altogether.

Mrs Elphinstone – that was the name of the woman in white – would listen to no reasoning, and kept calling upon 'George'; but her sister-in-law was astonishingly quiet and deliberate, and at last agreed to my brother's suggestion. So they went on towards Barnet, designing to cross the Great North Road, my brother leading the pony to save it as much as possible.

As the sun crept up the sky the day became excessively hot, and under foot a thick whitish sand grew burning and blinding, so that they travelled only very slowly. The hedges were grey with dust. And as they advanced towards Barnet, a tumultuous murmuring grew stronger.

They began to meet more people. For the most part these were staring before them, murmuring indistinct questions, jaded, haggard, unclean. One man in evening dress passed them on foot, his eyes on the ground. They heard his voice, and, looking back at him, saw one hand clutched in his hair and the other beating invisible things. His paroxysm[9] of rage over, he went on his way without once looking back.

As my brother's party went on towards the cross-roads to the south of Barnet, they saw a woman approaching the road across some fields on their left, carrying a child and with two other children, and then a man in dirty black, with a thick stick in one hand and a small portmanteau[10] in the other, passed. Then round the corner of the lane, from between the villas that guarded it at its confluence[11] with the highroad, came a little cart drawn by a sweating black pony and driven by a sallow youth in a bowler hat, grey with dust. There were three girls like East End factory girls, and a couple of little children, crowded in the cart.

'This'll tike us rahnd Edgware?' asked the driver, wild-eyed, white-faced; and when my brother told him it would if he turned to the left, he whipped up at once without the formality of thanks.

My brother noticed a pale grey smoke or haze rising among the houses in front of them, and veiling the white façade of a terrace beyond the road that appeared between the backs of the villas. Mrs Elphinstone suddenly cried out at a number of tongues of smoky red flame leaping up above the houses in front of them against the hot blue sky. The tumultuous noise resolved itself now into the disorderly mingling of many voices, the gride of many wheels, the creaking of wagons, and the staccato of hoofs. The lane came round sharply not fifty yards from the cross-roads.

'Good heavens!' cried Mrs Elphinstone. 'What is this you are driving us into?'

My brother stopped.

---

[9]**paroxysm**   a fit
[10]**portmanteau**   a leather travelling case
[11]**confluence**   where the two roads lead together

For the main road was a boiling stream of people, a torrent of human beings rushing northward, one pressing on another. A great bank of dust, white and luminous in the blaze of the sun, made everything within twenty feet of the ground grey and indistinct, and was perpetually renewed by the hurrying feet of a dense crowd of horses and men and women on foot, and by the wheels of vehicles of every description.

'Way!' my brother heard voices crying. 'Make way!'

It was like riding into the smoke of a fire to approach the meeting-point of the lane and road; the crowd roared like a fire, and the dust was hot and pungent. And, indeed, a little way up the road a villa was burning and sending rolling masses of black smoke across the road to add to the confusion.

Two men came past them. Then a dirty woman carrying a heavy bundle and weeping. A lost retriever dog with hanging tongue circled dubiously round them, scared and wretched, and fled at my brother's threat.

So much as they could see of the road Londonward, between the houses to the right, was a tumultuous stream of dirty, hurrying people pent in between the villas on either side; the black heads, the crowded forms, grew into distinctness as they rushed towards the corner, hurried past, and merged their individuality again in a receding multitude that was swallowed up at last in a cloud of dust.

'Go on! Go on!' cried the voices. 'Way! Way!'

One man's hands pressed on the back of another. My brother stood at the pony's head. Irresistibly attracted, he advanced slowly, pace by pace, down the lane.

Edgware had been a scene of confusion, Chalk Farm a riotous tumult, but this was a whole population in movement. It is hard to imagine that host. It had no character of its own. The figures poured out past the corner, and receded with their backs to the group in the lane. Along the margin came those who were on foot, threatened by the wheels, stumbling in the ditches, blundering into one another.

The carts and carriages crowded close upon one another, making little way for those swifter and more impatient vehicles that darted forward every now and then when an opportunity showed itself of doing so, sending the people scattering against the fences and gates of the villas.

'Push on!' was the cry. 'Push on! They are coming!'

In one cart stood a blind man in the uniform of the Salvation Army, gesticulating with his crooked fingers and bawling, 'Eternity! Eternity!' His voice was hoarse and very loud, so that my brother could hear him long after he was lost to sight in the northward dust. Some of the people who crowded in the carts whipped stupidly at their horses and quarrelled with other drivers; some sat motionless, staring at nothing with miserable eyes; some gnawed their hands with thirst or lay prostrate in the bottoms of their conveyances. The horses' bits were covered with foam, their eyes bloodshot.

There were cabs, carriages, shop-carts, wagons, beyond counting; a mail-cart, a road-cleaner's cart marked 'Vestry of St Pancras', a huge timber-wagon crowded with roughs. A brewer's dray[12] rumbled by with its two near wheels splashed with recent blood.

'Clear the way!' cried the voices. 'Clear the way!'

'Eter – nity! Eter – nity!' came echoing up the road.

There were sad, haggard women tramping by, well dressed, with children that cried and stumbled, their dainty clothes smothered in dust, their weary faces smeared with tears. With many of these came men, sometimes helpful, sometimes lowering and savage. Fighting side by side with them pushed some weary street outcast in faded black rags, wide-eyed, loud-voiced, and foul-mouthed. There were sturdy workmen thrusting their way along, wretched unkempt men clothed like clerks or shopmen, struggling spasmodically, a wounded soldier my brother noticed, men dressed in the clothes of railway porters, one wretched creature in a nightshirt with a coat thrown over it.

---

[12]**dray**   a low cart used for heavy loads

But, varied as its composition was, certain things all that host had in common. There was fear and pain on their faces, and fear behind them. A tumult up the road, a quarrel for a place in a wagon, sent the whole host of them quickening their pace; even a man so scared and broken that his knees bent under him was galvanized for a moment into renewed activity. The heat and dust had already been at work upon this multitude. Their skins were dry, their lips black and cracked. They were all thirsty, weary, and footsore. And amid the various cries one heard disputes, reproaches, groans of weariness and fatigue; the voices of most of them were hoarse and weak. Through it all ran a refrain:

'Way! Way! The Martians are coming!'

Few stopped and came aside from that flood. The lane opened slantingly into the main road with a narrow opening, and had a delusive appearance of coming from the direction of London. Yet a kind of eddy of people drove into its mouth; weaklings elbowed out of the stream, who for the most part rested but a moment before plunging into it again. A little way down the lane, with two friends bending over him, lay a man with a bare leg, wrapped about with bloody rags. He was a lucky man to have friends.

A little old man, with a grey military moustache and a filthy black frock-coat, limped out and sat down beside the trap, removed his boot – his sock was bloodstained – shook out a pebble, and hobbled on again; and then a little girl of eight or nine, all alone, threw herself under the hedge close by my brother, weeping.

'I can't go on! I can't go on!'

My brother woke from his torpor[13] of astonishment, and lifted her up, speaking gently to her, and carried her to Miss Elphinstone. So soon as my brother touched her she became quite still, as if frightened.

'Ellen!' shrieked a woman in the crowd, with tears in her voice. 'Ellen!' And the child suddenly darted away from my brother, crying: 'Mother!'

---

[13]**torpor**   state of being unable to move

'They are coming,' said a man on horseback, riding past along the lane.

'Out of the way, there!' bawled a coachman, towering high; and my brother saw a closed carriage turning into the lane.

The people crushed back on one another to avoid the horse. My brother pushed the pony and chaise back into the hedge, and the man drove by and stopped at the turn of the way. It was a carriage, with a pole for a pair of horses, but only one was in the traces.[14]

My brother saw dimly through the dust that two men lifted out something on a white stretcher, and put this gently on the grass beneath the privet hedge.

One of the men came running to my brother.

'Where is there any water?' he said. 'He is dying fast, and very thirsty. It is Lord Garrick.'

'Lord Garrick!' said my brother, 'The Chief Justice?'

'The water?' he said.

'There may be a tap,' said my brother, 'in some of the houses. We have no water. I dare not leave my people.'

The man pushed against the crowd towards the gate of the corner house.

'Go on!' said the people, thrusting at him. 'They are coming! Go on!'

Then my brother's attention was distracted by a bearded, eagle-faced man lugging a small handbag, which split even as my brother's eyes rested on it, and disgorged a mass of sovereigns that seemed to break up into separate coins as it struck the ground. They rolled hither and thither among the struggling feet of men and horses. The man stopped, and looked stupidly at the heap, and the shaft of a cab struck his shoulder and sent him reeling. He gave a shriek and dodged back, and a cartwheel shaved him narrowly.

'Way!' cried the men all about him. 'Make way!'

So soon as the cab had passed, he flung himself, with both hands open, upon the heap of coins, and began clutching

---

[14]**trace**   the chain or strap attaching a horse to a carriage

handfuls in his pockets. A horse rose close upon him, and in another moment he had half risen, and had been borne down under the horse's hoofs.

'Stop!' screamed my brother, and, pushing a woman out of his way, tried to clutch the bit of the horse.

Before he could get to it, he heard a scream under the wheels, and saw through the dust the rim passing over the poor wretch's back. The driver of the cart slashed his whip at my brother, who ran round behind the cart. The multitudinous shouting confused his ears. The man was writhing in the dust among his scattered money, unable to rise, for the wheel had broken his back, and his lower limbs lay limp and dead. My brother stood up and yelled the next driver, and a man on a black horse came to his assistance.

'Get him out of the road,' said he; and, clutching the man's collar with his free hand, my brother lugged him sideways. But he still clutched after his money, and regarded my brother fiercely, hammering at his arm with a handful of gold. 'Go on! Go on!' shouted angry voices behind. 'Way! Way!'

There was a smash as the pole of a carriage crashed into the cart that the man on horseback stopped. My brother looked up, and the man with the gold twisted his head round and bit the wrist that held his collar. There was a concussion, and the black horse came staggering sideways, and the cart-horse pushed beside it. A hoof missed my brother's foot by a hair's breadth. He released his grip on the fallen man and jumped back. He saw anger change to terror on the face of the poor wretch on the ground, and in a moment he was hidden and my brother was borne backward and carried past the entrance of the lane, and had to fight hard in the torrent to recover it.

He saw Miss Elphinstone covering her eyes, and a little child, with all a child's want of sympathetic imagination, staring with dilated eyes at a dusty something that lay black and still, ground and crushed under the rolling wheels. 'Let us go back!' he shouted, and began turning the pony round. 'We cannot cross this – hell,' he said; and they went back a hundred yards the way they had come, until the fighting crowd was hidden. As they passed the bend in the lane, my brother saw the face of the dying man in the ditch under the privet, deadly white and drawn, and shining with perspiration. The two women sat silent, crouching in their seats and shivering.

Then beyond the bend my brother stopped again. Miss Elphinstone was white and pale, and her sister-in-law sat weeping, too wretched even to call upon 'George'. My brother was horrified and perplexed. So soon as they had retreated, he realized how urgent and unavoidable it was to attempt this crossing. He turned to Miss Elphinstone suddenly, resolute.

'We must go that way,' he said, and led the pony round again.

For the second time that day this girl proved her quality. To force their way into the torrent of people, my brother plunged into the traffic and held back a cab-horse, while she drove the pony across its head. A wagon locked wheels for a moment, and ripped a long splinter from the chaise. In another moment they were caught and swept forward by the stream. My brother, with the cabman's whip-marks red across his face and hands, scrambled into the chaise, and took the reins from her.

'Point the revolver at the man behind,' he said giving it to her, 'if he presses us too hard. No! – point it at his horse.'

Then he began to look out for a chance of edging to the right across the road. But once in the stream, he seemed to lose volition,[15] to become a part of that dusty rout. They swept through Chipping Barnet with the torrent; they were nearly a mile beyond the centre of the town before they had fought across to the opposite side of the way. It was din and confusion indescribable; but in and beyond the town the road forks repeatedly, and this to some extent relieved the stress.

They struck eastward through Hadley, and there on either side of the road, and at another place farther on, they came upon a great multitude of people drinking at the stream, some fighting to come at the water. And farther on, from a hill near

---

[15]**volition**   will; ability to make a decision

East Barnet, they saw two trains running slowly one after the other without signal or order – trains swarming with people, with men even among the coals behind the engines – going northward along the Great Northern Railway. My brother supposes they must have filled outside London, for at that time the furious terror of the people had rendered the central termini impossible.

Near this place they halted for the rest of the afternoon, for the violence of the day had already utterly exhausted all three of them. They began to suffer the beginnings of hunger, the night was cold, and none of them dared to sleep. And in the evening many people came hurrying along the road near by their stopping-place, fleeing from unknown dangers before them and going in the direction from which my brother had come.

Further reading

Read chapter 17 of *The War of the Worlds* to find out what happens next in the story.

If you liked this, you might also like *The Time Machine* by H. G. Wells. Wells studied the science and technology of the day to make sure his stories were as grounded in fact as he could make them. In *The Time Machine* his central character is able to time-travel by the use of time as a fourth dimension, some years before Einstein published his own theories of space/time dimensions. *The Invisible Man* is another of Wells' science fiction adventures.

Activities

The Water Babies

Before you read

1   What do you think the job of a chimney sweep boy – a 'climbing boy' – involved? Note down your thoughts. You'll be able to compare your ideas with information given later on.

What's it about?

2   Draw a two-column table with the headings:
    What Tom did do   *What Tom didn't do*

    Use the first paragraph to help you find the information and write the details down under these two headings.

3   Write two sentences of your own describing Tom's life.

4   When Tom and Mr Grimes walked out of the town on their way to Harthover Place, what did Tom see? Make a list of those things and then describe them as if you are Tom. Try to show how different it all was for him.

5   Tom had never seen anything like the grand house and the little sleeping girl's bedroom. What do you think amazed him most? Choose three or four details and explain why they would have seemed so extraordinary.

Thinking about the text

6   Thomas Grimes, Tom's master, is a hard man. Pretend you are Tom: describe what it is like to work for him. Use the list you made in question 1 to help you, changing or adding details now you've read the text.

7   There are two worlds in this story: Tom's world; and the world of the little girl. How do they differ from each other? Choose and write down a quote that gives an example of each of the two different worlds. Draw two pictures with your quotes as captions.

8   The author wanted his readers to think about the real lives of climbing boys. Which word from the list below do you think best describe the reactions of Victorian readers? Explain why.

    angry   sad   indifferent

Around the World in Eighty Days

Before you read

1   Why was the voyage of the *Titanic* famous long before the ship sank? When was the first voyage in space? How long did it take Concorde to fly from London to New York? Share in class some of the most boundary-breaking travel stories you know about.

What's it about?

2   What has excited the members of the Reform Club that leads to the beginning of the whole adventure?

3   Stuart doubts that the journey-time for travelling around the world calculated in the *Morning Chronicle* is possible. In pairs, look at this calculation and reread the discussion between the men that follows. Then explain why Stuart may be right.

Thinking about the text

4   Fogg is calm, determined and unfazed by the prospect of the journey. He has a matter-of-fact style of speaking. In pairs, find the part where he informs Passepartout of the need to pack for the journey; act out the scene. Using Passepartout's characteristic style of speech, add one more thing that he might say to Fogg.

5   Trains and steamships made 19th-century travel the stuff of dreams. Imagine a Victorian child of the 1870s poring over a map of the world: write down what she or he might have longed to do.

How to Reach the Pole

Before you read

1   Look at the illustration below. What could go wrong? Write a list of the possible problems you think this plan could have.

What's it about?

2   Appoint a member of your class to be Commander Cheyne RN. Ask him to read out his plan, then use your list of potential problems to hot-seat him.

Thinking about the text

3   Imagine you are the person who is being asked to finance the plan. Write your response.

4   Commander Cheyne is one of many people who longed to reach the North and South Poles. Write about this particular dream as if you are the Commander: how far away the Pole is; the landscape; the climate; the adventure. Include not only the practical details but *why* you want to go. Your choice of language should be expressive as well as practical.

The proposed polar expedition – how to reach the north pole by balloons

Messages Without Wires

Before you read

1   Talk in class about how you communicate with your friends now (e.g. text-messaging, email, MSN). Try to imagine a time when writing letters was the only alternative to speaking face to face. Think about the advantages and disadvantages of both eras.

What's it about?

2   The first sentence of this account sounds unemotional. This is a scientist testing a theory using careful language and tone. But what do you think Marconi was feeling inside? Choose and copy out any three of the sentences in the account apart from the last one. Describe the emotions those steadily delivered words might be hiding.

3   The last sentence contains a phrase that might have been taken from a poem or a story: write it down and explain what it tells us about Marconi's excitement.

Thinking about the text

4   When people heard about Marconi's success, what do you think they thought? How was the world they knew about to change? Write down what families might have said to each other in their homes after reading the report in the newspapers. You could imagine a particular family with a relative living in another country. Write and act out your scenes in small groups.

A Lady's Life in the Rocky Mountains

Before you read

1   Anyone taking a trip to the Rocky Mountains in Victorian times would have had to prepare thoroughly. What do you think you would have to do? What would people advise you to do? What dangers do you think you might face? Discuss this in class.

What's it about?

2   While she likes to record the events of her days, Isabella Bird also records the beauty of the land: 'the pines, with their red stems, looked beautiful'. Find other examples.

3   The encounter with the bear was not a straightforward 'run for your life' moment. Write a paragraph explaining what was complicated about it.

Thinking about the text

4   'A story was current . . . ' You might think that this 'human body in a sack' story would have made Isabella Bird turn back. Tell this gruesome story as if you are the stable-owner and add some atmospheric detail. For example, 'The sun was going down when we heard the sound of hooves . . . '

5   Imagine you are Isabella, or a friend of hers. Explain the attraction of such a dangerous undertaking, especially for a woman in those times, and the reasons why you believe it is actually *less* dangerous than people may imagine.

The War of the Worlds

Before you read

1   In groups, talk about the films and books you've seen and read that have been about invasions from other worlds. Discuss the various plot lines and why this topic continues to excite readers and audiences.

What's it about?

2   Look at the descriptions of the total panic in London in the first paragraph: the 'roaring wave of fear' is one. Which others can you find? Write them down and search for others elsewhere in the chapter.

3   How did the narrator's brother find himself with 'a cut mouth, a bruised jaw and bloodstained knuckles'?

4   There is a huge crowd of people and vehicles that is growing bigger all the time. Describe the scene towards the end of the chapter through Miss Elphinstone's eyes.

Thinking about the text

5   'Invasion stories' were popular in Victorian times. They often used careful descriptions to make the stories seem more real. H. G. Wells remembered how he used to 'take his bicycle of an afternoon and note the houses and cottages and typical inhabitants to be destroyed after tea by the Heat Ray or smothered in red weed'.

    Test his method. Imagine this exodus from the place where you live. Like Wells, note down a list of details of houses, roads and people to make your description realistic. Then weave them into a description of one or more paragraphs.

6   Orson Welles, a famous film director, recast the story as a news programme on the radio on 30 October 1938, announcing the landing of Martians in America. It was so realistic that listeners fled their homes. Imagine you are a journalist writing a report for a radio news broadcast describing the invasion of London.

Compare and contrast

1   Tom's adventure in *The Water Babies* led him out of his working life as a chimney sweep and into another world: that of the upper classes. In 1842 a Royal Commission was set up to look into the working conditions of children of the working poor. You can read about it on page 125. Tom would have had a lot in common with the children working in the mines, the mills and the factories, but it would all have been unknown to the little sleeping girl.

Imagine that she entered *his* world by mistake. Write her story.

2   H. G. Wells played on his readers' excitement about other worlds and brought Martians to Earth. Mars was in the news in the 1890s: a light had been seen there and possibly patterns of canals. Might these be frightening evidence of other living beings?

If you could go round the world, if you could reach the North Pole, could you take humans to space? Look at Commander Cheyne's careful plans in *How to Reach the Pole*. Using his precise factual language and tone, prepare a Victorian expedition to Mars.

3   Marconi's astonishing breakthrough of 'messages without wires' scared people as well as thrilled them. *The Illustrated London News* reported him as having increased the means of naval warfare: 'a gunpowder magazine might be fired by electrical agency from a long distance'.

Fear, astonishment, anger and wonder are emotions that keep breaking through Victorian writing as the world changed. Find examples of these reactions in the texts in this section. Write them out and explain them.

4   Which of the writers of these texts would you have most liked to meet? What questions would you have liked to ask?

2 Childhood

The Victorians were among the first people to treat children as children rather than as little adults. They produced games and toys such as life-like doll's houses and lead soldiers. The greatest of children's classics were written then too: stories like *Alice's Adventures in Wonderland* by Lewis Carroll in 1865, R. L. Stevenson's *Treasure Island* in 1883, *Black Beauty* by Anna Sewell in 1877, to name just three. Children in homes where there were books and toys like the ones described above might be taught by a governess, or the boys might be sent away to boarding school. On page 95 you can read about Molly Hughes, who longed to go to school like her brothers – and did.

But what about the children of the poor? They might work hard from the age of three, or they might die young (you can read about this in the next section), or perhaps they had more benefits than some and went to ragged schools (see page 92). They wouldn't read *Treasure Island* and they wouldn't play with lead soldiers; they were lucky just to grow up.

Victorian mothers and fathers – especially fathers – in both rich and poor families believed in 'duty'. They expected a kind of obedience from their children and young people that we would find hard today. When you read this section, you may find yourself feeling that Victorian times are not just a century but a whole world away. Yet some of the feelings of love, expectation, anger, sadness and the need for action will probably seem very familiar.

Activities

1 Victorian children were often seen as obedient, quiet, punctual and well-mannered. Here is an example of how this information could be arranged as a spidergram:

Draw a spidergram using words to describe 21st-century children.

2 Make a list of some of the school rules that would be necessary to make sure Victorian children behaved well. Then write the list of rules that your school has in place today. What differences can you see?

3 Discuss the differences between Victorian and modern childhoods in class. How might they prepare you for different kinds of adulthood?

The Way of All Flesh

by Samuel Butler

Overton, a friend of the Pontifex family, makes a Sunday visit and witnesses something unexpected.

I was there on a Sunday, and observed the rigour[1] with which the young people were taught to observe the Sabbath;[2] they might not cut out things, nor use their paint-box on a Sunday, and this they thought rather hard, because their cousins the John Pontifexes might do these things. Their cousins might play with their toy train on Sunday, but though they had promised that they would run none but Sunday trains, all traffic had been prohibited. One treat only was allowed them – on Sunday evenings they might choose their own hymns.

[1]**rigour**   strictness
[2]**Sabbath**   the day of rest, in this case Sunday

In the course of the evening they came into the drawing room, and, as an especial treat, were to sing some of their hymns to me, instead of saying them, so that I might hear how nicely they sang. Ernest was to choose the first hymn, and he chose one about some people who were to come to the sunset tree. I am no botanist, and do not know what kind of tree a sunset tree is, but the words began, 'Come, come, come; come to the sunset tree for the day is past and gone.' The tune was rather pretty and had taken Ernest's fancy, for he was unusually fond of music and had a sweet little child's voice which he liked using.

He was, however, very late in being able to sound a hard 'c' or 'k,' and, instead of saying 'Come,' he said 'Tum, tum, tum.'

'Ernest,' said Theobald, from the arm-chair in front of the fire, where he was sitting with his hands folded before him, 'don't you think it would be very nice if you were to say "come" like other people, instead of "tum"?'

'I do say tum,' replied Ernest, meaning that he had said 'come.'

Theobald was always in a bad temper on Sunday evening. Whether it is that they are as much bored with the day as their neighbours, or whether they are tired, or whatever the cause may be, clergymen are seldom at their best on Sunday evening; I had already seen signs that evening that my host was cross; and was a little nervous at hearing Ernest say so promptly 'I do say tum,' when his papa had said he did not say it as he should.

Theobald noticed the fact that he was being contradicted in a moment. He got up from his arm-chair and went to the piano.

'No, Ernest, you don't,' he said, 'you say nothing of the kind, you say "tum," not "come." Now say "come" after me, as I do.'

'Tum,' said Ernest, at once; 'is that better?' I have no doubt he thought it was, but it was not.

'Now, Ernest, you are not taking pains; you are not trying as you ought to do. It is high time you learned to say "come," why, Joey can say "come," can't you, Joey?'

'Yeth, I can,' replied Joey; and he said something which was not far off 'come.'

'There, Ernest, do you hear that? There's no difficulty about it, nor shadow of difficulty. Now, take your own time, think about it, and say "come" after me.'

The boy remained silent a few seconds and then said 'tum' again.

I laughed, but Theobald turned to me impatiently and said, 'Please do not laugh, Overton; it will make the boy think it does not matter; and it matters a great deal;' then turning to Ernest he said, 'Now, Ernest, I will give you one more chance, and if you don't say "come," I shall know that you are self-willed and naughty.'

He looked very angry, and a shade came over Ernest's face, like that which comes upon the face of a puppy when it is being scolded without understanding why. The child saw well what was coming now, was frightened, and, of course, said 'tum' once more.

'Very well, Ernest,' said his father, catching him angrily by the shoulder. 'I have done my best to save you, but if you will have it so, you will,' and he lugged the little wretch, crying by anticipation, out of the room. A few minutes more and we could hear screams coming from the dining-room, across the hall which separated the drawing-room from the dining-room, and knew that poor Ernest was being beaten.

'I have sent him up to bed,' said Theobald, as he returned to the drawing-room, 'and now, Christina, I think we will have the servants in to prayers,' and he rang the bell for them, red-handed as he was.

Further reading

Chapter 23 of *The Way of All Flesh* will tell you what happened afterwards, and the next few chapters are about Ernest and his life at school. Samuel Butler was reflecting his cheerless childhood as the son of a clergyman in a strictly religious household. He had very outspoken views about childhood and religion.

During the 1860s and 1870s, there were many arguments about the place of religion in society because Charles Darwin had written his theory of the 'survival of the fittest', casting doubt on the generally accepted idea that God had created everything simply 'in one go'. Darwin found himself no longer welcome in society and Butler enjoyed joining in this massive debate.

Another book by Butler to try is *Erewhon* (an anagram of 'nowhere'), which is a satirical look at Victorian society.

The Adventures of Huckleberry Finn
by Mark Twain

Huck is 13. He's a clever lad, but uneducated, and loves to run wild with his good friend, Tom Sawyer. He's been adopted by the kindly Widow Douglas, who does her best to 'sivilize' him. Everything is going as well as can be expected until his father, the local drunk, turns up . . .

I had shut the door to. Then I turned around, and there he was. I used to be scared of him all the time, he tanned me so much. I reckoned I was scared now, too; but in a minute I see I was mistaken. That is, after the first jolt, as you may say, when my breath sort of hitched – he being so unexpected; but right away after, I see I warn't scared of him worth bothering about.

He was most fifty, and he looked it. His hair was long and tangled and greasy, and hung down, and you could see his eyes shining through like he was behind vines. It was all black, no gray: so was his long, mixed-up whiskers. There warn't no color in his face, where his face showed; it was white; not like another man's white, but a white to make a body sick, a white to make a body's flesh crawl – a tree-toad white, a fish-belly white. As for his clothes – just rags, that was all. He had one ankle resting on t'other knee; the boot on that foot was busted, and two of his toes stuck through, and he worked them now and then. His hat was laying on the floor; an old black slouch[1] with the top caved in, like a lid.

I stood a-looking at him; he sat there a-looking at me, with his chair tilted back a little. I set the candle down. I noticed the window was up; so he had clumb in by the shed. He kept a-looking me all over. By-and-by he says:

'Starchy clothes – very. You think you're a good deal of a big-bug, *don't* you?'

---

[1]**slouch**   a hat with a big brim you can pull down over your ears

'Maybe I am, maybe I ain't,' I says.

'Don't you give me none o' your lip,' says he. 'You've put on considerble many frills since I been away. I'll take you down a peg before I get done with you. You're educated, too, they say; can read and write. You think you're better'n your father, now, don't you, because he can't? I'll take it out of you. Who told you you might meddle with such hifalut'n foolishness, hey? – who told you you could?'

'The widow. She told me.'

'The widow, hey? – and who told the widow she could put in her shovel about a thing that ain't none of her business?'

'Nobody never told her.'

'Well, I'll learn her how to meddle. And looky here – you drop that school, you hear? I'll learn people to bring up a boy to put on airs over his own father and let on to be better'n what *he* is. You lemme catch you fooling around that school again, you hear? Your mother couldn't read, and she couldn't write, nuther, before she died. None of the family couldn't, before *they* died. *I* can't; and here you're a-swelling yourself up like this. I ain't the man to stand it – you hear? Say – lemme hear you read.'

I took up a book and begun something about General Washington[2] and the wars. When I'd read about a half a minute, he fetched the book a whack with his hand and knocked it across the house. He says:

'It's so. You can do it. I had my doubts when you told me. Now looky here; you stop that putting on frills. I won't have it. I'll lay for you, my smarty; and if I catch you about that school I'll tan you good. First you know you'll get religion, too. I never see such a son.'

He took up a little blue and yaller picture of some cows and a boy, and says:

'What's this?'

'It's something they give me for learning my lessons good.'

He tore it up, and says –

---

[2]**General Washington**   first president of the USA, 1789–97

'I'll give you something better – I'll give you a cowhide.'

He set there a-mumbling and a-growling a minute, and then he says –

'*Ain't* you a sweet-scented dandy,³ though? A bed; and bed-clothes; and a look'n-glass; and a piece of carpet on the floor – and your own father got to sleep with the hogs in the tanyard. I never see such a son. I bet I'll take some o' these frills out o' you before I'm done with you. Why there ain't no end to your airs – they say you're rich. Hey? – how's that?'

'They lie – that's how.'

'Looky here – mind how you talk to me; I'm a-standing about all I can stand, now – so don't gimme no sass. I've been in town two days, and I hain't heard nothing but about you bein' rich. I heard about it away down the river, too. That's why I come. You git me that money to-morrow – I want it.'

'I hain't got no money.'

'It's a lie. Judge Thatcher's got it. You got it. I want it.'

'I hain't got no money, I tell you. You ask Judge Thatcher; he'll tell you the same.'

'All right. I'll ask him; and I'll make him pungle,⁴ too, or I'll know the reason why. Say – how much you got in your pocket? I want it.'

'I hain't got only a dollar, and I want that to – '

'It don't make no difference what you want it for – you just shell it out.'

He took it and bit it to see if it was good, and then he said he was going down town to get some whisky; said he hadn't had a drink all day. When he had got out of the shed, he put his head in again, and cussed me for putting on frills and trying to be better than him; and when I reckoned he was gone, he come back and put his head in again, and told me to mind about that school, because he was going to lay for me and lick⁵ me if I didn't drop that.

---

³**dandy**   a man who likes to dress in expensive, fashionable clothes and is very interested in his own appearance

⁴**pungle**   pay

⁵**lick**   beat

Next day he was drunk, and he went to Judge Thatcher's and bullyragged him and tried to make him give up the money, but he couldn't, and then he swore he'd make the law force him.

The judge and the widow went to law to get the court to take me away from him and let one of them be my guardian; but it was a new judge that had just come, and he didn't know the old man: so he said courts mustn't interfere and separate families if they could help it; said he'd druther not take a child away from its father. So Judge Thatcher and the widow had to quit on the business.

That pleased the old man till he couldn't rest. He said he'd cowhide me till I was black and blue if I didn't raise some money for him. I borrowed three dollars from Judge Thatcher, and pap took it and got drunk and went a-blowing around and cussing and whooping and carrying on; and he kept it up all over town, with a tin pan, till most midnight; then they jailed him, and next day they had him before court, and jailed him again for a week. But he said *he* was satisfied; said he was boss of his son, and he'd make it warm for *him*.

When he got out the new judge said he was agoing to make a man of him. So he took him to his own house, and dressed him up clean and nice, and had him to breakfast and dinner and supper with the family, and was just old pie to him, so to speak. And after supper he talked to him about temperance[6] and such things till the old man cried, and said he'd been a fool, and fooled away his life; but now he was agoing to turn over a new leaf and be a man nobody wouldn't be ashamed of, and he hoped the judge would help him and not look down on him. The judge said he could hug him for them words; so *he* cried, and his wife she cried again; pap said he'd been a man that had always been misunderstood before, and the judge said he believed it. The old man said that what a man wanted that was down, was sympathy; and the judge said it was so; so they cried again. And when it was bedtime, the old man rose up and held out his hand, and says:

---

[6]**temperance**   giving up drink

'Look at it, gentlemen, and ladies all; take ahold of it; shake it. There's a hand that was the hand of a hog; but it ain't so no more; it's the hand of a man that's started in on a new life, and 'll die before he'll go back. You mark them words – don't forget I said them. It's a clean hand now; shake it – don't be afeard.'

So they shook it, one after the other, all around, and cried. The judge's wife she kissed it. Then the old man he signed a pledge – made his mark. The judge said it was the holiest time on record, or something like that. Then they tucked the old man into a beautiful room, which was the spare room, and in the night sometime he got powerful thirsty and clumb out onto the porch-roof and slid down a stanchion[7] and traded his new coat for a jug of forty-rod,[8] and clumb back again and had a good old time; and towards daylight he crawled out again, drunk as a fiddler, and rolled off the porch and broke his left arm in two places and was most froze to death when somebody found him after sun-up. And when they come to look at that spare room, they had to take soundings before they could navigate it.

The judge he felt kind of sore. He said he reckoned a body could reform the ole man with a shot-gun, maybe, but he didn't know no other way.

Further reading

Chapter 6 of *The Adventures of Huckleberry Finn* will tell you what happens next. You could also try *The Adventures of Tom Sawyer*, which Mark Twain wrote first. Both boys figure as main characters in the stories, which are set against a background of slavery in the Deep South. Another book of the times with slavery at its heart is *Uncle Tom's Cabin* by Harriet Beecher Stowe, although this is a very different one. It's interesting to read as a period piece, but it's considered by many people to be unintentionally racist, as Beecher Stowe worked within, rather than beyond, the language and ideas of the age.

---

[7]**stanchion**   a post
[8]**forty-rod**   a whisky powerful enough to throw a person off his/her feet a distance of forty rods (about 200 yards)

David Copperfield

by Charles Dickens

> Mr Murdstone has become David Copperfield's stepfather and David has arrived home after a short holiday to find life utterly changed. His gentle mother, Clara, stays downstairs. The kindly servant, Peggotty, is told to leave the room. David faces Mr Murdstone with fear.

When we two were left alone, he shut the door, and sitting on a chair, and holding me standing before him, looked steadily into my eyes. I felt my own attracted, no less steadily, to his. As I recall our being opposed thus, face to face, I seem again to hear my heart beat fast and high.

'David,' he said, making his lips thin, by pressing them together, 'if I have an obstinate horse or dog to deal with, what do you think I do?'

'I don't know.'

'I beat him.'

I had answered in a kind of breathless whisper, but I felt, in my silence, that my breath was shorter now.

'I make him wince, and smart. I say to myself, "I'll conquer that fellow;" and if it were to cost him all the blood he had, I should do it. What is that upon your face?'

'Dirt,' I said.

He knew it was the mark of tears as well as I. But if he had asked the question twenty times, each time with twenty blows, I believe my baby heart would have burst before I would have told him so.

'You have a good deal of intelligence for a little fellow,' he said, with a grave smile that belonged to him, 'and you understood me very well, I see. Wash that face, sir, and come down with me.'

He pointed to the washing-stand, which I had made out to be like Mrs Gummidge, and motioned me with his head to obey him directly. I had little doubt then, and I have less doubt now, that he would have knocked me down without the least compunction, if I had hesitated.

'Clara, my dear,' he said, when I had done his bidding, and he walked me into the parlour, with his hand still on my arm; 'you will not be made uncomfortable any more, I hope. We shall soon improve our youthful humours.'

God help me, I might have been improved for my whole life, I might have been made another creature perhaps, for life, by a kind word at that season. A word of encouragement and explanation, of pity for my childish ignorance, of welcome home, of reassurance to me that it *was* home, might have made me dutiful to him in my heart henceforth, instead of in my hypocritical outside, and might have made me respect instead of hate him. I thought my mother was sorry to see me standing in the room so scared and strange, and that, presently, when I stole to a chair, she followed me with her eyes more sorrowfully still – missing, perhaps, some freedom in my childish tread – but the word was not spoken, and the time for it was gone.

We dined alone, we three together. He seemed to be very fond of my mother – I am afraid I liked him none the better for that – and she was very fond of him. I gathered from what they said, that an elder sister of his was coming to stay with them, and that she was expected that evening. I am not certain whether I found out then or afterwards, that, without being actively concerned in any business, he had some share in, or some annual charge upon the profits of, a wine-merchant's house in London, with which his family had been connected from his great-grandfather's time, and in which his sister had a similar interest; but I may mention it in this place, whether or no.

After dinner, when we were sitting by the fire, and I was meditating an escape to Peggotty without having the hardihood to slip away, lest it should offend the master of the house, a coach drove up to the garden-gate, and he went out to receive the visitor. My mother followed him. I was timidly following her, when she turned round at the parlour-door, in the dusk, and taking me in her embrace as she had been used to do, whispered me to love my new father and be obedient to him. She did this hurriedly and secretly, as if it were wrong, but tenderly; and, putting out her hand behind her, held mine in it, until we came near to where he was standing in the garden, where she let mine go, and drew hers through his arm.

It was Miss Murdstone who was arrived, and a gloomy-looking lady she was; dark, like her brother, whom she greatly resembled in face and voice; and with very heavy eyebrows, nearly meeting over her large nose, as if, being disabled by the wrongs of her sex from wearing whiskers, she had carried them to that account. She brought with her two uncompromising hard black boxes,[1] with her initials on the lids in hard brass nails. When she paid the coachman she took her money out of

---

[1] **boxes**   travel-cases

a hard steel purse, and she kept the purse in a very jail of a bag which hung upon her arm by a heavy chain, and shut up like a bite. I had never, at that time, seen such a metallic lady altogether as Miss Murdstone was.

She was brought into the parlour with many tokens of welcome, and there formally recognised my mother as a new and near relation. Then she looked at me, and said:

'Is that your boy, sister-in-law?'

My mother acknowledged me.

'Generally speaking,' said Miss Murdstone, 'I don't like boys. How d'ye do, boy?'

Under these encouraging circumstances, I replied that I was very well, and that I hoped she was the same; with such an indifferent grace, that Miss Murdstone disposed of me in two words:

'Wants manners!'

Having uttered which with great distinctness, she begged the favour of being shown to her room, which became to me from that time forth a place of awe and dread, wherein the two black boxes were never seen open or known to be left unlocked, and where (for I peeped in once or twice when she was out) numerous little steel fetters and rivets, with which Miss Murdstone embellished herself when she was dressed, generally hung upon the looking-glass in formidable array.

As well as I could make out, she had come for good, and had no intention of ever going again. She began to 'help' my mother next morning, and was in and out of the store-closet all day, putting things to rights, and making havoc in the old arrangements. Almost the first remarkable thing I observed in Miss Murdstone was her being constantly haunted by a suspicion that the servants had a man secreted somewhere on the premises. Under the influence of this delusion, she dived into the coal-cellar at the most untimely hours, and scarcely ever opened the door of a dark cupboard without clapping it to again, in the belief that she had got him.

Though there was nothing very airy about Miss Murdstone, she was a perfect Lark in point of getting up. She was up (and, as I believe to this hour, looking for that man) before anybody in the house was stirring. Peggotty gave it as her opinion that she even slept with one eye open; but I could not concur in this idea; for I tried it myself after hearing the suggestion thrown out, and found it couldn't be done.

On the very first morning after her arrival she was up and ringing her bell at cock-crow. When my mother came down to breakfast and was going to make the tea, Miss Murdstone gave her a kind of peck on the cheek, which was her nearest approach to a kiss, and said:

'Now, Clara, my dear, I am come here, you know, to relieve you of all the trouble I can. You're much too pretty and thoughtless' – my mother blushed but laughed, and seemed not to dislike this character – 'to have any duties imposed upon you that can be undertaken by me. If you'll be so good as to give me your keys, my dear, I'll attend to all this sort of thing in future.'

From that time, Miss Murdstone kept the keys in her own little jail all day, and under her pillow all night, and my mother had no more to do with them than I had.

My mother did not suffer her authority to pass from her without a shadow of protest. One night when Miss Murdstone had been developing certain household plans to her brother, of which he signified his approbation,[2] my mother suddenly began to cry, and said she thought she might have been consulted.

'Clara!' said Mr Murdstone sternly. 'Clara! I wonder at you.'

'Oh, it's very well to say you wonder, Edward!' cried my mother, 'and it's very well for you to talk about firmness, but you wouldn't like it yourself.'

Firmness, I may observe, was the grand quality on which both Mr and Miss Murdstone took their stand. However I might

---

[2]**signified his approbation**   showed approval

have expressed my comprehension of it at that time, if I had been called upon, I nevertheless did clearly comprehend in my own way, that it was another name for tyranny; and for a certain gloomy, arrogant, devil's humour, that was in them both. The creed, as I should state it now, was this. Mr Murdstone was firm; nobody in his world was to be so firm as Mr Murdstone; nobody else in his world was to be firm at all, for everybody was to be bent to his firmness. Miss Murdstone was an exception. She might be firm, but only by relationship, and in an inferior and tributary³ degree. My mother was another exception. She might be firm, and must be; but only in bearing their firmness, and firmly believing there was no other firmness upon earth.

'It's very hard,' said my mother, 'that in my own house – '

'*My* own house?' repeated Mr Murdstone. 'Clara!'

'*Our* own house, I mean,' faltered my mother, evidently frightened – 'I hope you must know what I mean, Edward – it's very hard that in *your* own house I may not have a word to say about domestic matters. I am sure I managed very well before we were married. There's evidence,' said my mother sobbing; 'ask Peggotty if I didn't do very well when I wasn't interfered with!'

'Edward,' said Miss Murdstone, 'let there be an end of this. I go to-morrow.'

'Jane Murdstone,' said her brother, 'be silent! How dare you to insinuate that you don't know my character better than your words imply?'

'I am sure,' my poor mother went on at a grievous disadvantage, and with many tears, 'I don't want anybody to go. I should be very miserable and unhappy if anybody was to go. I don't ask much. I am not unreasonable. I only want to be consulted sometimes. I am very much obliged to anybody who assists me, and I only want to be consulted as a mere form, sometimes. I thought you were pleased, once, with my being a

---

³**tributary** a stream that leads into another one: Miss Murdstone's firmness feeds into her brother's

little inexperienced and girlish, Edward – I am sure you said so – but you seem to hate me for it now, you are so severe.'

'Edward,' said Miss Murdstone, again, 'let there be an end of this. I go to-morrow.'

'Jane Murdstone,' thundered Mr Murdstone. 'Will you be silent? How dare you?'

Miss Murdstone made a jail-delivery of her pocket-hand-kerchief, and held it before her eyes.

'Clara,' he continued, looking at my mother, 'you surprise me! You astound me! Yes, I had a satisfaction in the thought of marrying an inexperienced and artless person, and forming her character, and infusing into it some amount of that firmness and decision of which it stood in need. But when Jane Murdstone is kind enough to come to my assistance in this endeavour, and to assume, for my sake, a condition something like a housekeeper's, and when she meets with a base return – '

'Oh, pray, pray, Edward,' cried my mother, 'don't accuse me of being ungrateful. I am sure I am not ungrateful. No one ever said I was before. I have many faults, but not that. Oh, don't, my dear!'

'When Jane Murdstone meets, I say,' he went on, after waiting until my mother was silent, 'with a base return, that feeling of mine is chilled and altered.'

'Don't, my love, say that!' implored my mother very piteously. 'Oh, don't, Edward! I can't bear to hear it. Whatever I am, I am affectionate. I know I am affectionate. I wouldn't say it, if I wasn't sure that I am. Ask Peggotty. I am sure she'll tell you I'm affectionate.'

'There is no extent of mere weakness, Clara,' said Mr Murdstone in reply, 'that can have the least weight with me. You lose breath.'

'Pray let us be friends,' said my mother, 'I couldn't live under coldness or unkindness. I am so sorry. I have a great many defects, I know, and it's very good of you, Edward, with your strength of mind, to endeavour to correct them for me. Jane, I don't object to anything. I should be quite broken-hearted if you thought of leaving – ' My mother was too much overcome to go on.

'Jane Murdstone,' said Mr Murdstone to his sister, 'any harsh words between us are, I hope, uncommon. It is not my fault that so unusual an occurrence has taken place to-night. I was betrayed into it by another. Nor is it your fault. You were betrayed into it by another. Let us both try to forget it. And as this,' he added, after these magnanimous⁴ words, 'is not a fit scene for the boy – David, go to bed!'

I could hardly find the door, through the tears that stood in my eyes. I was so sorry for my mother's distress; but I groped my way out, and groped my way up to my room in the dark, without even having the heart to say good night to Peggotty, or to get a candle from her. When her coming up to look for me, an hour or so afterwards, awoke me, she said that my mother had gone to bed poorly, and that Mr and Miss Murdstone were sitting alone.

Going down next morning rather earlier than usual, I paused outside the parlour-door, on hearing my mother's voice. She was very earnestly and humbly entreating Miss Murdstone's pardon, which that lady granted, and a perfect reconciliation took place. I never knew my mother afterwards to give an opinion on any matter, without first appealing to Miss Murdstone, or without having first ascertained by some sure means, what Miss Murdstone's opinion was; and I never saw Miss Murdstone, when out of temper (she was infirm that way), move her hand towards her bag as if she were going to take out the keys and offer to resign them to my mother, without seeing that my mother was in a terrible fright.

The gloomy taint that was in the Murdstone blood darkened the Murdstone religion, which was austere and wrathful. I have thought, since, that its assuming that character was a necessary consequence of Mr Murdstone's firmness, which wouldn't allow him to let anybody off from the utmost weight of the severest penalties he could find any excuse for. Be this as it may,

---

⁴**magnanimous** generous

I well remember the tremendous visages[5] with which we used to go to church, and the changed air of the place. Again the dreaded Sunday comes round, and I file into the old pew first, like a guarded captive brought to a condemned service. Again, Miss Murdstone, in a black velvet gown, that looks as if it had been made out of a pall,[6] follows close upon me; then my mother; then her husband. There is no Peggotty now, as in the old time. Again, I listen to Miss Murdstone mumbling the responses, and emphasising all the dread words with a cruel relish. Again, I see her dark eyes roll round the church when she says 'miserable sinners,' as if she were calling all the congregation names. Again, I catch rare glimpses of my mother, moving her lips timidly between the two, with one of them muttering at each ear like low thunder. Again, I wonder with a sudden fear whether it is likely that our good old clergyman can be wrong, and Mr and Miss Murdstone right, and that all the angels in Heaven can be destroying angels. Again, if I move a finger or relax a muscle of my face, Miss Murdstone pokes me with her prayer-book, and makes my side ache.

Yes, and again, as we walk home, I note some neighbours looking at my mother and at me, and whispering. Again, as the three go on arm-in-arm, and I linger behind alone, I follow some of those looks, and wonder if my mother's step be really not so light as I have seen it, and if the gaiety of her beauty be really almost worried away. Again, I wonder whether any of the neighbours call to mind, as I do, how we used to walk home together, she and I; and I wonder stupidly about that, all the dreary, dismal day.

There had been some talk on occasions of my going to boarding-school. Mr and Miss Murdstone had originated it, and my mother had of course agreed with them. Nothing, however, was concluded on the subject yet. In the meantime I learnt lessons at home.

---

[5]**visages**   faces
[6]**pall**   a cloth covering a coffin

Shall I ever forget those lessons! They were presided over nominally[7] by my mother, but really by Mr Murdstone and his sister, who were always present, and found them a favourable occasion for giving my mother lessons in that miscalled firmness, which was the bane of both our lives. I believe I was kept at home for that purpose. I had been apt enough to learn, and willing enough, when my mother and I had lived alone together. I can faintly remember learning the alphabet at her knee. To this day, when I look upon the fat black letters in the primer, the puzzling novelty of their shapes, and the easy good-nature of O and Q and S, seem to present themselves again before me as they used to do. But they recall no feeling of disgust or reluctance. On the contrary, I seem to have walked along a path of flowers as far as the crocodile-book, and to have been cheered by the gentleness of my mother's voice and manner all the way. But these solemn lessons which succeeded those, I remember as the death-blow at my peace, and a grievous daily drudgery and misery. They were very long, very numerous, very hard – perfectly unintelligible, some of them, to me – and I was generally as much bewildered by them as I believe my poor mother was herself.

Let me remember how it used to be, and bring one morning back again.

I come into the second-best parlour after breakfast, with my books, and an exercise-book, and a slate. My mother is ready for me at her writing-desk, but not half so ready as Mr Murdstone in his easy-chair by the window (though he pretends to be reading a book), or as Miss Murdstone, sitting near my mother stringing steel beads. The very sight of these two has such an influence over me, that I begin to feel the words I have been at infinite pains to get into my head, all sliding away, and going I don't know where. I wonder where they *do go*, by-the-by?

---

[7]**nominally**   in name only

I hand the first book to my mother. Perhaps it is a grammar, perhaps a history or geography. I take a last drowning look at the page as I give it into her hand, and start off aloud at a racing pace while I have got it fresh. I trip over a word. Mr Murdstone looks up. I trip over another word. Miss Murdstone looks up. I redden, tumble over half-a-dozen words, and stop. I think my mother would show me the book if she dared, but she does not dare, and she says softly:

'Oh, Davy, Davy!'

'Now, Clara,' says Mr Murdstone, 'be firm with the boy. Don't say, "Oh, Davy, Davy!" That's childish. He knows his lesson, or he does not know it.'

'He does *not* know it,' Miss Murdstone interposes awfully.

'I am really afraid he does not,' says my mother.

'Then, you see, Clara,' returns Miss Murdstone, 'you should just give him the book back, and make him know it.'

'Yes, certainly,' says my mother; 'that is what I intend to do, my dear Jane. Now, Davy, try once more, and don't be stupid.'

I obey the first clause of the injunction by trying once more, but am not so successful with the second, for I am very stupid. I tumble down before I get to the old place, at a point where I was all right before, and stop to think. But I can't think about the lesson. I think of the number of yards of net in Miss Murdstone's cap, or of the price of Mr Murdstone's dressing-gown, or any such ridiculous problem that I have no business with, and don't want to have anything at all to do with. Mr Murdstone makes a movement of impatience which I have been expecting for a long time. Miss Murdstone does the same. My mother glances submissively at them, shuts the book, and lays it by as an arrear to be worked out when my other tasks are done.

There is a pile of these arrears very soon, and it swells like a rolling snowball. The bigger it gets, the more stupid *I* get. The case is so hopeless, and I feel that I am wallowing in such a bog of nonsense, that I give up all idea of getting out, and abandon myself to my fate. The despairing way in which my mother and

I look at each other, as I blunder on, is truly melancholy. But the greatest effect in these miserable lessons is when my mother (thinking nobody is observing her) tries to give me the cue by the motion of her lips. At that instant, Miss Murdstone, who has been lying in wait for nothing else all along, says in a deep warning voice:

'Clara!'

My mother starts, colours, and smiles faintly. Mr Murdstone comes out of his chair, takes the book, throws it at me or boxes my ears with it, and turns me out of the room by the shoulders.

Even when the lessons are done, the worst is yet to happen, in the shape of an appalling sum. This is invented for me, and delivered to me orally by Mr Murdstone, and begins, 'If I go into a cheesemonger's shop, and buy five thousand double-Gloucester cheeses at fourpence-halfpenny each, present payment' – at which I see Miss Murdstone secretly overjoyed. I pore over these cheeses without any result or enlightenment until dinner-time, when, having made a Mulatto[8] of myself by getting the dirt of the slate into the pores of my skin, I have a slice of bread to help me out with the cheeses, and am considered in disgrace for the rest of the evening.

It seems to me, at this distance of time, as if my unfortunate studies generally took this course. I could have done very well if I had been without the Murdstones; but the influence of the Murdstones upon me was like the fascination of two snakes on a wretched young bird. Even when I did get through the morning with tolerable credit, there was not much gained but dinner; for Miss Murdstone never could endure to see me untasked, and if I rashly made any show of being unemployed, called her brother's attention to me by saying, 'Clara, my dear, there's nothing like work – give your boy an exercise;' which caused me to be clapped down to some new labour there and

---

[8] **mulatto**   light brown; originally a 16th-century Spanish word for a person of mixed race

then. As to any recreation with other children of my age, I had very little of that; for the gloomy theology of the Murdstones made all children out to be a swarm of little vipers (though there *was* a child once set in the midst of the Disciples), and held that they contaminated one another.

The natural result of this treatment, continued, I suppose, for some six months or more, was to make me sullen, dull, and dogged. I was not made the less so by my sense of being daily more and more shut out and alienated from my mother. I believe I should have been almost stupefied but for one circumstance.

It was this. My father had left a small collection of books in a little room up-stairs, to which I had access (for it adjoined my own) and which nobody else in our house ever troubled. From that blessed little room, Roderick Random, Peregrine Pickle, Humphrey Clinker, Tom Jones, the Vicar of Wakefield, Don Quixote, Gil Blas, and Robinson Crusoe, came out, a glorious host, to keep me company. They kept alive my fancy, and my hope of something beyond that place and time, – they, and the Arabian Nights, and the Tales of the Genii, – and did me no harm; for whatever harm was in some of them was not there for me; *I* knew nothing of it. It is astonishing to me now, how I found time, in the midst of my porings and blunderings over heavier themes, to read those books as I did. It is curious to me how I could ever have consoled myself under my small troubles (which were great troubles to me), by impersonating my favourite characters in them – as I did – and by putting Mr and Miss Murdstone into all the bad ones – which I did too. I have been Tom Jones (a child's Tom Jones, a harmless creature) for a week together. I have sustained my own idea of Roderick Random for a month at a stretch, I verily believe. I had a greedy relish for a few volumes of Voyages and Travels – I forget what, now – that were on those shelves; and for days and days I can remember to have gone about my region of our house, armed with the centre-piece out of an old set of boot-trees – the perfect realisation of Captain Somebody, of the Royal British Navy, in danger of being beset by savages, and resolved to sell his life at a great price. The Captain never lost dignity, from having his ears boxed with the Latin Grammar. I did; but the Captain was a Captain and a hero, in despite of all the grammars of all the languages in the world, dead or alive.

This was my only and my constant comfort. When I think of it, the picture always rises in my mind, of a summer evening, the boys at play in the churchyard, and I sitting on my bed, reading as if for life. Every barn in the neighbourhood, every stone in the church, and every foot of the churchyard, had some association of its own, in my mind, connected with these books, and stood for some locality made famous in them. I have seen Tom Pipes go climbing up the church-steeple; I have watched Strap, with the knapsack on his back, stopping to rest himself upon the wicket-gate; and I *know* that Commodore Trunnion held that club with Mr Pickle, in the parlour of our little village alehouse.

The reader now understands, as well as I do, what I was when I came to that point of my youthful history to which I am now coming again.

One morning when I went into the parlour with my books, I found my mother looking anxious, Miss Murdstone looking firm, and Mr Murdstone binding something round the bottom of a cane – a lithe and limber cane, which he left off binding when I came in, and poised and switched in the air.

'I tell you, Clara,' said Mr Murdstone, 'I have been often flogged myself.'

'To be sure; of course,' said Miss Murdstone.

'Certainly, my dear Jane,' faltered my mother, meekly. 'But – but do you think it did Edward good?'

'Do you think it did Edward harm, Clara?' asked Mr Murdstone, gravely.

'That's the point,' said his sister.

To this my mother returned, 'Certainly, my dear Jane,' and said no more.

I felt apprehensive that I was personally interested in this dialogue, and sought Mr Murdstone's eye as it lighted on mine.

'Now, David,' he said – and I saw that cast again as he said it – 'you must be far more careful today than usual.' He gave the cane another poise, and another switch; and having finished his preparation of it, laid it down beside him, with an impressive look, and took up his book.

This was a good freshener to my presence of mind, as a beginning. I felt the words of my lessons slipping off, not one by one, or line by line, but by the entire page; I tried to lay hold of them; but they seemed, if I may so express it, to have put skates on, and to skim away from me with a smoothness there was no checking.

We began badly, and went on worse. I had come in with an idea of distinguishing myself rather, conceiving that I was very well prepared; but it turned out to be quite a mistake. Book after book was added to the heap of failures, Miss Murdstone being firmly watchful of us all the time. And when we came at last to the five thousand cheeses (canes he made it that day, I remember), my mother burst out crying.

'Clara!' said Miss Murdstone, in her warning voice.

'I am not quite well, my dear Jane, I think,' said my mother.

I saw him wink, solemnly, at his sister, as he rose and said, taking up the cane:

'Why, Jane, we can hardly expect Clara to bear, with perfect firmness, the worry and torment that David has occasioned her to-day. That would be stoical.[9] Clara is greatly strengthened and improved, but we can hardly expect so much from her. David, you and I will go up-stairs, boy.'

As he took me out at the door, my mother ran towards us. Miss Murdstone said, 'Clara! are you a perfect fool?' and interfered. I saw my mother stop her ears then, and I heard her crying.

He walked me up to my room slowly and gravely – I am certain he had a delight in that formal parade of executing justice – and when we got there, suddenly twisted my head under his arm.

---

[9]**stoical**   resigned; submitting to your destiny, determined not to show your pain or your feelings

'Mr Murdstone! Sir!' I cried to him. 'Don't! Pray don't beat me! I have tried to learn, sir, but I can't learn while you and Miss Murdstone are by. I can't indeed!'

'Can't you, indeed, David?' he said. 'We'll try that.'

He had my head as in a vice, but I twined round him some-how, and stopped him for a moment, entreating him not to beat me. It was only for a moment that I stopped him, for he cut me heavily an instant afterwards, and in the same instant I caught the hand with which he held me in my mouth, between my teeth, and bit it through. It sets my teeth on edge to think of it.

He beat me then as if he would have beaten me to death. Above all the noise we made, I heard them running up the stairs, and crying out – I heard my mother crying out – and Peggotty. Then he was gone; and the door was locked outside; and I was lying, fevered and hot, and torn, and sore, and raging in my puny way, upon the floor.

How well I recollect, when I became quiet, what an unnat-ural stillness seemed to reign through the whole house! How well I remember, when my smart and passion began to cool, how wicked I began to feel!

I sat listening for a long while, but there was not a sound. I crawled up from the floor, and saw my face in the glass, so swollen, red, and ugly that it almost frightened me. My stripes were sore and stiff, and made me cry afresh, when I moved; but they were nothing to the guilt I felt. It lay heavier on my breast than if I had been a most atrocious criminal, I dare say.

It had begun to grow dark, and I had shut the window (I had been lying, for the most part, with my head upon the sill, by turns crying, dozing, and looking listlessly out), when the key was turned, and Miss Murdstone came in with some bread and meat, and milk. These she put down upon the table with-out a word, glaring at me the while with exemplary firmness, and then retired, locking the door after her.

Long after it was dark I sat there, wondering whether any-body else would come. When this appeared improbable for that night, I undressed, and went to bed; and there, I began to wonder fearfully what would be done to me. Whether it was a criminal act that I had committed? Whether I should be taken into custody, and sent to prison? Whether I was at all in danger of being hanged?

I never shall forget the waking next morning; the being cheerful and fresh for the first moment, and then the being weighed down by the stale and dismal oppression of remembrance. Miss Murdstone reappeared before I was out of bed; told me, in so many words, that I was free to walk in the garden for half an hour and no longer; and retired, leaving the door open, that I might avail myself of that permission.

I did so, and did so every morning of my imprisonment, which lasted five days. If I could have seen my mother alone, I should have gone down on my knees to her and besought her forgiveness; but I saw no one, Miss Murdstone excepted, during the whole time – except at evening prayers in the parlour; to which I was escorted by Miss Murdstone after everybody else was placed; where I was stationed, a young outlaw, all alone by myself near the door; and whence I was solemnly conducted by my jailer, before any one arose from the devotional posture. I only observed that my mother was as far off from me as she could be, and kept her face another way, so that I never saw it; and that Mr Murdstone's hand was bound up in a large linen wrapper.

The length of those five days I can convey no idea of to any one. They occupy the place of years in my remembrance. The way in which I listened to all the incidents of the house that made themselves audible to me; the ringing of bells, the opening and shutting of doors, the murmuring of voices, the footsteps on the stairs; to any laughing, whistling, or singing, outside, which seemed more dismal than anything else to me in my solitude and disgrace – the uncertain pace of the hours, especially at night, when I would wake thinking it was morning, and find that the family were not yet gone to bed, and that all the length of night had yet to come – the depressed dreams and nightmares I had – the return of day, noon, afternoon, evening, when the boys played in the churchyard, and I watched them from a distance within the room, being ashamed to show myself at the window lest they should know I was a prisoner – the strange sensation of never hearing myself speak – the fleeting intervals of something like cheerfulness, which came with eating and drinking, and went away with it – the setting in of rain one evening, with a fresh smell, and its coming down faster and faster between me and the church, until it and gathering night seemed to quench me in gloom, and fear, and remorse – all this appears to have gone round and round for years instead of days, it is so vividly and strongly stamped on my remembrance.

On the last night of my restraint, I was awakened by hearing my own name spoken in a whisper. I started up in bed, and putting out my arms in the dark, said:

'Is that you, Peggotty?'

There was no immediate answer, but presently I heard my name again, in a tone so very mysterious and awful, that I think I should have gone into a fit, if it had not occurred to me that it must have come through the keyhole.

I groped my way to the door, and putting my own lips to the keyhole, whispered:

'Is that you, Peggotty dear?'

'Yes, my own precious Davy,' she replied. 'Be as soft as a mouse, or the Cat'll hear us.'

I understood this to mean Miss Murdstone, and was sensible of the urgency of the case; her room being close by.

'How's mama, dear Peggotty? Is she very angry with me?'

I could hear Peggotty crying softly on her side of the keyhole, as I was doing on mine, before she answered. 'No. Not very.'

'What is going to be done with me, Peggotty dear? Do you know?'

'School. Near London,' was Peggotty's answer. I was obliged to get her to repeat it, for she spoke it the first time quite down my throat, in consequence of my having forgotten to take my mouth away from the keyhole and put my ear there; and though her words tickled me a good deal, I didn't hear them.

'When, Peggotty?'

'To-morrow.'

'Is that the reason why Miss Murdstone took the clothes out of my drawers?' which she had done, though I have forgotten to mention it.

'Yes,' said Peggotty. 'Box.'

'Shan't I see mama?'

'Yes,' said Peggotty. 'Morning.'

Then Peggotty fitted her mouth close to the keyhole, and delivered these words through it with as much feeling and earnestness as a keyhole has ever been the medium of communicating, I will venture to assert: shooting in each broken little sentence in a convulsive little burst of its own.

'Davy, dear. If I ain't been azackly as intimate with you. Lately, as I used to be. It ain't because I don't love you. Just as well and more, my pretty poppet. It's because I thought it better for you. And for some one else besides. Davy, my darling, are you listening? Can you hear?'

'Ye—ye—ye—yes, Peggotty!' I sobbed.

'My own!' said Peggotty, with infinite compassion. 'What I want to say, is. That you must never forget me. For I'll never forget you. And I'll take as much care of your mama, Davy. As ever I took of you. And I won't leave her. The day may come when she'll be glad to lay her poor head. On her stupid, cross, old Peggotty's arm again. And I'll write to you, my dear. Though I ain't no scholar. And I'll – I'll – ' Peggotty fell to kissing the keyhole, as she couldn't kiss me.

'Thank you, dear Peggotty!' said I. 'Oh, thank you! Thank you! Will you promise me one thing, Peggotty? Will you write and tell Mr Peggotty and little Em'ly, and Mrs Gummidge and Ham, that I am not so bad as they might suppose, and that I sent 'em all my love – especially to little Em'ly? Will you, if you please, Peggotty?'

The kind soul promised, and we both of us kissed the keyhole with the greatest affection – I patted it with my hand, I recollect, as if it had been her honest face – and parted. From that night there grew up in my breast a feeling for Peggotty which I cannot very well define. She did not replace my mother; no one could do that; but she came into a vacancy in my heart, which closed upon her, and I felt towards her something I have never felt for any other human being. It was a sort of comical affection, too; and yet if she had died, I cannot think what I should have done, or how I should have acted out the tragedy it would have been to me.

In the morning Miss Murdstone appeared as usual, and told me I was going to school; which was not altogether such news to me as she supposed. She also informed me that when I was dressed, I was to come down-stairs into the parlour, and have my breakfast. There I found my mother, very pale and with red eyes: into whose arms I ran, and begged her pardon from my suffering soul.

'Oh, Davy!' she said. 'That you could hurt any one I love! Try to be better, pray to be better! I forgive you; but I am so grieved, Davy, that you should have such bad passions in your heart.'

They had persuaded her that I was a wicked fellow, and she was more sorry for that than for my going away. I felt it sorely. I tried to eat my parting breakfast, but my tears dropped upon my bread-and-butter, and trickled into my tea. I saw my mother look at me sometimes, and then glance at the watchful Miss Murdstone, and then look down, or look away.

'Master Copperfield's box! there!' said Miss Murdstone, when wheels were heard at the gate.

I looked for Peggotty, but it was not she; neither she nor Mr Murdstone appeared. My former acquaintance, the carrier, was at the door; the box was taken out to his cart, and lifted in.

'Clara!' said Miss Murdstone, in her warning note.

'Ready, my dear Jane,' returned my mother. 'Good-bye, Davy. You are going for your own good. Good-bye, my child. You will come home in the holidays, and be a better boy.'

'Clara!' Miss Murdstone repeated.

'Certainly, my dear Jane,' replied my mother, who was holding me. 'I forgive you, my dear boy. God bless you!'

'Clara!' Miss Murdstone repeated.

Miss Murdstone was good enough to take me out to the cart, and to say on the way that she hoped I would repent, before I came to a bad end; and then I got into the cart, and the lazy horse walked off with it.

Further reading

Chapter 7 of *David Copperfield* tells you what happened next. If you like Charles Dickens' writing, you could try the early chapters of *Oliver Twist* and *Great Expectations* for other glimpses of Victorian boyhoods. The description of a small boy called Pip meeting an escaped convict out in the marshes at the start of *Great Expectations* is one of the most famous and exciting scenes in Victorian literature.

Ragged Schools

from *The Illustrated London News* 11 April 1846

> Ragged Schools were charitable schools set up to educate destitute
> children. The first one was opened in 1818 by John Pounds, a
> Portsmouth shoemaker. By the middle of the century, with Lord
> Shaftesbury's strong support, there were 200 of them. They were
> one of the most hopeful signs that society wanted to change the
> lives of poor children. *The Illustrated London News* championed their
> cause.

Mr Charles Dickens, in an eloquent Letter addressed to the
Editors of the *Daily News*, describes the places which bear the
above name, as an effort 'to introduce among the most miserable and neglected outcasts in London some knowledge of the
commonest principles of morality and religion; to commence
their recognition as immortal human creatures, before the Gaol
Chaplain[1] becomes their only schoolmaster . . . This attempt is
being made in certain of the most obscure and squalid parts of
the Metropolis;[2] where rooms are opened at night, for the gra-
tuitous instruction of all comers, children or adults, under the
title of "RAGGED SCHOOLS". The name implies the purpose.
They who are too ragged, wretched, filthy, and forlorn, to enter
any other place: who could gain admission into no charity
school, and who would be driven from any churchdoor: are
invited to come in here and find some people not depraved,
willing to teach them something, and show them some
sympathy . . . '

We have selected the School in Jurston street, Oakley street,
Lambeth. The School is opened on Sunday evenings at six o'clock;
and the year's average attendance has been 250 children and 25
teachers. We gather from a lecture recently delivered by the

---

[1]**Gaol Chaplain**   clergyman working in a prison
[2]**Metropolis**   a main city (in this case, London)

Rev. Mr Ainslie, that at Windsor a school on 'the Ragged' principle has been established by a poor chimney-sweep 'who had himself been a bad and abandoned man, but who was reclaimed, and
who now sat there, with his dirty face, teaching and doing more
good than thousands of others of ten times his capacity.'

Lambeth Ragged School – girls

Lambeth Ragged School – boys

Further reading

Charles Dickens wrote an article about his experiences when visiting ragged schools which you can read on the Maybole Ragged School website: http://www.maybole.org/history/articles/mayboleragged-school.htm. The website also includes pages transcribed from an original collection of handwritten journals, probably kept by a minister, about the lives of the children who went there.

Visits are welcomed at the Ragged School Museum, 46–50 Copperfield Road, London E3 4RR http://www.raggedschoolmuseum.org.uk/. The museum also publishes a book about ragged schools, called *Ragged Schools, Ragged Children* by Claire Seymour.

A London Child of the Seventies

by Molly Vivian Hughes

> Molly is desperate to follow her four older brothers and go to school. But will it be what she expects?

To be allowed to see a real classroom, where boys behaved badly, with desks all inky and carved with names, a desk where the master sat, and a noticeboard; to run out on the great green, where the masters were swishing about in gowns and hoods, being agreeable to mothers, and where the grand senior boys were still walking about in the stage clothes in which they had been acting – all this was a kind of awful delight.

It is hardly surprising that I cast longing thoughts on going to school myself. So in my twelfth year mother decided to send me to an 'Establishment for Young Ladies' about a mile from home. It must have been to give me some companionship, for I can conceive no other rational motive for the step. Indeed, I have come to think that the main value of school life is to prevent one's getting on too fast in the natural surroundings of home.

My first day is photographed in my memory. Of course I was delirious with excitement, and sped along Highbury New Park as though on air. I was placed in the lowest class with three other little girls of my own age, who were reading aloud the story of Richard Arkwright. I say 'reading', but unless I had had a book I should have understood not a word of their jerky mumblings. Meanwhile I got interested in this barber who out-did his rivals by shaving people for a half-penny, and when my turn came to read I held forth delightedly. Soon there was a whispered consultation with the Authorities, and I was removed then and there into a higher class. Here were three or four big girls. They seemed to me so big as almost to be of the 'aunt' type. But my fear of them soon disappeared, for the sounds coming from them purporting to be French were even worse than the English reading had been. Again I sailed ahead, and was asked by the teacher if I had been to France. 'No,' said I, 'but my mother has a lot.' (I need hardly say that I soon found it best to fall in with the pronunciation used by the others, much to poor mother's chagrin.[1])

At lunch-time I was questioned by the girls as to my full name, what my father was, how many brothers I had, and how big a house. After this came instructions for the next day and the acquisition of lovely new exercise-books and a new history book, and then I fled triumphantly home, to find mother waiting for me with the front door open. She embraced me as though I had come from Australia or some great peril, breathed the word 'darling', and no more.

My sense of triumph and complacency was short-lived, for the next day, as you may guess, there was an arithmetic lesson. Absurd as it may seem, it is the cold truth that I had done plenty of shopping and had managed the change, and yet in my twelfth year I had never seen an £ s. d. sum laid out, and had to be told what the symbols stood for. Hill Difficulty[2] was nothing to the task of turning farthings into pence, pence into shillings, and shillings into pounds. Then I was expected to take a halfpenny from a farthing, which seemed the height of absurdity. The other girls went to work with easy assurance, raising the eyebrow a little at my dismay. Worse was in store, for there followed something they called 'mental arithmetic', of which I had never heard. The mistress stood up and gave forth sums from her head, and, without any slate to work them out on, the girls shouted the answers. One kind of sum smacked to me of black magic: 'Twelve articles at fourpence three farthings each, how much altogether?' Hardly were the words out of the teacher's mouth before the answer came. A kind girl next me told me in a hurried whisper to keep the pence and turn the farthings into threepences. But why? And what were the 'articles' that one could buy so quickly? And supposing you only wanted ten?

---

[1]**chagrin**   annoyance, feeling mortified
[2]**Hill Difficulty**   a reference to a difficult place encountered by the main
    character, 'Christian', in John Bunyan's *The Pilgrim's Progress*, 1678

However, I soon learnt not to ask for explanations, for the explanations were far worse than the original difficulty. For instance, we had object lessons, one day on a snail, another day on a candle, each time a pleasant surprise. The teacher read them out of a little book. 'How a pin is made' greatly attracted me. I had used pins without ever thinking, and now I suddenly saw that it must need quite an effort to make one. So I attended carefully. Still there were gaps in my grasp of the process, and I went to the mistress in our lunch-interval, and begged her to explain it to me. 'Oh, yes, dear,' said she, and opening her book read aloud to me very slowly and emphatically just what she had said before. 'You see now, don't you, dear?' 'Oh, yes, I see now, thank you,' said I brightly, lest she should read it again.

Similar assertions of perfect understanding were ready after an explanation of the treatment of remainders in short division. Short! Surely the word was used in sarcasm. I always 'did it by long'. No one bothered about method or understanding or anything as long as you got the answer. A kind of sum that gave me immense trouble was this: 'A man has £85 13s. 4½d. To how many children can he give £7 16s. 1¾d?' Well, I proceeded to dole it out, subtracting and subtracting, until my paper ran short. Even when, after an hour's work, the man was reduced to practically nothing more, I never could be sure of the number of his beneficiaries ticked off on the many bits of paper. One evening at home Dym caught me at this task, and began to laugh.

'Good Lord!' he exclaimed. 'Don't they teach you how to . . . Look here, darling, can you do simple long division?'

'Oh, yes, Dym,' said I hopefully, for that was my long suit.

He breathed something about fractions, but seeing my blank face, showed me how to bring everything to farthings, and then see how many times I could take the little heap from the big heap – by division.

'And will the answer be in children?' said I; 'because it's got to be.'

'Of course,' said he. And when I got to school it was right. This incident was a Rosetta Stone,[3] for I at last understood why one had had to do reduction, which had seemed to me a silly waste of time.

Not that time mattered. In school 'time was all withdrawn'. This was brought home to me by a curious experience one dreary morning. I was seated with my school-fellows at a long table, copying again and again 'Alfred Tennyson is a poet', my writing getting steadily worse as the hated statement was repeated. Doubt began – perhaps people had denied that he was a poet? Glancing up at the school clock to see how far off it still was to the lunch-interval at a quarter to eleven, I beheld a miracle. As I looked, the big hand slipped from ten past ten to twenty past! If the sun had done a similar turn in the sky I could not have been more astonished. And it was not an answer to a prayer like Joshua's,[4] though it might well have been. I watched to see what would happen next: the clock resumed its usual duty at twenty past, and nobody noticed anything. We had lunch-time by the clock, and I was too glad of this to point out what I had seen. But thenceforward all clocks for me lost something of their authority. At home we all 'went' by the dining-room clock, which was regularly kept at ten minutes fast, 'to be on the safe side', as mother said. She also confided to me once that it caused visitors to go a little earlier than they otherwise might to catch a train, for she had observed that they never trusted their own watches. I can hear her saying, 'Our clock is most reliable,' which of course was perfectly true.

I have no recollection of any time-table at school, and I rather think that the authorities yielded to clamour oftener than we suspected. But it was usual to do a little Scripture every

---

[3]**Rosetta Stone**   a carved rock discovered in 1799 at Rosetta which provided the key to deciphering Ancient Egyptian texts

[4]**a prayer like Joshua's**   a reference to the Bible, book of Joshua, chapter 10. Joshua prayed for the sun to stand still to give his people time to chase their enemies. The sun stood still and so did the moon, helping the people to catch their enemies up.

morning. This consisted in writing out and reciting a verse or two, fortunately without religious comment. One day we were told as a great treat that we might for the following day learn *any* text we like, and recite it as a little surprise.

'I know which I shall choose,' I whispered to my neighbour. Alas! I had been overheard by the lady at the head of the table.

'I fear, Mary dear, that you are being irreverent. I know which text you mean – a very short one.'

I felt disgraced, but when I came to think of it, how did she guess which one I meant if she hadn't been a bit irreverent herself?

My new history book was *Little Arthur,* which one could read like a delightful story. The general spirit of the author about unpleasant things seemed to be that they happened so long ago that they probably never happened at all. Anyhow, we gained a fair idea of the flow of events and the stories of leading people without boredom. Alongside of this we were drilled in the dates of the kings and queens, and could say them off like the multiplication table, for which I have ever been grateful.

What demon invented 'freehand copies'? And why this name? Anything less free it would be hard to imagine. While Charles was being encouraged to plunge away and paint at Merchant Taylors', we poor girls used to waste the precious hours labelled 'Drawing' in slavishly copying the design of a vase, or a fancy scroll, printed on a card. The only trouble was to get both sides exactly alike. It was 'corrected', rubbed out, improved, and finally 'clear-lined', that is firmly and fiercely drawn over with a freshly sharpened pencil. It might take two hours to complete one of these horrors; then you turned a new page and were given another. Nothing else was done until you got to the top class, where the big girls copied shaded cottages.

By far the best part of those school-days was the play-time, for the other girls were a jolly lot, whose names and faces and peculiarities I remember as though it were yesterday. Our liberal lunch-intervals were spent in games of tip-and-run and rounders in the big garden, from which we came in all hot and panting. And we hatched schemes of small wickednesses, in which I was always made to take the lead, 'because you always look so innocent, Mary, she'll never guess it's you'.

Of bosom friends I had none at all, but kept several of my school-fellows in fee. The walk home was long and boring, so I would induce any one 'coming my way' to accompany me, or more often to go out of their way to do so. I would ask them to hold my books 'just while I get my gloves on'. On the principle of the Arabian Nights[5] those gloves were never completely buttoned, while I distracted the attention of the book-carrier with the doings of the boys or with stories about the siege of Troy. My victim would sometimes protest, but generally ended by carrying my books almost to my door, and agitated next day for a similar job if I would go on with the story. For some curious reason my memory always failed me if my arms were cumbered up with books.

One big girl, in a long skirt and with her hair done up, hated me. I had once openly set her right on a horrible pronunciation of a French word, and thenceforth she snubbed me whenever she could. One day I could bear this no longer, and with all my force let fly a blow at her most accessible spot, which annoyed me by its mere size. Holding herself as though in great pain she went straight to the head mistress and lodged a complaint. This turn of events was quite new to me – telling! Whatever would happen next? I was summoned to the drawing-room and told that such a blow might be very serious, might set up a terrible internal disease and cause perchance *death*. Never shall I forget that afternoon and evening. Suppose Louisa Roberts were to die? For me then the gallows. Disgrace and a harrowing end faced me. I had to practise my music, but what was the good when I had to die so soon? I didn't dare to tell mother, lest she should begin recriminations.[6] I looked long-

---

[5]**Arabian Nights**   a collection of about 200 stories. Scheherazade tells these stories to the King, Shahriyar, to put off the moment of her death. By the time she has finished, after 1,001 nights, he has fallen in love with her.
[6]**recriminations**   arguments between people who are blaming each other

ingly at Charles, who would make light of even the Judgement Day, but again dreaded that even he would be horrified at having a murderer for a sister. All through tea-time I could think of nothing but the gallows, and I don't know how I got through the evening and long night. As early as decently possible the next morning I rushed off to school. Racing along Highbury New Park I passed the school and made for the road towards Louisa's house, so that I might know the worst. Expecting to see something in the nature of a funeral, or straw laid down in the street, what was my astonishment at seeing Louisa herself, bouncing along, swinging her books by the strap, red in the face as usual! 'Hullo, Mary, good morning,' says she. 'You're rather early, aren't you?' My relief was so great that I came near giving her another blow for her heartlessness. Probably it is the memory of that dreadful experience that has made me doubtful of the wisdom of 'reasoning' with children instead of giving them a short sharp punishment.

Further reading

Molly Hughes later trained as a teacher and eventually became a schools inspector. After this book, she wrote two sequels telling the story of her life, each in the same warm detail as this extract. The great rush of school stories had not yet begun. (Angela Brazil was a particular favourite from 1912 onwards – such stories as *The Luckiest Girl in the School* are good period pieces.) At around the same time in America, the *Anne of Green Gables* stories were being written by L. M. Montgomery and the *Pollyanna* stories by Eleanor H. Porter. But in Britain, most of the school stories were only about boys, of which *Tom Brown's Schooldays* by Thomas Hughes is the most famous.

You're a Brick, Angela! by Mary Cadogan and Patricia Craig is a lively and funny study of girls' stories written between 1839 and 1985 and published by Girls Gone By Ltd, 2003.

A Horseman in the Sky

by Ambrose Bierce

The American Civil War was a conflict between two parts of the United States of America. Eleven southern states, known as the South or Confederacy, fought to preserve black slavery. The northern states, known as the North or the Union, opposed slavery and fought to preserve the union of all the states in the USA.

In this story, Carter Druse is fighting for the Union or Federal Army. It is 1861 and he is on sentry duty high up on a mountainside, guarding the Federal infantry which lies below.

One sunny afternoon in the autumn of the year 1861, a soldier lay in a clump of laurel by the side of a road in Western Virginia. He lay at full length, upon his stomach, his feet resting upon the toes, his head upon the left forearm. His extended right hand loosely grasped his rifle. But for the somewhat methodical disposition of his limbs and a slight rhythmic movement of the cartridge box at the back of his belt, he might have been thought to be dead. He was asleep at his post of duty. But if detected he would be dead shortly afterward, that being the just and legal penalty of his crime.

The clump of laurel in which the criminal lay was in the angle of a road which, after ascending, southward, a steep acclivity[1] to that point, turned sharply to the west, running along the summit for perhaps one hundred yards. There it turned southward again and went zigzagging downward through the forest. At the salient[2] of that second angle was a large flat rock, jutting out from the ridge to the northward, overlooking the deep valley from which the road ascended. The rock capped a high cliff; a stone dropped from its outer edge would have fallen sheer downward one thousand feet to the

---

[1] **acclivity**   an upward slope
[2] **salient**   the point that juts outwards

tops of the pines. The angle where the soldier lay was on another spur of the same cliff. Had he been awake he would have commanded a view, not only of the short arm of the road and the jutting rock but of the entire profile of the cliff below it. It might well have made him giddy to look.

The country was wooded everywhere except at the bottom of the valley to the northward, where there was a small natural meadow, through which flowed a stream scarcely visible from the valley's rim. This open ground looked hardly larger than an ordinary door-yard, but was really several acres in extent. Its green was more vivid than that of the inclosing forest. Away beyond it rose a line of giant cliffs similar to those upon which we are supposed to stand in our survey of the savage scene, and through which the road had somehow made its climb to the summit. The configuration of the valley, indeed, was such that from our point of observation it seemed entirely shut in, and one could not but have wondered how the road which found a way out of it had found a way into it, and whence came and whither went the waters of the stream that parted the meadow two thousand feet below.

No country is so wild and difficult but men will make it a theatre of war; concealed in the forest at the bottom of that military rat trap, in which half a hundred men in possession of the exits might have starved an army to submission, lay five regiments of Federal infantry. They had marched all the previous day and night and were resting. At nightfall they would take to the road again, climb to the place where their unfaithful sentinel now slept, and, descending the other slope of the ridge, fall upon a camp of the enemy at about midnight. Their hope was to surprise it, for the road led to the rear of it. In case of failure their position would be perilous in the extreme; and fail they surely would should accident or vigilance apprise the enemy of the movement.

The sleeping sentinel in the clump of laurel was a young Virginian[3] named Carter Druse. He was the son of wealthy

---

[3]**Virginian**   someone from the State of Virginia

parents, an only child, and had known such ease and cultivation and high living as wealth and taste were able to command in the mountain country of Western Virginia. His home was but a few miles from where he now lay. One morning he had risen from the breakfast table and said, quietly but gravely: 'Father, a Union regiment has arrived at Grafton. I am going to join it.'

The father lifted his leonine head, looked at the son a moment in silence, and replied: 'Go, Carter, and, whatever may occur, do what you conceive to be your duty. Virginia, to which you are a traitor, must get on without you. Should we both live to the end of the war, we will speak further of the matter. Your mother, as the physician has informed you, is in a most critical condition; at the best she cannot be with us longer than a few weeks, but that time is precious. It would be better not to disturb her.'

So Carter Druse, bowing reverently to his father, who returned the salute with a stately courtesy which masked a breaking heart, left the home of his childhood to go soldiering. By conscience and courage, by deeds of devotion and daring, he soon commended himself to his fellows and his officers; and it was to these qualities and to some knowledge of the country that he owed his selection for his present perilous duty at the extreme outpost. Nevertheless, fatigue had been stronger than resolution, and he had fallen asleep. What good or bad angel came in a dream to rouse him from his state of crime, who shall say? Without a movement, without a sound, in the profound silence and the languor[4] of the late afternoon, some invisible messenger of fate touched with unsealing finger the eyes of his consciousness – whispered into the ear of his spirit the mysterious awakening word which no human lips have ever spoken, no human memory ever has recalled. He quietly raised his forehead from his arm and looked between the masking stems of the laurels, instinctively closing his right hand about the stock of his rifle.

---

[4]**languor**   heaviness; stillness

His first feeling was a keen artistic delight. On a colossal pedestal, the cliff, motionless at the extreme edge of the capping rock and sharply outlined against the sky, was an equestrian[5] statue of impressive dignity. The figure of the man sat the figure of the horse, straight and soldierly, but with the repose of a Grecian god carved in the marble which limits the suggestion of activity. The gray costume harmonised with its aerial background; the metal of accoutrement[6] and comparison was softened and subdued by the shadow; the animal's skin had no points of high light. A carbine,[7] strikingly foreshortened, lay across the pommel of the saddle, kept in place by the right hand grasping it at the 'grip'; the left hand, holding the bridle rein, was invisible. In silhouette against the sky, the profile of the horse was cut with the sharpness of a cameo;[8] it looked across the heights of air to the confronting cliffs beyond. The face of the rider, turned slightly to the left, showed only an outline of temple and beard; he was looking downward to the bottom of the valley. Magnified by its lift against the sky and by the soldier's testifying sense of the formidableness of a near enemy, the group appeared of heroic, almost colossal, size.

For an instant Druse had a strange, half-defined feeling that he had slept to the end of the war and was looking upon a noble work of art reared upon that commanding eminence to commemorate the deeds of an heroic past of which he had been an inglorious part. The feeling was dispelled by a slight movement of the group; the horse, without moving its feet, had drawn its body slightly backward from the verge; the man remained immobile as before. Broad awake and keenly alive to the significance of the situation, Druse now brought the butt of his rifle against his cheek by cautiously pushing the barrel forward through the bushes, cocked the piece, and, glancing through the

---

[5]**equestrian**   a person on horseback
[6]**accoutrement**   equipment worn by soldiers
[7]**carbine**   short-barrelled shoulder rifle used by cavalry
[8]**cameo**   a carving where the background is a different colour from the raised design

sights, covered a vital spot of the horseman's breast. A touch upon the trigger and all would have been well with Carter Druse. At that instant the horseman turned his head and looked in the direction of his concealed foeman – seemed to look into his very face, into his eyes, into his brave compassionate heart.

Is it, then, so terrible to kill an enemy in war – an enemy who has surprised a secret vital to the safety of one's self and comrades – an enemy more formidable for his knowledge than all his army for its numbers? Carter Druse grew deathly pale; he shook in every limb, turned faint, and saw the statuesque group before him as black figures, rising, falling, moving unsteadily in arcs of circles in a fiery sky. His hand fell away from his weapon, his head slowly dropped until his face rested on the leaves in which he lay. This courageous gentleman and hardy soldier was near swooning from intensity of emotion.

It was not for long; in another moment his face was raised from earth, his hands resumed their places on the rifle, his forefinger sought the trigger; mind, heart, and eyes were clear, conscience and reason sound. He could not hope to capture that enemy; to alarm him would but send him dashing to his camp with his fatal news. The duty of the soldier was plain: the man must be shot dead from ambush – without warning, without a moment's spiritual preparation, with never so much as an unspoken prayer, he must be sent to his account. But no – there is a hope; he may have discovered nothing – perhaps he is but admiring the sublimity[9] of the landscape. If permitted he may turn and ride carelessly away in the direction whence he came. Surely it will be possible to judge at the instant of his withdrawing whether he knows. It may well be that his fixity of attention – Druse turned his head and looked below, through the deeps of air downward, as from the surface to the bottom of a translucent sea. He saw creeping across the green meadow a sinuous line of figures of men and horses – some foolish commander was permitting the soldiers of his

---

[9]**sublimity**   beauty so wonderful it lifts the heart

escort to water their beasts in the open, in plain view from a hundred summits!

Druse withdrew his eyes from the valley and fixed them again upon the group of man and horse in the sky, and again it was through the sights of his rifle. But this time his aim was at the horse. In his memory, as if they were a divine mandate, rang the words of his father at their parting. 'Whatever may occur, do what you conceive to be your duty.' He was calm now. His teeth were firmly but not rigidly closed; his nerves were as tranquil as a sleeping babe's – not a tremor affected any muscle of his body; his breathing, until suspended in the act of taking aim, was regular and slow. Duty had conquered; the spirit had said to the body: 'Peace, be still.' He fired.

At that moment an officer of the Federal force, who, in a spirit of adventure or in quest of knowledge, had left the hidden *bivouac*[10] in the valley, and, with aimless feet, had made his way to the lower edge of a small open space near the foot of the cliff, was considering what he had to gain by pushing his exploration further. At a distance of a quarter-mile before him, but apparently at a stone's throw, rose from its fringe of pines the gigantic face of rock, towering to so great a height above him that it made him giddy to look up to where its edge cut a sharp, rugged line against the sky. At some distance away to his right it presented a clean, vertical profile against a background of blue sky to a point half of the way down, and of distant hills hardly less blue thence to the tops of the trees at its base. Lifting his eyes to the dizzy altitude of its summit, the officer saw an astonishing sight – a man on horseback riding down into the valley through the air!

Straight upright sat the rider, in military fashion, with a firm seat in the saddle, a strong clutch upon the rein to hold his charger from too impetuous a plunge. From his bare head his long hair streamed upward, waving like a plume. His right hand was concealed in the cloud of the horse's lifted mane. The animal's body was as level as if every hoof stroke encountered the resistant

---

[10]**bivouac**   a temporary encampment

earth. Its motions were those of a wild gallop, but even as the officer looked they ceased, with all the legs thrown sharply forward as in the act of alighting from a leap. But this was a flight!

Filled with amazement and terror by this apparition of a horseman in the sky – half believing himself the chosen scribe of some new Apocalypse,[11] the officer was overcome by the intensity of his emotions; his legs failed him and he fell. Almost at the same instant he heard a crashing sound in the trees – a sound that died without an echo, and all was still.

The officer rose to his feet, trembling. The familiar sensation of an abraded shin recalled his dazed faculties. Pulling himself together, he ran rapidly obliquely away from the cliff to a point a half-mile from its foot; thereabout he expected to find his man; and thereabout he naturally failed. In the fleeting instant of his vision his imagination had been so wrought upon by the apparent grace and ease and intention of the marvellous performance that it did not occur to him that the line of march of aerial cavalry is directed downward, and that he could find the objects of his search at the very foot of the cliff. A half hour later he returned to camp.

This officer was a wise man; he knew better than to tell an incredible truth. He said nothing of what he had seen. But when the commander asked him if in his scout he had learned anything of advantage to the expedition, he answered:

'Yes, sir; there is no road leading down into this valley from the southward.'

The commander, knowing better, smiled.

After firing his shot private Carter Druse reloaded his rifle and resumed his watch. Ten minutes had hardly passed when a Federal sergeant crept cautiously to him on hands and knees. Druse neither turned his head nor looked at him, but lay without motion or sign of recognition.

'Did you fire?' the sergeant whispered.

'Yes.'

---

[11]**apocalypse**   an event of great importance

'At what?'

'A horse. It was standing on yonder rock – pretty far out. You see it is no longer there. It went over the cliff.'

The man's face was white but he showed no other sign of emotion. Having answered, he turned away his face and said no more. The sergeant did not understand.

'See here, Druse,' he said, after a moment's silence, 'it's no use making a mystery. I order you to report. Was there anybody on the horse?'

'Yes.'

'Who?'

'My father.'

The sergeant rose to his feet and walked away. 'Good God!' he said.

Further reading

If you liked this, you might like other short stories by Ambrose Bierce. Try *An Occurence at Owl Creek Bridge*. Other stories with unexpected endings are the *Sherlock Holmes* tales by Sir Arthur Conan Doyle, strange tales such as *The Pit and the Pendulum* by Edgar Allen Poe and several of the short stories by Guy de Maupassant.

War and Peace

by Leo Tolstoy

> The young Petya longs to see action in war-time and may be about to have his dream come true. It is 1812 and Napoleon is fighting a campaign in Russia. Deep in a forest, Russian soldiers are preparing to fight under the command of Denisov. Petya excitedly joins them on what he sees as a great adventure.

Leaving his people after their departure from Moscow, Petya had joined his regiment and was soon taken on as orderly by the general of a large guerrilla detachment.[1] From the time he received his commission, and especially after his transfer into the army in the field, and his introduction to active service at Vyazma, Petya had been in a constant state of blissful excitement at being grown-up, and chronically eager not to miss the slightest chance of covering himself with glory. He was highly delighted with what he saw and experienced in the army but at the same time it seemed to him that the really heroic exploits were always being performed just where he did not happen to be. And he was always in a hurry to get where he was not.

When on the 21st of October his general expressed a wish to send somebody to Denisov's detachment, Petya had begged so piteously to go that the general could not refuse. But as he was seeing him off he recalled Petya's foolhardy behaviour at the battle of Vyazma, where instead of keeping to the road Petya had galloped across the front line of sharpshooters under the fire of the French, and had there discharged a couple of pistol-shots. So in letting him go the general explicitly forbade Petya to take part in any enterprise whatever that Denisov might be planning. This was why Petya had blushed and been disconcerted when Denisov asked him if he could stay. Until he reached the outskirts of the forest Petya had fully intended to

---

[1] **guerrilla detachment**   irregular armed force that fights a stronger regular army

carry out his instructions to the letter and return at once. But when he saw the French and met Tikhon, and learned that there would certainly be an attack that night, he decided, with the swiftness with which young people change their opinions, that the general for whom up to that moment he had had the greatest respect was a rubbishy German, that Denisov was a hero, the hetman[2] a hero, and Tikhon a hero too, and that it would be shameful of him to desert them at a critical moment.

It was growing dark when Denisov, Petya and the hetman rode up to the forester's hut. In the twilight they could see saddled horses, and Cossacks and hussars[3] rigging up rough shelters in the clearing and kindling a glowing fire in a hollow where the smoke would not be seen by the French. In the entrance of the little watch-house a Cossack with sleeves rolled up was cutting up a sheep. In the hut itself three officers of Denisov's were converting a door into a table-top. Petya pulled off his wet clothes, gave them to be dried, and at once set to work helping the officers to fix up the dinner-table.

In ten minutes the table was ready, covered with a napkin, and spread with vodka, a flask of rum, white bread, roast mutton and salt.

Sitting at the table with the officers and tearing the fat, savoury mutton with greasy fingers, Petya was in an ecstatic childlike state of melting love for all men and a consequent belief that in the same way they loved him.

'So what do you think, Vasili Fiodorovich?' he said to Denisov. 'It won't matter my staying just one day with you, will it?' And not waiting for Denisov to reply he supplied an answer for himself: 'You see, I was told to find out – well, I am finding out . . . Only do let me into the very . . . into the real . . . I don't care about rewards and decorations . . . I just want . . . '

Petya clenched his teeth and looked about him, tossing his head and waving his arm.

---

[2]**hetman**   headman
[3]**hussars**   light cavalry

'The real thing . . . ' Denisov said with a smile.

'Only please give me a command, just the smallest command to command myself,' Petya went on. 'What difference could it make to you? Oh, is it a knife you want?' he said to an officer who was trying to sever himself a piece of mutton. And he handed him his clasp-knife.

The officer admired the blade.

'Please keep it! I have several others like it . . . ' said Petya, blushing. 'Heavens! I was quite forgetting,' he cried suddenly. 'I have some wonderful raisins with me – you know, those seedless ones. Our new sutler[4] has such first-rate things. I bought ten pounds. I always like sweet things. Will you have some? . . . ' And Petya ran out to his Cossack in the passage and returned with baskets containing about five pounds of raisins. 'Help yourselves, gentlemen, help yourselves.'

'Don't you need a coffee-pot?' he said to the hetman. 'I got a marvellous one from our sutler. His things are first-rate. And he's very honest. That's the great thing. I'll be sure and send it to you. Or perhaps your flints are giving out, or you are out of them – that does happen sometimes. I've got some here' – he pointed to the baskets – 'a hundred flints. I bought them dirt cheap. Do take them – have as many as you want, all of them if you like . . . '

Then suddenly, dismayed at the thought that he had let his tongue run away with him, Petya stopped short and blushed.

He tried to remember whether he had been guilty of any other folly. And passing the events of the day in review he remembered the French drummer-boy. 'We are very snug here, but what of him? Where have they put him? Have they given him anything to eat? I hope they aren't being nasty to him?' he wondered. But, having caught himself saying too much about the flints, he was afraid to speak now.

'I have a great mind to ask,' he thought. 'But won't they say: "He's a boy himself, so of course he feels for the other boy"? I'll show them tomorrow whether I'm a boy! Would I be

---

[4]**sutler**   someone who sold provisions to an army

embarrassed to ask?' Petya wondered. 'Oh well, I don't care,' and on the spur of the moment, colouring and looking anxiously at the officers to see if they would laugh at him, he said:

'May I call in that boy who was taken prisoner? Give him something to eat, perhaps? . . . '

'Yes, poor little chap,' said Denisov, who evidently saw nothing to be ashamed of in this thought. 'Fetch him in. His name is Vincent Bosse. Fetch him in.'

'I'll go,' said Petya.

'Yes, yes, do. Poor little chap,' said Denisov again.

Petya was standing at the door when Denisov said this. He slipped in between the officers and went up to Denisov.

'I must embrace you for that, my dear fellow!' he exclaimed. 'Oh, how good of you, how kind!'

And having embraced Denisov he ran out of the hut.

'Bosse! Vincent!' called Petya, stopping outside the door.

'Who is it you want, sir?' asked a voice from the darkness.

Petya explained that he wanted the French lad who had been taken prisoner that day.

'Oh, Vesenny?' said a Cossack.

The boy's name, Vincent, had already been transformed by the Cossacks into Vesenny, and by the peasants and the soldiers into Vesenya, and both these words which have to do in Russian with the spring-time seemed appropriate to the young lad who was little more than a child.

'He's warming himself by the fire there. Hey, Vesenya! Vesenya! – Vesenny!' laughing voices called, catching up the cry one after another.

'He's a sharp little fellow,' remarked an hussar standing near Petya. 'We gave him a meal not long ago. He was frightfully hungry!'

There was the sound of footsteps in the darkness, and the drummer-boy came towards the door, bare feet splashing through the mud.

'Ah, there you are!' said Petya in French. 'Would you like some food? Don't be afraid, no one will hurt you,' he added, shyly laying a friendly hand on his arm. 'Come along, come in.'

'*Merci, monsieur,*' said the drummer-boy in a trembling, almost childish voice, and he began wiping his muddy feet against the threshold. Petya had a great many things he longed to say to the drummer-boy but he did not dare. He stood irresolutely beside him in the passage. Then he took the boy's hand in the darkness and pressed it.

'Come along, come in!' he repeated in an encouraging whisper.

'Oh, I wonder what I could do for him?' he thought, and opening the door he ushered the boy in before him.

When the drummer-boy was in the hut Petya sat down at some distance from him, feeling that it would be lowering his dignity to take much notice of him. But he was fingering the money in his pocket and asking himself whether it would seem ridiculous if he gave some to the little prisoner.

Further reading

Chapters 10 and 11 in Book 14 of *War and Peace* will tell you about what happened to Petya. (Have you guessed?) The whole story of *War and Peace* is a long one, but well worth trying in full one day.

'If I were told that what I shall write will be read in 20 years by the children of today and that they will weep and smile over it and will fall in love with life, I would devote all my life and all my strengths, to it.'

Activities

The Way of All Flesh

Before you read

1   Look at the photograph on page 63. Victorian families would have thought the room looked very beautiful. How is it different from your own home? Write a few notes.

2   Many children of disciplined middle-class Victorian families in this kind of home were not allowed to play, paint or draw on Sundays, the day on which this incident takes place. Compare experiences in class about what Sunday means to you.

What's it about?

3   If you were one of Ernest's cousins, what would you think about his special Sunday treat?

4   How is Theobald's reaction to Ernest's difficulty in pronouncing 'come' different from Overton's?

5   Ernest looked like a scolded puppy when he saw how angry his father was. What does this comparison tell us about how he feels?

6   The whole household would have heard Ernest's screams and known that he was being beaten. What have we learnt about Theobald from this passage that suggests no one would have been surprised?

Thinking about the text

7   Ernest was not trying to be naughty and he struggled to do what he was told. If you had been there, how would you have reacted? Write a playscript using the words Ernest and Theobald say to each other but adding your own interruptions. Think hard about whether or not you will have the power to change what happens.

8   We have the saying 'caught red-handed' when someone is found in the act of doing wrong. Why is Theobald literally red-handed at the end?

9   Explain what the author wants us to think and feel about what Theobald has done by adding a few lines to the end of this chapter, writing down Ernest's thoughts as he cries upstairs in his bedroom.

The Adventures of Huckleberry Finn

Before you read

1   Huck is a boy with money and an absent father. In pairs, discuss what might happen when his father turns up.

2   Think of the fathers you've read about in stories and met in real life. Draw up a list of ideal characteristics for fathers in the first of three columns.

3   In the second column, write all the opposites. (Leave the third column empty.)

What's it about?

4   The author establishes Huck's father's appearance and character in one fell swoop. Check the lists of characteristics you made before reading the text. Now fill in the third column: Huck's father.

5   Huck wants to get on in life. Find a sentence that shows that:

   ● he's not scared of his father any more

   ● he's prepared to defy him.

Thinking about the text

6   The author uses Huck's voice, his natural language. For example, 'my breath sort of hitched . . .'. This means he catches his breath, just like you might hitch your trousers up – and you can almost see him do it. Huck's voice helps us to see what happens from his point of view.

   a   Write down a couple of phrases Huck uses that describe his father's eyes and skin when he first sees him.

   b   These descriptions tell us more about Huck's father than just his appearance. In your own words, what is Huck really saying?

7   What does the story suggest about Huck's future with his father? Write down his thoughts.

David Copperfield

Before you read

1   Mr Murdstone is David's new stepfather. What kind of character does this name conjure up to you? Write down the words that spring to your mind.

What's it about?

2   David is frightened by the vivid language that Mr Murdstone uses. What do you think Mr Murdstone means by his reference to horses and dogs?

3   Create a spidergram with the information given in the paragraph beginning 'It was Miss Murdstone who was arrived . . . ', where the author makes it very clear that David must expect no help from this newcomer. (You could draw Miss Murdstone in the middle.)

4   Mr Murdstone is 'firm'. He does not give way. He and Miss Murdstone stand together like a high wall between David and any hope of loving kindness and understanding. Draw this wall and write on the bricks the words that you wrote down in question 1. Add any others that now come to your mind.

Thinking about the text

5   David's mother, Clara, fails to stand up for her son. Do you sympathise with her or feel she fails as a parent?
    a   In groups, discuss her role in the story.
    b   Choose one member of the class to take the part of Clara. Put Clara in the 'hot seat' and get her to account for her part in the story.

6   Peggotty is a servant; she is the least powerful person in the household, but the author uses her to show David that love does exist and can comfort him. Imagine that Peggotty goes back to the kitchen when David leaves for school and rants and raves about the Murdstones. If this were a film, how would you show this? Write the dialogue and think particularly about expression, tone of voice and gestures.

Ragged Schools

Before you read

1   Look at the pictures. What sort of teaching and learning is going on here? On a separate sheet of paper write speech bubbles for some of the adults and children in both pictures.

2   Imagine you are a journalist for this paper. Your brief is to go to Lambeth in London and see a Ragged School for yourself. What are you expecting to see? Write down the questions that might help you to prepare for your report.

What's it about?

3   The children are described as 'miserable and neglected'; they are outcasts from society. Write down some other adjectives in the report that describe their appearance.

4   The children are taught the principles of two subjects. What are they and why do you think they have been chosen?

Thinking about the text

5   The novelist Charles Dickens was also a fierce campaigner for better lives for poorer children. He wrote articles for newspapers and magazines, he visited schools, and he worked hard to make the public aware of what it could be like for children who lived on the streets. He also worried that many of the Ragged Schools were badly run.

In groups, discuss what challenges these Ragged Schools face and how you might set about meeting them. Then have a class debate based around the statement: 'Ragged Schools are the only way forward to save the children of the poor!'

A London Child of the Seventies

Before you read

1   When you are older and look back on your schooldays, what do you think you'll remember most clearly? Your first day? Particular teachers, friends, games, lessons? In pairs, share the memories you already have, then choose one of the most memorable and write about it. You could share these memories with the rest of the class.

What's it about?

2   Molly had clearly daydreamed about the joys of going to school. Re-read the first paragraph and write her thoughts in a big thought bubble.

3   Explain how the name of the school, the Establishment for Young Ladies, contains clues about what Molly might expect to do there.

4   Molly puts inverted commas around 'reading' and 'drawing', which writers often do to show that this use of the word doesn't completely fit the way it is usually used. What does this tell you about how she reads and draws at home?

5   'Brightly' is an adverb that writers often use when they want a character to sound cheerful in order to hide desperation. Why does Molly answer 'brightly' when the teacher asks, 'You see now, don't you, dear?' about the lesson on how a pin is made?

Thinking about the text

6   Molly was not unhappy at school; it was just different from what she had excitedly imagined. Draw two columns. In one, write some of Molly's hopes; in the other, write some of the things that actually happened.

7   *How I wish I were a boy! . . . My father's slogan was that boys should go everywhere and know everything and that a girl should stay at home and know nothing.* Molly wrote this in an earlier chapter. Imagine that she time-travelled to your school: write what she finds there and describe her reactions.

A Horseman in the Sky

Before you read

1   'Duty' – a task or action that a person is bound to perform for moral or legal reasons – is not a word we often use any more. It has an old-fashioned feel to it. But do we still have duties to other people? Discuss this in groups and then share your conclusions with the rest of your class.

What's it about?

2   Draw a diagram of this scene, showing the features of the landscape, the roads and the positions of Carter Druse, the regiments and the horseman.

3   Write the order that Carter Druse must have been given before the start of the story.

4   Carter bows 'reverently to his father' and shows 'conscience and courage, by deeds of devotion and daring'. His father has 'stately courtesy which masked a breaking heart'. At this point in the story, which man do you like best? Why?

5   Two completely different thoughts must have been at war in Carter's head before he fired his gun. Write them down.

6   The father's death is described in slow motion.
    a   Look at the details as if you are directing this part of the story on film. Draw and describe frame by frame what you want the audience to see and focus on.
    b   In pairs, look back through the story for clues to its ending.

Thinking about the text

7   Was Carter right to pull the trigger? Why was his aim at the horse? What made him suddenly calm? Hot-seat him: test his resolve under pressure.

8   Put yourself in Carter Druse's shoes. How have you been changed by what you did that day? Write your answer in the form of a letter written afterwards, a diary entry or a prayer.

War and Peace

Before you read

1 'When you're old enough . . . ' 'You're not old enough yet . . . '
   'When you're grown up . . . ' are statements that adults often make
   to children and teenagers. In groups, discuss the kinds of issues
   that cause these arguments.

What's it about?

2 'Petya had been in a constant state of blissful excitement at being
   grown-up . . . '. But there are several examples of how he acts like
   a child. Choose one and describe what he does or says.

3 Petya uses lively questions and emphatic statements as if he can't
   get over the excitement of being in the forest. Write down two.

4 The adults around him get on with what they have to do. What do
   you think life is really like for them? Write down what a soldier
   might be thinking as Petya dashes around.

Thinking about the text

5 Petya and the French drummer-boy might have been friends if they
   weren't on opposite sides in the war. If Petya had decided to give
   the money to Vincent, what might they have said to each other?
   Write their whispered conversation as a playscript and act it out.

6 Moments of sympathy between opposing sides in wars are not
   uncommon. (For example, there was a famous Christmas truce in
   World War I when the soldiers from Britain and Germany played
   football and sang carols together.) Write a paragraph about the
   message that Tolstoy might be giving in this chapter.

Compare and contrast

1 The fathers in *The Way of All Flesh* and *David Copperfield* are both cruel. Do they mean to be? In your view, which one is worse?

Read the texts again, making notes as you go. Use your notes to write three paragraphs: describe Theobald's cruelty; then describe Mr Murdstone's; then write your conclusion, taking care to explain your opinion.

2 David Copperfield and Huckleberry Finn are both shocked by what happens to them but they are different characters and react differently from one another. Would Huck have let himself be locked up by Mr Murdstone? Would David have stood up to Huck's father? What kinds of boys have the authors created? Draw columns for each of the boys and compare their qualities, quoting evidence from the texts. Include their:

- courage
- quick-wittedness
- sense of humour
- determination
- and any others . . .

3 The young soldiers Carter Druse and Petya Rostov share a view of duty in battle, although the serious Carter Druse is filled with a solemn sense of duty and the irrepressible Petya is filled with notions of glory. Write about how these two young men tackle their jobs. What would it be like to fight alongside them? Which of them might make a better job of supporting and protecting you? What do you think soldiers *need* to be like?

4 In writing autobiographically in a *London Child of the Seventies*, Molly gives us her version of what happens at school. This is also what authors do when they create 'first-person' narratives, as in the stories of Huckleberry Finn and David Copperfield. Re-read the *Ragged Schools* text and imagine one of the children is explaining to you how she or he ended up there. Write down exactly what she or he says to you.

3 Urbanisation

'Two nations – who are as ignorant of each other's habits, thoughts and feelings as if they were dwellers in different zones, or inhabitants of different planets. The rich and the poor.'

This is how Benjamin Disraeli, a famous Victorian prime minister, described Britain in 1845.

Parliament set the 1842 Royal Commission the great task of finding out about the lives and conditions of poor children. In this way, faces were seen and voices heard that would otherwise have stayed buried in the darkness of the pits, the tumult of the factories and the whirl of the mills. The Commission's report led to new laws being created and the 'two nations' drew a little closer together.

Meanwhile, sackmakers worked to fill overnight orders by gathering under streetlamps, weary seamstresses stitched shirts for the rich day and night, little chimney-sweep boys got stuck in chimneys . . . The years passed and change came slowly for poor people. Samuel Smiles's book *Self-Help* in 1859 was a much-read collection of biographies of people who had achieved financial success by their own efforts, and the common saying was 'Heaven helps those who help themselves'. So if you were poor, the common thought was that perhaps you deserved it.

But some men and women did help. Lord Shaftesbury's passionate words in parliament had brought about the 1842 Royal Commission; Octavia Hill raised money to build houses for poor families; and many, many more individuals you can find out about committed their lives to social change. Mr Thomas Clarke, a chimney sweep in Nottingham, said of the boys who died at work, 'They go off just as quietly as you might fall asleep in the chair, by the fire there.' When you heard the evidence – if you had any conscience – you had to act. Some didn't wait; they marched (the Chartists), or they went on strike (the Match Girls in 1888).

This was also an age of huge achievements. It was a fabulous age for scientific and technological advancement and the 1851 Great Exhibition was its showcase. The Exhibition building itself was a marvel. It had a steel frame of 3,300 columns, 2,300 girders, nearly 300,000 panes of glass, and Queen Victoria herself officially opened it to a fanfare of trumpets. It dazzled the world. Charles Kingsley (the author of *The Water Babies*) was moved to tears. He said he was 'going into a sacred place'. It made the Victorians believe they could overcome all the evils and despairs of their times.

Activities

1   Do you know the age at which children are allowed to work today and under what conditions (minimum wage and length of time spent at work)? If not, take a guess and then find out the facts. Discuss in class what you think the terms and conditions should be.

2   The English class system used to be clear and rigid. Being working, middle or upper class (and even with grades of how 'middle' class you were) meant that you knew where you had been born in the class system and where you were expected to stay. If you married 'out of your class', or started to earn a great deal of money, there were difficulties: would you cope, and would others accept you? Discuss in groups whether you think we still have a class system that divides people today.

3   Make lists of all the reasons why:
   • people should look after themselves
   • the government should look after people
   • individuals with money, time and opportunities in life should help others.

From your knowledge of the Victorian age so far, where do you think poor people looked to for help? Talk about this in class.

Children in the Coal Mines: The 1842 Report

by R. H. Horne

The 1842 Royal Commission was set up to look at how children worked: how old they were, where they worked and under what conditions. It is astonishing to read today about how little responsibility employers had to take, not only for children's well-being, but for their very lives.

In 1840 it was decided to set up a Commission to inquire into the state of children in mines and manufactories. The Commissioners were Thomas Tooke and Dr Southwood Smith, who had been Commissioners in the Factory Commission of 1833, and two factory inspectors, Leonard Horner and R. J. Saunders. Some twenty sub-commissioners were appointed to make the necessary inquiries, collect evidence, etc.

The first report appeared in May 1842, and covered the employment of children and young persons (and also women) in mines.

LORD SHAFTESBURY VISITING THE COAL MINES OF THE BLACK COUNTRY, 1840-42

Picture used by Herbert Ingram as part of his campaign in *The Illustrated London News* to bring an end to child labour in the mines

The 1842 Report

From the whole of the evidence which has been collected, and of which we have thus endeavoured to give a digest,[1] we find – In regard to COAL MINES –

1   That instances occur in which Children are taken into these mines to work as early as four years of age, sometimes at five, and between five and six, not unfrequently between six and seven, and often from seven to eight, while from eight to nine is the ordinary age at which employment in these mines commences.

2   That a very large proportion of the persons employed in carrying on the work of these mines is under thirteen years of age; and a still larger proportion between thirteen and eighteen.

3   That in several districts female Children begin to work in these mines at the same early ages as the males.

4   That a great body of the Children and Young Persons employed in these mines are of the families of the adult workpeople engaged in the pits, or belong to the poorest population in the neighbourhood, and are hired and paid in some districts by the workpeople, but in others by the proprietors or contractors.

* * *

7   That the nature of the employment which is assigned to the youngest Children, generally that of 'trapping',[2] requires that they should be in the pit as soon as the work of the day commences, and, according to the present system, that they should not leave the pit before the work of the day is at an end.

8   That although this employment scarcely deserves the name of labour, yet, as the Children engaged in it are commonly excluded from light and are always without companions, it would, were it not for the passing and repassing of the coal carriages, amount to solitary confinement of the worst order.

---

[1]**digest**   summary
[2]**trapping**   opening and shutting the ventilation doors in a mine

9 That in those districts in which the seams of coal are so thick that horses go direct to the workings, or in which the side passages from the workings to the horseways are not of any great length, the lights in the main ways render the situation of these Children comparatively less cheerless, dull, and stupefying;[3] but that in some districts they remain in solitude and darkness during the whole time they are in the pit, and, according to their own account, many of them never see the light of day for weeks together during the greater part of the winter season, excepting on those days in the week when work is not going on, and on the Sundays.

10 That at different ages, from six years old and upwards, the hard work of pushing and dragging the carriages of coal from the workings to the main ways, or to the foot of the shaft, begins; a labour which all classes of witnesses concur[4] in stating requires the unremitting exertion[5] of all the physical power which the young workers possess.

* * *

20 That one of the most frequent causes of accidents in these mines is the want of superintendence by overlookers or otherwise to see to the security of the machinery for letting down and bringing up the workpeople, the restriction of the number of persons who ascend and descend at a time, the state of the mine as to the quantity of noxious gas in it, the efficiency of the ventilation, the exactness with which the air-door keepers perform their duty, the places into which it is safe or unsafe to go with a naked lighted candle, and the security of the proppings to uphold the roof, etc.

21 That another frequent cause of fatal accidents in coal mines is the almost universal practice of intrusting the closing of the air-doors to very young Children.

---

[3]**stupefying**   making you bored to the point of being barely conscious
[4]**concur**   agree
[5]**unremitting exertion**   endless effort

22 That there are many mines in which the most ordinary precautions to guard against accidents are neglected, and in
which no money appears to be expended[6] with a view to
secure the safety, much less the comfort, of the workpeople.

The experiences of three children of the time:
Sarah, Mary and William

'I daren't sing in the dark'

Sarah Gooder, age 8: I'm a trapper in the Gawber pit. It does not
tire me, but I have to trap without a light, and I'm scared.
Sometimes I sing when I have a light, but not in the dark; I dare
not sing then. I don't like being in the pit.

I go to Sunday-schools and read Reading made Easy. (She
knows her letters and can read little words.) They teach me to
pray. (She repeated the Lord's Prayer, not very perfectly, and ran
on with the following addition: – 'God bless my father and
mother, and sister and brother, uncles and aunts and cousins, and
everybody else, and God bless me and make me a good servant.
Amen.'). I have heard tell of Jesus many a time. I don't know why
he came to earth, I'm sure, and I don't know why he died, but he
had stones for his head to rest on. I would like to be at school far
better than in the pit.

Her lamp had gone out

Mary Davis, near seven years old, keeper of an air-door in a pit
in South Wales, was described by Sub-Commissioner Franks
as, 'A very pretty little girl, who was fast asleep under a piece
of rock near the air-door below ground. Her lamp had gone
out for want of oil; and upon waking her, she said the rats or
some one had run away with her bread and cheese, so she
went to sleep. The oversman, who was with me, thought she
was not so old, though he felt sure she had been below near
18 months.'

---

[6]**expended**   spent

Little boy lost

I imagine one of the first questions an anxious mother would ask would be, 'Is there not a great danger of little boys of ten years of age being lost in the passages of the dark mine?'

Formerly there was great danger of this kind, with very little boys, under ten, or even eight years old. But, on the whole, very few cases of this kind have occurred in the northern pits. The trappers are stationary, and if found away from their doors are thumped and threatened . . . Many sit there, too, in fear of the hobgoblins to be met with in the pit; and the reputation of hobgoblins is sustained[7] for their good behaviour. Some friend, if not the father, takes them to the door, and probably comes for them at 'kenner' or 'lose' time.[8]

Very recently a little boy was lost in one of the Welsh pits. His name was William Withers, and on a Friday morning he went to work with his father as usual. On arriving at the pit, he found that he had forgotten his lamp, and returned for the purpose of getting it, intending to follow his father into the mine. As he, however, proceeded along the subterranean road, he lost his light, and as a consequence his way, and wandered into some old works. From that time till Monday morning he was not seen or heard of. He was then found by the hauliers in a very weak state, and taken home . . . His own account is as follows:

'After I lost my light, I found that I was lost, and in a strange road. I could hear my father at work all Friday, I knocked the side, and made as much noise as I possibly could, but no one answered me. They all went out that night, leaving me there; I cried very much. I thought I saw the stars two or three times, although I was 100 yards under ground. I saved my dinner as much as I could, only eating a bit at a time, not knowing whether I should ever be found. The pit broke (work) on Saturday morning, so there was no work until Monday morning.

---

[7]**sustained**   kept going, prolonged
[8]**'kenner' or 'lose' time**   unpaid time, such as a meal break

The whole time I had been wandering about in the dark, when I heard the hauliers, and I made my way to them.'

When asked what day it was, the poor little fellow did not know, but thought he had been lost seven or eight days.

Further reading

If you would like to find out more about working children's experiences in Victorian times, have a look at the first chapter of *The Timetraveller's Guide to Victorian London* by Natasha Narayan (Watling Street Publishing, 2004). For an insight into the working world outside London, have a look at the CD-ROM *Victorian Britain*, published by Cambridge University Press in 2004, which follows a working-class family in Burton-upon-Trent in 1881.

The Cry of the Children
by Elizabeth Barrett Browning

Elizabeth Barrett Browning wrote this poem in response to the 1842 Report, which had been written by her friend R. H. Horne. It was published in *Blackwood's Magazine* a year later. (Many novelists and poets had their work first published in popular magazines and journals and consequently made their name there.)

Poetry reached some audiences in ways that parliamentary reports did not. When people read this poem, perhaps they were touched in a different way. Certainly Elizabeth Barrett Browning hoped so.

Do ye hear the children weeping, O my brothers,
    Ere[1] the sorrow comes with years?
They are leaning their young heads against their mothers –
    And that cannot stop their tears.
The young lambs are bleating in the meadows;
    The young birds are chirping in the nest;
The young fawns are playing with the shadows;
    The young flowers are blowing toward the west –
But the young, young children, O my brothers,
    They are weeping bitterly!
They are weeping in the playtime of the others,
    In the country of the free.

'For oh,' say the children, 'we are weary,
    And we cannot run or leap –
If we cared for any meadows, it were merely
    To drop down in them and sleep.
Our knees tremble *sorely* in the *stooping* –
    We fall upon our faces, trying to go;

---

[1]**Ere**   before

And, underneath our heavy eyelids drooping,
    The reddest flower would look as pale as snow.
For, all day, we drag our burden tiring,
    Through the coal-dark, underground –
Or, all day, we drive the wheels of iron
    In the factories, round and round.

'For all day, the wheels are droning, turning –
    Their wind comes in our faces –
Till our hearts turn, – our heads, with pulses burning,
    And the walls turn in their places –
Turns the *sky* in the *high* window blank and reeling –
    Turns the long light that droppeth down the wall –
Turns the black flies that crawl along the ceiling –
    All are turning, all the day, and we with all! –

And all day, the iron wheels are droning;
    And sometimes we could pray,
'O ye wheels,' (breaking out in a mad moaning)
    'Stop! be silent for to-day!'
Ay! be silent! Let them hear each other breathing
    For a moment, mouth to mouth –
Let them touch each other's hands, in a fresh wreathing[2]
    Of their tender human youth!
Let them feel that this cold metallic motion
    Is not all the life God fashions or reveals –
Let them prove their inward souls against the notion
    That they live in you, or under you, O wheels! –
Still, all day, the iron wheels go onward,
    As if Fate in each were stark;[3]
And the children's souls, which God is calling sunward,
    Spin on blindly in the dark.

---

[2]**wreathing**   taking the shape of a wreath – a band of flowers
[3]**stark**   blunt, clear

They look up, with their pale and sunken faces,
      And their look is dread to see,
For they think you see their angels in their places,
      With eyes meant for Deity;[4] –
'How long,' they say, 'how long, O cruel nation,
      Will you stand, to move the world, on a child's heart,
Stifle down with a mailed heel[5] its palpitation,
      And tread onward to your throne amid the mart?
Our blood splashes upward, O our tyrants,
      And your purple shews[6] your path;
But the child's sob curseth deeper in the silence
      Than the strong man in his wrath!'

Further reading

If you would be interested to read another of Elizabeth Barrett Browning's poems, you could try her *Sonnets from the Portuguese* which include the famous *How Do I Love Thee? Let Me Count the Ways*. Her husband was Robert Browning, and one of his most famous poems is *The Pied Piper of Hamelin*.

---

[4]**Deity**   God
[5]**mailed heel**   a shoe with metal rivets
[6]**shews**   shows

Narrative of a Pickpocket

by Henry Mayhew

Imagine being ten years old, falling out with your family and ending up living on the streets. It still happens today. But in 1840 when this young man's account begins, Mayhew said there were 'thousands of neglected children loitering about the low neighbourhoods of the metropolis and prowling about the streets'.

'As we endeavoured to inspire him with hope in an honest career,' Mayhew writes in this chapter, 'he mournfully shook his head . . . and began his tale.'

After being several times spoken to by my father about my quarrelsome disposition[1] with my brothers and sister, I threatened, young as I was, to burn the house down the first opportunity I got. This threat, though not uttered in my father's hearing, came to his ear, and he gave me a severe beating for it, the first time he ever corrected me. This was in the summer of 1840, in the end of May. I determined to leave home, and took nothing away but what belonged to me. I had four sovereigns[2] of pocket money, and the suit of clothes I had on, and a shirt. I walked to Shrewsbury and took the coach to London. When I got to London I had neither friend nor acquaintance. I first put up in a coffee-shop in the Mile End Road, and lodged there for seven weeks, till my money was nearly all spent.

During this time my clothes had been getting shabby and dirty, having no one to look after me. After being there for seven weeks I went to a mean lodging-house at Field Lane, Holborn. There I met with characters I had never seen before, and heard language that I had not formerly heard. This was about July, 1840, and I was about ten years of age the ensuing October.

---

[1]**disposition**   temperament, frame of mind
[2]**sovereign**   a gold coin then worth a pound sterling

I stopped there about three weeks doing nothing. At the end of that time I was completely destitute.[3]

The landlady took pity on me as a poor country boy who had been well brought up, and kept me for some days longer after my money was done. During these few days I had very little to eat, except what was given me by some of the lodgers when they got their own meals. I often thought at that time of my home in the country, and of what my father and mother might be doing, as I had never written to them since the day I had first left my home.

I sometimes was almost tempted to write to them and let them know the position I was in, as I knew they would gladly send me up money to return home, but my stubborn spirit was not broke then. After being totally destitute for two or three days, I was turned out of doors, a little boy in the great world of London, with no friend to assist me, and perfectly ignorant of the ways and means of getting a living in London.

I was taken by several poor ragged boys to sleep in the dark arches of the Adelphi. I often saw the boys follow the male passengers when the halfpenny boats came to the Adelphi stairs, i.e., the part of the river almost opposite to the Adelphi Theatre. I could not at first make out the meaning of this, but I soon found they generally had one or two handkerchiefs when the passengers left. At this time there was a prison-van in the Adelphi arches, without wheels, which was constructed different from the present prison-van, as it had no boxes in the interior. The boys used to take me with them into the prison-van. There we used to meet a man my companions called 'Larry'. I knew him by no other name for the time. He used to give almost what price he liked for the handkerchiefs. If they refused to give them at the price he named, he would threaten them in several ways. He said he would get the other boys to drive them away, and not allow them to get any more handkerchiefs there.

---

[3]**destitute**   totally poor

If this did not intimidate them, he would threaten to give them in charge, so that at last they were compelled to take whatever price he liked to give them.

I have seen handkerchiefs I afterwards found out to be of the value of four or five shillings, sold him lumped together at 9*d*. each.

The boys, during this time, had been very kind to me, sharing what they got with me, but always asking why I did not try my hand, till at last I was ashamed to live any longer upon the food they gave me without doing something for myself. One of the boys attached himself to me more than the others, whom we used to call Joe Muckraw, who was afterwards transported,[4] and is now in a comfortable position in Australia.

Joe said to me, that when the next boat came in, if any man came out likely to carry a good handkerchief, he would let me have a chance at it. I recollect when the boat came in that evening: I think it was the last one, about nine o'clock. I saw an elderly gentleman step ashore, and a lady with him. They had a little dog, with a string attached to it, that they led along. Before Joe said anything to me, he had 'fanned' the gentleman's pocket, i.e., had felt the pocket and knew there was a handkerchief.

He whispered to me, "Now, Dick, have a try," and I went to the old gentleman's side, trembling all the time, and Joe standing close to me in the dark, and went with him up the steep hill of the Adelphi. He had just passed an apple-stall there, Joe still following us, encouraging me all the time, while the old gentleman was engaged with the little dog. I took out a green 'kingsman' (handkerchief), next in value to a black silk handkerchief. (They are used a good deal as neckerchiefs by costermongers.[5]) The gentleman did not perceive his loss. We immediately went to the arches and entered the van where Larry was, and Joe said to him, "There is Dick's first trial, and

---

[4]**transported**   exiled to a penal colony, a working prison in a foreign country, often Australia
[5]**costermonger**   someone who sells fruit, vegetables or fish from a stall

you must give him a 'ray' for it," i.e., 1s. 6d. After a deal of pressing we got 1s. for it.

After that I gained confidence, and in the course of a few
weeks I was considered the cleverest of the little band, never
missing one boat coming in, and getting one or two handkerchiefs on each occasion. During the time we knew there were no
boats coming we used to waste our money on sweets, and fruits,
and went often in the evenings to the Victoria Theatre, and
Bower Saloon, and other places. When we came out at twelve, or
half-past twelve at night, we went to the arches again, and slept
in the prison-van. This was the life I led till January, 1841.

During that month several men came to us. I did not know,
although I afterwards heard they were brought by 'Larry' to
watch me, as he had been speaking of my cleverness at the 'tail,'
i.e., stealing from the tails of gentlemen's coats, and they used
to make me presents. It seemed they were not satisfied altogether with me, for they did not tell me what they wanted, nor
speak their mind to me. About the middle of the month I was
seized by a gentleman, who caught me with his handkerchief in
my hand. I was taken to Bow Street police station and got two
months in Westminster Bridewell.

I came out in March, and when outside the gate of
Westminster Bridewell there was a cab waiting for me, and two
of the men standing by who had often made me presents and
spoken to me in the arches. They asked me if I would go with
them, and took me into the cab. I was willing to go anywhere to
better myself, and went with them to Flower-and-Dean Street,
Brick Lane, Whitechapel. They took me to their own home. One
of them had the first floor of a house there, the other had the
second. Both were living with women, and I found out shortly
afterwards that these men had lately had a boy, but he was
transported about that time, though I did not know this then.
They gave me plenty to eat, and one of the women, by name
'Emily', washed and cleansed me, and I got new clothes to put
on. For three days I was not asked to do anything, but in the
meantime they had been talking to me of going with them, and

having no more to do with the boys at the Adelphi, or with the 'tail,' but to work at picking ladies' pockets.

I thought it strange at first, but found afterwards that it was more easy to work on a woman's pocket than upon a man's, for this reason: More persons work together, and the boy is well surrounded by companions older than himself, and is shielded from the eyes of the passers-by; and, besides, it pays better.

It was on a Saturday, in company with three men, I set out on an excursion from Flower-and-Dean Street along Cheapside. They were young men, from nineteen to twenty-five years of age, dressed in fashionable style. I was clothed in the suit given me when I came out of prison, a beaver-hat,[6] a little surtout-coat[7] and trousers, both of black cloth, and a black silk necktie and collar, dressed as a gentleman's son. We went into a pastrycook's shop in St Paul's Churchyard about half-past two in the afternoon, and had pastry there, and they were watching the ladies coming into the shop, till at last they followed one out, taking me with them.

As this was my first essay in having anything to do in stealing from a woman, I believe they were nervous themselves, but they had well tutored me during the two or three days I had been out of prison. They had stood against me in the room while Emily walked to and fro, and I had practised on her pocket by taking out sometimes a lady's clasp purse, termed a 'portemonnaie,' and other articles out of her pocket, and thus I was not quite ignorant of what was expected of me. One walked in front of me, one on my right hand, and the other in the rear, and I had the lady on my left hand. I immediately 'fanned' her (felt her pocket) as she stopped to look in at a hosier's window, when I took her purse and gave it to one of them, and we immediately went to a house in Giltspur Street. We there examined what was in the purse. I think there was a sovereign, and about 17s.; I cannot speak positively how much. The purse was

---

[6]**beaver-hat**   a hat made of beaver fur
[7]**surtout-coat**   a man's overcoat

thrown away, as is the general rule, and we went down Newgate
Street, into Cheapside, and there we soon got four more purses
that afternoon, and went home by five o'clock p.m. I recollect
how they praised me afterwards that night at home for my cleverness.

I think we did not go out again till the Tuesday, and that
and the following day we had a good pull. It amounted to about
£19 each. They always take care to allow the boy to see what is
in the purse, and to give him his proper share equal with the
others, because he is their sole support. If they should lose him
they would be unable to do anything till they got another. Out
of my share, which was about £19, I bought a silver watch and
a gold chain, and about this time I also bought an overcoat, and
carried it on my left arm to cover my movements.

A few weeks after this we went to Surrey Gardens, and I got two purses from ladies. In one of them were some French coins and a ring, that was afterwards advertised as either lost or stolen in the garden. We did very well that visit, and were thinking of going again, when I was caught in Fleet Street, and they had no means of getting me away, though they tried all they could to secure my escape. They could not do it without exposing themselves to too much suspicion. I was sentenced to three months' imprisonment in Bridge Street Bridewell, Blackfriars, termed by the thieves the Old Horse.

Further reading

The most famous pickpocket in literature is in the novel *Oliver Twist* by Charles Dickens. The Artful Dodger and a gang of other boys are trained by Fagin to make a living by picking pockets. Dickens knew that many children in real life ended up like the boys in Mayhew's book.

Song of the Shirt

by Thomas Hood

This was one of the most quoted and anthologised poems of the
19th century. It influenced many people to see that the conditions
under which poor women were forced to sew were truly evil, and that
they must stop. Thomas Hood was so fond of this powerful description of the miseries of the poor that he wished to have one single line
inscribed on his tombstone: 'He sang the "Song of the Shirt"'.

With fingers weary and worn,
    With eyelids heavy and red,
A woman sat, in unwomanly rags,
    Plying[1] her needle and thread –
      Stitch! stitch! stitch!
In poverty, hunger, and dirt,
    And still, with a voice of dolorous[2] pitch,
She sang the 'Song of the Shirt.'

    'Work! work! work!
While the cock is crowing aloof!
    And work – work – work,
Till the stars shine through the roof!
It's oh! to be a slave
    Along with the barbarous Turk,
Where woman has never a soul to save,
    If this is Christian work!

    'Work – work – work,
Till the brain begins to swim,
    Work – work – work,
Till the eyes are heavy and dim!

---

[1]**Plying**   working with, using
[2]**dolorous pitch**   a sad tone

Seam, and gusset, and band,
 Band, and gusset, and seam,
Till over the buttons I fall asleep,
 And sew them on in a dream.

'Oh! men with sisters dear!
 Oh, men with mothers and wives!
It is not linen you're wearing out,
 But human creatures' lives!
 Stitch – stitch – stitch,
 In poverty, hunger, and dirt,
Sewing at once, with a double thread,
 A shroud³ as well as a shirt.

'But why do I talk of death,
 That phantom of grisly bone?
I hardly fear his terrible shape,
 It seems so like my own –
 It seems so like my own,
 Because of the fasts I keep.
O God! that bread should be so dear,
 And flesh and blood so cheap!

 'Work – work – work,
 My labour never flags;
And what are its wages? A bed of straw,
 A crust of bread, – and rags –
That shattered roof, – and this naked floor –
 A table, – a broken chair –
And a wall so blank, my shadow I thank
 For sometimes falling there!

 'Work – work – work!
From weary chime to chime!

---

³**shroud**   cloth used to wrap a dead body

Work – work – work!
As prisoners work for crime!
    Band, and gusset, and seam,
    Seam, and gusset, and band,
Till the heart is sick, and the brain benumbed,
    As well as the weary hand.

'Work – work – work,
In the dull December light,
    And work – work – work,
When the weather is warm and bright –
While underneath the eaves
    The brooding swallows cling,
As if to show me their sunny backs,
    And twit me with the Spring.

'Oh, but to breathe the breath
    Of the cowslip and primrose sweet –
With the sky above my head,
    And the grass beneath my feet;
For only one sweet hour!
    To feel as I used to feel,
Before I knew the woes of want,
    And the walk that costs a meal;

'Oh, but for one short hour!
    A respite,[4] however brief!
No blessed leisure for love or hope,
    But only time for grief!
A little weeping would ease my heart,
    But in their briny[5] bed
My tears must stop, for every drop
    Hinders needle and thread!'

---

[4]**respite** rest
[5]**briny** salty

With fingers weary and worn,
    With eyelids heavy and red,
A woman sat, in unwomanly rags,
    Plying her needle and thread –
        Stitch! stitch! stitch!
    In poverty, hunger, and dirt,
And still, with a voice of dolorous pitch –
Would that its tone could reach the Rich! –
    She sang this 'Song of the Shirt.'

Further reading

If you enjoyed reading this, you might like to read another poem by Hood – a popular one is *I Remember, I Remember*.

Mary Barton
by Mrs Gaskell

John Barton, the heroine's father, is about to take part in the Chartist demonstration of 1839.

The Chartists were largely working-class men and women who used petitions and marches to agitate parliament to give every man the vote. They believed this would make everyone's lives better. Laws might then be passed that would help the poor.

Here we see that John and his friends trust 'the parliament people' to help them. All John will have to do, they think, is put their case clearly. They have no idea of the struggles that still lie ahead.

For three years past, trade had been getting worse and worse, and the price of provisions[1] higher and higher. This disparity[2] between the amount of the earnings of the working classes, and the price of their food, occasioned in more cases than could well be imagined, disease and death. Whole families went through a gradual starvation. They only wanted a Dante[3] to record their sufferings. And yet even his words would fall short of the awful truth; they could only present an outline of the tremendous facts of the destitution[4] that surrounded thousands upon thousands in the terrible years 1839, 1840, and 1841. Even philanthropists[5] who had studied the subject, were forced to own themselves perplexed in the endeavour to ascertain[6] the real causes of the misery; the whole matter was of so complicated a nature that it became next to impossible to understand it thoroughly. It need excite no surprise then to learn

---

[1]**provisions**   food
[2]**disparity**   difference
[3]**Dante**   Dante Alighieri, the great Italian poet (1265–1321) who wrote an account of a journey through Hell, Purgatory and Paradise in *The Divine Comedy*.
[4]**destitution**   the state of being very poor, lacking everything necessary to live such as food, clothing and shelter
[5]**philanthropists**   people concerned to do good for society
[6]**perplexed in the endeavour to ascertain**   confused in the attempt to find out

that a bad feeling between working-men and the upper classes became very strong in this season of privation.[7] The indigence[8] and sufferings of the operatives[9] induced a suspicion in the minds of many of them, that their legislators, their magistrates, their employers, and even the ministers of religion, were, in general, their oppressors and enemies; and were in league for their prostration and enthralment.[10] The most deplorable and enduring evil that arose out of the period of commercial depression to which I refer, was this feeling of alienation between the different classes of society. It is so impossible to describe, or even faintly to picture, the state of distress which prevailed in the town at that time, that I will not attempt it; and yet I think again that surely, in a Christian land, it was not known even so feebly as words could tell it, or the more happy and fortunate would have thronged with their sympathy and their aid. In many instances the sufferers wept first, and then they cursed. Their vindictive[11] feelings exhibited themselves in rabid[12] politics. And when I hear, as I have heard, of the sufferings and privations of the poor, or provision shops where ha'porths of tea, sugar, butter, and even flour, were sold to accommodate the indigent, – of parents sitting in their clothes by the fire-side during the whole night for seven weeks together, in order that their only bed and bedding might be reserved for the use of their large family, – of others sleeping upon the cold hearth-stone for weeks in succession, without adequate means of providing themselves with food or fuel (and this in the depth of winter), – of others being compelled to fast for days together, uncheered by any hope of better fortune, living, moreover, or rather starving, in a crowded garret, or damp cellar, and gradually sinking under the pressure of want and despair into a premature grave; and when this has been confirmed by the evidence of their careworn looks, their excited feelings, and their desolate homes, – can I wonder that many of

---

[7]**privation**   lack of the necessities of life
[8]**indigence**   poverty
[9]**operatives**   the workers of the machines
[10]**prostration and enthralment**   helplessness and enslavement
[11]**vindictive**   vengeful
[12]**rabid**   angry

The Chartist demonstration on Kennington Common, April 1848

them, in such times of misery and destitution, spoke and acted with ferocious precipitation?[13]

An idea was now springing up among the operatives, that originated with the Chartists, but which came at last to be cherished as a darling child by many and many a one. They could not believe that government knew of their misery: they rather chose to think it possible that men could voluntarily assume the office of legislators[14] for a nation ignorant of its real state; as who should make domestic rules for the pretty behaviour of children without caring to know that these children had been kept for days without food. Besides, the starving multitudes had heard that the very existence of their distress had been denied in Parliament; and though they felt this strange and inexplicable, yet the idea that their misery had still to be revealed in all its depths, and that then some remedy would be found, soothed their aching hearts, and kept down their rising fury.

So a petition was framed, and signed by thousands in the bright spring days of 1839, imploring Parliament to hear witnesses

---

[13]**ferocious precipitation**   very angry and impulsive actions
[14]**office of legislators**   parliament

who could testify to the unparalleled destitution of the manufacturing districts. Nottingham, Sheffield, Glasgow, Manchester, and
many other towns were busy appointing delegates[15] to convey this
petition, who might speak, not merely of what they had seen and
had heard, but from what they had borne and suffered. Life-worn,
gaunt, anxious, hunger-stamped men, were those delegates.

One of them was John Barton. He would have been
ashamed to own the flutter of spirits his appointment gave him.
There was the childish delight of seeing London – that went a
little way, and but a little way. There was the vain idea of speaking out his notions before so many grand folk – that went a little further; and last, there was the really pure gladness of heart
arising from the idea that he was one of those chosen to be
instruments in making known the distresses of the people, and
consequently in procuring them some grand relief, by means of
which they should never suffer want or care any more. He hoped
largely, but vaguely, of the results of his expedition. An argosy[16]
of the precious hopes of many otherwise despairing creatures,
was that petition to be heard concerning their sufferings.

The night before the morning on which the Manchester delegates were to leave for London, Barton might be said to hold a
levée,[17] so many neighbours came dropping in. Job Legh had
early established himself and his pipe by John Barton's fire, not
saying much, but puffing away, and imagining himself of use in
adjusting the smoothing-irons[18] that hung before the fire, ready
for Mary when she should want them. As for Mary, her employment was the same as that of Beau Tibbs' wife, 'Just washing her
father's two shirts,' in the pantry back-kitchen; for she was anxious about his appearance in London. (The coat had been

---

[15] **delegates**   people chosen to represent others
[16] **argosy**   a ship or fleet of merchant ships: John Barton and his friends are
    going on a journey to London carrying important cargo – their information
[17] **levée**   a formal reception held when a monarch first got up in the morning;
    the use of the word here is to show John Barton is 'holding court',
    though he does this in a very humble way
[18] **smoothing-irons**   irons for pressing clothes which are heated by putting
    them in front of a fire

redeemed,[19] though the silk handkerchief was forfeited.[20]) The door stood open, as usual, between the house-place and back-kitchen, so she gave her greeting to their friends as they entered.

'So, John, yo're bound for London, are yo?' said one.

'Ay, I suppose I mun[21] go,' answered John, yielding to necessity as it were.

'Well, there's many a thing I'd like yo to speak on to the parliament people. Thou'lt not spare 'em, John, I hope. Tell 'em our minds; how we're thinking we've been clemmed[22] long enough, and we donnot see whatten good they'n been doing, if they can't give us what we're all crying for sin' the day we were born.'

'Ay, ay! I'll tell 'em that, and much more to it, when it gets to my turn; but thou knows there's many will have their word afore me.'

'Well, thou'lt speak at last. Bless thee, lad, do ask 'em to make th' masters break th' machines. There's never been good times sin' spinning-jennies[23] came up.'

'Machines is th' ruin of poor folk,' chimed in several voices.

'For my part,' said a shivering, half-clad[24] man, who crept near the fire, as if ague-stricken,[25] 'I would like thee to tell 'em to pass th' short-hours' bill. Flesh and blood gets wearied wi' so much work; why should factory hands work so much longer nor other trades? Just ask 'em that, Barton, will ye?'

Barton was saved the necessity of answering, by the entrance of Mrs Davenport, the poor widow he had been so kind to; she looked half-fed, and eager, but was decently clad. In her hand she brought a little newspaper parcel, which she took to Mary, who opened it, and then called out, dangling a shirt collar from her soapy fingers:

---

[19]**redeemed**   recovered
[20]**forfeited**   lost, given-up
[21]**mun**   must
[22]**clemmed**   starving
[23]**spinning jennies**   an early type of spinning-frame invented by James
     Hargreaves in 1764
[24]**half-clad**   half-dressed
[25]**ague-stricken**   ill

'See, father, what a dandy[26] you'll be in London! Mrs Davenport has brought you this; made new cut, all after the fashion. – Thank you for thinking on him.'

'Eh, Mary!' said Mrs Davenport, in a low voice. 'Whatten's all I can do, to what he's done for me and mine? But, Mary, sure I can help ye, for you'll be busy wi' this journey.'

'Just help me wring these out, and then I'll take 'em to th' mangle.'[27]

So Mrs Davenport became a listener to the conversation; and after a while joined in.

'I'm sure, John Barton, if yo are taking messages to the parliament folk, yo'll not object to telling 'em what a sore trial it is, this law o' theirs, keeping childer fra' factory work, whether they be weakly or strong. There's our Ben; why, porridge seems to go no way wi' him, he eats so much; and I han gotten no money to send him t' school, as I would like; and there he is, rampaging about th' streets a' day, getting hungrier and hungrier, and picking up a' manner o' bad ways; and th' inspector won't let him in to work in th' factory, because he's not right age; though he's twice as strong as Sankey's little ritling[28] of a lad, as works till he cries for his legs aching so, though he is right age, and better.'

'I've one plan I wish to tell John Barton,' said a pompous, careful-speaking man, 'and I should like him for to lay it afore the honourable house. My mother comed out o' Oxfordshire, and were under-laundry-maid in Sir Francis Dashwood's family; and when we were little ones, she'd tell us stories of their grandeur: and one thing she named were, that Sir Francis wore two shirts a day. Now he were all as one as a parliament man; and many on 'em, I han no doubt, are like extravagant. Just tell 'em, John, do, that they'd be doing th' Lancashire weavers a great kindness, if they'd ha' their shirts a' made o' calico;[29] 'twould make trade brisk, that would, wi' the power o' shirts they wear.'

---

[26]**dandy**   a man who likes to dress well
[27]**mangle**   a machine for wringing the wetness out of washed clothes
[28]**ritling**   a child who suffers from rickets (a lack of vitamins softens bones and children with rickets were common: their legs made a bow-shape)
[29]**calico**   white or unbleached cotton

Job Legh now put in his word. Taking the pipe out of his mouth, and addressing the last speaker, he said:

'I'll tell ye what, Bill, and no offence mind ye; there's but hundreds of them parliament folk as wear so many shirts to their back; but there's thousands and thousands o' poor weavers as han only gotten one shirt i' th' world; ay, and don't know where t' get another when that rag's done, though they're turning out miles o' calico every day; and many o' mile o't is lying in warehouses, stopping up trade for want o' purchasers. Yo take my advice, John Barton, and ask parliament to set trade free, so as workmen can earn a decent wage, and buy their two, ay and three, shirts a year; that would make weaving brisk.'

He put his pipe in his mouth again, and redoubled his puffing to make up for lost time.

'I'm afeard, neighbours,' said John Barton, 'I've not much chance o' telling 'em all yo say; what I think on, is just speaking out about the distress, that they say is nought. When they hear o' children born on wet flags, without a rag t' cover 'em, or a bit o' food for th' mother; when they hear of folk lying down to die i' th' streets, or hiding their want i' some hole o' a cellar till death come to set 'em free; and when they hear o' all this plague, pestilence, and famine, they'll surely do somewhat wiser for us than we can guess at now. Howe'er, I han no objection, if so be there's an open-ing to speak up for what yo say; anyhow, I'll do my best, and yo see now, if better times don't come after Parliament knows all.'

Some shook their heads, but more looked cheery: and then one by one dropped off, leaving John and his daughter alone.

Further reading

If you liked reading about a character who turns the tables on someone richer and more confident, you might like to try a chapter in Anthony Trollope's *The Last Chronicle of Barset*, where a poor curate is almost undone by a woman called Mrs Proudie.

Mrs Gaskell also wrote *North and South*, a novel about the effects of industrialisation, and *Wives and Daughters*, a novel about women. Charles Dickens's novel *Hard Times* is a brilliant depiction of life in the manufac-turing districts of the north of England, with the dreadful Mr Gradgrind as the headmaster of a school.

The Disturbances in the Manufacturing Districts

from *The Illustrated London News* 20 August 1842

The paper's journalists were on the spot, as usual, and reported exactly what they saw. Here, danger on the streets is brewing.

We have [August 1842] to record the disastrous occurrence of a turn-out of manufacturing labourers in and about Manchester, which must be regarded with sorrow by wise and thoughtful men. It would appear that the sudden and turbulent display of congregated thousands, leaving their daily employment – marching upon mills, forcing willing and unwilling alike to join them and, in a moment, paralysing the whole activity of the natural enterprise of their neighbourhood, – arose, in the first instance, from a reduction of wages in one quarter, given almost without notice, and taken by the men as the omen of a general intention on the part of the masters everywhere else. At once, with a desperation of purpose, they gathered in half-starved thousands, resolved to abjure[1] work, unless they can have 'a fair day's pay for a fair day's labour'; and partly with riot, partly with invective,[2] partly with threat, plunged the sober population into fear, and created anxieties, natural to these troublous times, from one end to the other of the land.

All the manufacturing districts have been up in arms; at Preston the insurgents[3] were fired upon, and some of them wounded mortally. At Stockport, where there are upwards of 20,000 persons out of employment who have no resources but those of plunder and beggary, a large body of rioters broke open and pillaged the workhouses of food and clothing, and mobs robbed the provision shops. Troops, guards,

---

[1] **abjure**   give up under oath
[2] **invective**   bitter accusations
[3] **insurgents**   rebels

and artillery have been poured in upon the shocking scene of insurrection;[4] and there seems to have been a spreading organization of a most formidable and disciplined character. The fact that troops had been ordered off to the disturbed districts soon became publicly known, and produced an intense feeling of alarm and excitement in the mind of individuals generally.

The anti-corn-law leaguer[5] and the chartist are, we fear, responsible for these agitations – responsible, as we think, to their Queen, their country, and their God. We are no partisans;[6] we do not oppose, abstractedly for their peculiar doctrines,[7] either the chartist or the anti-corn-law leaguer; we leave all political opinion, however violent, its fair play; but we despise the infamous diplomacy which would make its game out of the miseries of the people. Nothing can more excite our indignant rebuke than the revolutionary villain or the quack preacher of politics, who says, 'I have a charter to achieve here, or a corn-law to repeal there, and, now that the people are starving and in tatters, I will convert their rags into banners of rebellion, and their hunger into the sign of blood.' Yet this, we believe, is the course that *was* pursued, furnishing the key to all the riots and seditions[8] that disturbed the land.

Every way we lament the dismal occurrences that have transpired, from which, because they are destitute of social peace and order, even the justification of injury is taken away. Heaven knows that our cause is with the poor, and strongly have we reasoned and remonstrated on their behalf; but we set up JUSTICE and HUMANITY as our household gods, and for neither rich nor poor will we despoil their altars. There is no justice, there is no

---

[4]**insurrection**   rebellion
[5]**anti-corn-law leaguer**   a person who was against the laws between 1400 and 1846 to control the price of corn in England, who wanted to have free trade
[6]**partisans**   keen members of a cause
[7]**doctrine**   a description of the teachings of a religious, political or philosophical group
[8]**seditions**   fights against the authority of the country

humanity, in the late revolts; and although we rest their blame and guilt more upon the inciters than the enactors of the crime, yet we will not take the part of the latter because we execrate the former.

Further particulars of the disturbances

Reports stated that immense bodies of rioters from Wigan, Chorley, and the district of the collieries, some making them as numerous as 15,000, armed with axes, spades, bludgeons etc., were on their way to Preston. It was reported that a large cotton factory at Bamberbridge was partially destroyed by the mob. From the church steeple and the North Union Railway bridge, which commanded extensive views of the various roads to Preston, it was soon ascertained that the mob were in a body on their road towards the town of Chorley. However, the police and military were all brought together, and took up their station near Walton-bridge, the police being in the turnpike road, and the Rifles on each side concealed behind the hedges. About three o'clock in the afternoon a mob of about 1,000 persons, chiefly armed with iron truncheons, reached Walton, passed through the village, and were about entering the town, when the police force attempted to prevent them, and in consequence a battle commenced. Several of the police were severely wounded, one of whom had two fingers nearly severed from his hand by a blow with an iron bar. It soon became evident that the police force would be defeated, and the appearance of the mob became so alarming that orders were given to the military, who instantly burst through the hedges on each side of the road, and presented a bold front to the mob. The sudden appearance of the Rifles spread consternation and dismay in the ranks of the insurgents, who fled in all directions.

The more remarkable features of the proceedings at Stockport were the extortion of money from mill-owners as well as shop keepers, and an attack on the New Union Workhouse, Shaw-heath, where the mob forced an entrance and immediately commenced to help themselves to bread and money. Information of this was conveyed to the authorities, and they hastened to the spot with the constables, and infantry and captured about forty of the rioters.

Further reading

The 'danger' of the working classes rebelling was quite a subject of debate amongst well-to-do Victorians. If you're interested in the way the upper classes reacted to incidents like the Disturbances in the Manufacturing Districts, you could try reading Elizabeth Gaskell's *North and South*. Joan Aiken has written some adventure stories where the central characters join the struggle for survival in industrial towns much like those in Victorian England – try *Black Hearts in Battersea* (1964) or *Midnight is a Place* (1974).

1851; or the Adventures of Mr and Mrs Sandboys

by Henry Mayhew

The full title of Mayhew's book is: *1851; or the Adventures of Mr and Mrs Sandboys and family, who came up to London to 'enjoy themselves', and to see the Great Exhibition.*

At the close of the Great Exhibition in October, almost four and a half million visitors had come on 'shilling days', when the working classes were invited to see the wonders in the Crystal Palace. This document by the author of *London Labour and the London Poor* is seen as one of the first studies of the working class in Britain.

But if the other parts of the Great Exhibition are curious and instructive, the machinery, which has been from the first the grand focus of attraction, is, on the 'shilling days,' the most peculiar sight of the whole. Here every other man you rub against is habited[1] in a corduroy jacket, or a blouse, or leathern gaiters;[2] and round every object more wonderful than the rest, the people press, two and three deep, with their heads stretched out, watching intently the operations of the moving mechanism. You see the farmers, their dusty hats telling of the distance they have come, with their mouths wide agape, leaning over the bars to see the self-acting mills at work, and smiling as they behold the frame spontaneously draw itself out, and then spontaneously run back again. Some, with great smockfrocks, were gazing at the girls in their long pinafores engaged at the doubling-machines.

But the chief centres of curiosity are the power-looms,[3] and in front of these are gathered small groups of artisans,[4] and labourers, and young men whose red coarse hands tell you they do something for their living, all eagerly listening to the attendant, as he explains the operations, after stopping the loom. Here, too, as you pass along, you meet, now a member of the National Guard, in his

---

[1]**habited**   dressed
[2]**gaiters**   cloths covering or protecting legs
[3]**power-loom**   mechanical apparatus for weaving yarn (threads) into cloth
[4]**artisans**   workers

peculiar conical hat, with its little ball on top, and horizontal peak, and his red worsted epaulettes and full-plaited trowsers; then you come to a long, thin, and bilious[5]-looking Quaker,[6] with his tidy and clean-looking Quakeress by his side; and the next minute, may be, you encounter a school of charity-girls, in their large white collars and straw bonnets, with the mistress at their head, instructing the children as she goes. Round the electro-plating and the model diving-bell are crowds jostling one another for a foremost place. At the steam brewery, crowds of men and women are continually ascending and descending the stairs; youths are watching the model carriages moving along the new pneumatic railway; young girls are waiting to see the hemispherical lamp-shades made out of a flat sheet of paper; indeed, whether it be the noisy flax[7]-crushing machine, or the splashing centrifugal pump, or the clatter of the Jacquard lace machine, or the bewildering whirling of the cylindrical steam-press, – round each and all these are anxious, intelligent, and simple-minded artisans, and farmers, and servants, and youths, and children clustered, endeavouring to solve the mystery of its complex operations.

---

[5]**bilious**   bad-tempered
[6]**Quaker**   a member of the Society of Friends: a Christian sect who live and worship very simply
[7]**flax**   a plant: fibres from the stalks are spun into thread

For many days before the 'shilling people' were admitted to the building, the great topic of conversation was the probable behaviour of the people. Would they come sober? will they destroy the things? will they want to cut their initials, or scratch their names on the panes of the glass lighthouses? But they have surpassed in decorum the hopes of their well-wishers. The fact is, the Great Exhibition is to them more of a school than a show. The working-man has often little book-learning, but of such knowledge as constitutes[8] the education of life – viz.,[9] the understanding of human motives, and the acquisition[10] of power over natural forces, so as to render them subservient[11] to human happiness – of such knowledge as this, we repeat, the working-man has generally a greater share than those who are said to belong to the 'superior classes'. Hence it is, that what was a matter of tedium, and became ultimately more a lounge, for gentlefolks, is used as a place of instruction by the people.

We have been thus prolix[12] on the classes attending the Great Exhibition, because it is the influence that this institution is likely to exercise upon labour which constitutes its most interesting and valuable feature. If we really desire the improvement of our social state, (and surely we are far from perfection yet,) we must address ourselves to the elevation of the people;[13] and it is because the Great Exhibition is fitted to become a special instrument towards this end, that it forms one of the most remarkable and hopeful characteristics of our time.

Further reading

You could have a look at *World for a Shilling: How the Great Exhibition of 1851 Shaped a Nation* by Michael Leapman (2001). It is also worth visiting the National Art Library in the V&A which has been collecting children's publications since the mid-nineteenth century and has some interesting material on the Great Exhibition.

---

[8]**constitutes**   makes
[9]**viz.**   abbreviation of *videlicet:* that is to say
[10]**acquisition**   gaining
[11]**subservient**   helpful to
[12]**prolix**   long-winded
[13]**elevation of the people**   raising up the people, making their lives better

Bleak House

by Charles Dickens

> Mrs Pardiggle is one of Charles Dickens' superb characters. She is terrifying in her will to do good. 'There were two classes of charitable people,' says someone earlier in the chapter. 'One, the people who did a little and made a great deal of noise; the other, the people who did a great deal and made no noise at all . . . '

She was a formidable style of lady, with spectacles, a prominent nose, and a loud voice, who had the effect of wanting a great deal of room. And she really did, for she knocked down little chairs with her skirts that were quite a great way off. As only Ada and I were at home, we received her timidly; for she seemed to come in like cold weather, and to make the little Pardiggles blue as they followed.

'These, young ladies,' said Mrs Pardiggle, with great volubility,[1] after the first salutations,[2] 'are my five boys. You may have seen their names in a printed subscription list[3] (perhaps more than one), in the possession of our esteemed friend Mr Jarndyce. Egbert, my eldest (twelve), is the boy who sent out his pocket-money, to the amount of five-and-threepence, to the Tockahoopo Indians. Oswald, my second (ten-and-a-half), is the child who contributed two-and-ninepence to the Great National Smithers Testimonial. Francis, my third (nine), one-and-sixpence-halfpenny; Felix, my fourth (seven), eightpence to the Superannuated Widows; Alfred, my youngest (five), has voluntarily enrolled himself in the Infant Bonds of Joy,[4] and is pledged never, through life, to use tobacco in any form.'

---

[1]**volubility**   talking easily, readily and at length
[2]**salutations**   greetings
[3]**subscription list**   a list of the names of people who have promised to give money to a charity
[4]**Bonds of Joy**   children who promised they would never drink alcohol were formed into these bands or groups

We had never seen such dissatisfied children. It was not merely that they were weazen and shrivelled – though they were certainly that too – but they looked absolutely ferocious with discontent. At the mention of the Tockahoopo Indians, I could really have supposed Egbert to be one of the most baleful[5] members of that tribe, he gave me such a savage frown. The face of each child, as the amount of his contribution was mentioned, darkened in a peculiarly vindictive manner, but his was by far the worst. I must except, however, the little recruit into the Infant Bonds of Joy, who was stolidly and evenly miserable.

'You have been visiting, I understand,' said Mrs Pardiggle, 'at Mrs Jellyby's?'

We said yes, we had passed one night there.

'Mrs Jellyby,' pursued the lady, always speaking in the same demonstrative, loud, hard tone, so that her voice impressed my fancy as if it had a sort of spectacles on too – and I may take the opportunity of remarking that her spectacles were made the less engaging by her eyes being what Ada called 'choking eyes,' meaning very prominent: 'Mrs Jellyby is a benefactor to society, and deserves a helping hand. My boys have contributed to the African project – Egbert, one-and-six, being the entire allowance of nine weeks; Oswald, one-and-a-penny-halfpenny, being the same; the rest, according to their little means. Nevertheless, I do not go with Mrs Jellyby in all things. I do not go with Mrs Jellyby in her treatment of her young family. It has been noticed. It has been observed that her young family are excluded from participation in the objects to which she is devoted. She may be right, she may be wrong; but, right or wrong, this is not my course with *my* young family. I take them everywhere.'

I was afterwards convinced (and so was Ada) that from the ill-conditioned eldest child, these words extorted a sharp yell. He turned it off into a yawn, but it began as a yell.

---

[5]**baleful**　menacing

'They attend Matins[6] with me (very prettily done), at half-past six o'clock in the morning all the year round, including of course the depth of winter,' said Mrs Pardiggle rapidly, 'and they are with me during the revolving duties of the day. I am a School lady, I am a Visiting lady, I am a Reading lady, I am a Distributing lady; I am on the local Linen Box Committee, and many general Committees; and my canvassing alone is very extensive – perhaps no one's more so. But they are my companions everywhere; and by these means they acquire that knowledge of the poor, and that capacity of doing charitable business in general – in short, that taste for the sort of thing – which will render them in after life a service to their neighbours, and a satisfaction to themselves. My young family are not frivolous;[7] they expend the entire amount of their allowance, in subscriptions, under my direction; and they have attended as many public meetings, and listened to as many lectures, orations,[8] and discussions, as generally fall to the lot of few grown people. Alfred (five), who, as I mentioned, has of his own election joined the Infant Bonds of Joy, was one of the very few children who manifested consciousness on that occasion, after a fervid[9] address of two hours from the chairman of the evening.'

Alfred glowered at us as if he never could, or would, forgive the injury of that night.

'I do not understand what it is to be tired; you cannot tire me if you try!' said Mrs Pardiggle. 'The quantity of exertion (which is no exertion to me), the amount of business (which I regard as nothing) that I go through, sometimes astonishes myself. I have seen my young family, and Mr Pardiggle, quite worn out with witnessing it, when I may truly say I have been as fresh as a lark!'

If that dark-visaged eldest boy could look more malicious than he had already looked, this was the time when he

---

[6]**Matins**   morning prayers
[7]**frivolous**   not serious
[8]**orations**   formal public speeches
[9]**fervid**   intensely passionate

did it. I observed that he doubled his right fist, and delivered a secret blow into the crown of his cap, which was under his left arm.

'This gives me a great advantage when I am making my rounds,' said Mrs Pardiggle. 'If I find a person unwilling to hear what I have to say, I tell that person directly, "I am incapable of fatigue, my good friend, I am never tired, and I mean to go on until I have done." It answers admirably! Miss Summerson, I hope I shall have your assistance in my visiting rounds immediately, and Miss Clare's very soon?'

At first I tried to excuse myself, for the present, on the general ground of having occupations to attend to, which I must not neglect. But as this was an ineffectual protest, I then said, more particularly, that I was not sure of my qualifications. That I was inexperienced in the art of adapting my mind to minds very differently situated, and addressing them from suitable points of view. That I had not that delicate knowledge of the heart which must be essential to such a work. That I had much to learn, myself, before I could teach others, and that I could not confide in my good intentions alone. For these reasons, I thought it best to be as useful as I could, and to render what kind services I could, to those immediately about me; and to try to let that circle of duty gradually and naturally expand itself. All this I said, with anything but confidence; because Mrs Pardiggle was much older than I, and had great experience, and was so very military in her manners.

'You are wrong, Miss Summerson,' said she: 'but perhaps you are not equal to hard work, or the excitement of it; and that makes a vast difference. If you would like to see how I go through my work, I am now about – with my young family – to visit a brick-maker in the neighbourhood (a very bad character), and shall be glad to take you with me. Miss Clare also, if she will do me the favour.'

Ada and I interchanged looks, and, as we were going out in any case, accepted the offer. When we hastily returned from putting on our bonnets, we found the young family languishing[10] in a corner, and Mrs Pardiggle sweeping about the room, knocking down nearly all the light objects it contained. Mrs Pardiggle took possession of Ada, and I followed with the family.

Ada told me afterwards that Mrs Pardiggle talked in the same loud tone (that, indeed, I overheard), all the way to the brick-maker's, about an exciting contest which she had for two or three years waged against another lady, relative to the bringing in of their rival candidates for a pension somewhere. There had been a quantity of printing, and promising, and proxying, and polling;[11] and it appeared to have imparted great liveliness to all concerned, except the pensioners – who were not elected yet.

I am very fond of being confided in by children, and am happy in being usually favoured in that respect, but on this occasion it gave me great uneasiness. As soon as we were out of doors, Egbert, with the manner of a little footpad,[12] demanded a shilling of me, on the ground that his pocket-money was 'boned'[13] from him. On my pointing out the great impropriety of the word, especially in connexion with his parent (for he added sulkily 'By her!'), he pinched me and said, 'O then! Now! Who are you! *You* wouldn't like it, I think? What does she make a sham[14] for, and pretend to give me money, and take it away again? Why do you call it *my* allowance, and never let me spend it?' These exasperating questions so inflamed his mind, and the minds of Oswald and Francis, that they all pinched me at once, and in a dreadfully expert way: screwing up such little pieces of my arms that I could hardly forbear crying out. Felix, at the same time, stamped upon my toes. And the Bond of Joy, who, on account of always having the whole of his little income anticipated, stood in fact pledged to abstain from cakes as well as

---

[10]**languishing**   lying around without any energy
[11]**proxying and polling**   women couldn't vote but these ladies still fiercely campaigned in other ways
[12]**footpad**   thief
[13]**boned**   stolen
[14]**sham**   pretence

tobacco, so swelled with grief and rage when we passed a pastry-cook's shop, that he terrified me by becoming purple. I never underwent so much, both in body and mind, in the course of a walk with young people, as from these unnaturally constrained children, when they paid me the compliment of being natural.

I was glad when we came to the brickmaker's house; though it was one of a cluster of wretched hovels in a brickfield, with pigsties close to the broken windows, and miserable little gardens before the doors, growing nothing but stagnant pools. Here and there, an old tub was put to catch the droppings of rain-water from a roof, or they were banked up with mud into a little pond like a large dirt-pie. At the doors and windows, some men and women lounged or prowled about, and took little notice of us, except to laugh to one another, or to say something as we passed, about gentlefolks minding their own business, and not troubling their heads and muddying their shoes with coming to look after other people's.

Mrs Pardiggle, leading the way with a great show of moral determination, and talking with much volubility about the untidy habits of the people (though I doubted if the best of us could have been tidy in such a place), conducted us into a cottage at the farthest corner, the ground-floor room of which we nearly filled. Besides ourselves, there were in this damp offensive room – a woman with a black eye, nursing a poor little gasping baby by the fire; a man, all stained with clay and mud, and looking very dissipated,[15] lying at full length on the ground, smoking a pipe; a powerful young man, fastening a collar on a dog; and a bold girl, doing some kind of washing in very dirty water. They all looked up at us as we came in, and the woman seemed to turn her face towards the fire, as if to hide her bruised eye; nobody gave us any welcome.

'Well, my friends,' said Mrs Pardiggle; but her voice had not a friendly sound, I thought; it was much too business-like and

---

[15]**dissipated**   exhausted, hung-over

systematic. 'How do you do, all of you? I am here again. I told you, you couldn't tire me, you know. I am fond of hard work, and am true to my word.'

'There an't,' growled the man on the floor; whose head rested on his hand as he stared at us, 'any more on you to come in, is there?'

'No, my friend,' said Mrs Pardiggle, seating herself on one stool, and knocking down another. 'We are all here.'

'Because I thought there warn't enough of you, perhaps?' said the man, with his pipe between his lips, as he looked round upon us.

The young man and the girl both laughed. Two friends of the young men whom we had attracted to the doorway, and who stood there with their hands in their pockets, echoed the laugh noisily.

'You can't tire me, good people,' said Mrs Pardiggle to these latter. 'I enjoy hard work; and the harder you make mine, the better I like it.'

'Then make it easy for her!' growled the man upon the floor. 'I wants it done, and over. I wants a end of these liberties took with my place. I wants a end of being drawed like a badger.[16] Now you're a going to poll-pry and question according to custom – I know what you're a going to be up to. Well! You haven't got no occasion to be up to it. I'll save you the trouble. Is my daughter a washin? Yes, she *is* a washin. Look at the water. Smell it! That's wot we drinks. How do you like it, and what do you think of gin, instead! An't my place dirty? Yes, it is dirty – it's nat'rally dirty, and it's nat'rally onwholesome;[17] and we've had five dirty and onwholesome children, as is all dead infants, and so much the better for them, and for us besides. Have I read the little book wot you left? No, I an't read the little book wot you left. There an't nobody here as knows how to read it; and if there wos, it wouldn't be suitable to me. It's a book fit for a

---

[16]**drawed like a badger**   dragged from his set (his home) in hunting
[17]**onwholesome**   old-fashioned version of the modern 'unwholesome', meaning unhealthy

babby, and I'm not a babby. If you was to leave me a doll, I should-n't nuss it. How have I been conducting of myself? Why, I've been drunk for three days; and I'd a been drunk four, if I'd a had the money. Don't I never mean for to go to church? No, I don't never mean for to go to church. I shouldn't be expected there, if I did; the beadle's[18] too genteel for me. And how did my wife get that black eye? Why, I giv' it her; and if she says I didn't, she's a Lie!'

He had pulled his pipe out of his mouth to say all this, and he now turned over on his other side, and smoked again. Mrs Pardiggle, who had been regarding him through her spectacles with a forcible composure, calculated, I could not help think-ing, to increase his antagonism, pulled out a good book, as if it were a constable's staff, and took the whole family into custody. I mean into religious custody, of course; but she really did it, as if she were an inexorable[19] moral Policeman carrying them all off to a station house.

Ada and I were very uncomfortable. We both felt intrusive and out of place; and we both thought that Mrs Pardiggle would have got on infinitely better, if she had not had such a mechani-cal way of taking possession of people. The children sulked and stared; the family took no notice of us whatever, except when the young man made the dog bark: which he usually did, when Mrs Pardiggle was most emphatic. We both felt painfully sensi-ble that between us and these people there was an iron barrier, which could not be removed by our new friend. By whom, or how, it could be removed, we did not know; but we knew that. Even what she read and said, seemed to us to be ill chosen for such auditors, if it had been imparted ever so modestly and with ever so much tact. As to the little book to which the man on the floor had referred, we acquired a knowledge of it after-wards; and Mr Jarndyce said he doubted if Robinson Crusoe[20]

---

[18]**beadle**   a minor official in the parish
[19]**inexorable**   relentless
[20]**Robinson Crusoe**   the hero of a novel (published in 1719) by Daniel
    Defoe, who was the sole survivor of a shipwreck and lived on a desert
    island for many years

could have read it, though he had had no other on his desolate island.

We were much relieved, under these circumstances, when Mrs Pardiggle left off. The man on the floor then turning his head round again, said morosely,[21]

'Well! You've done, have you?'

'For to-day, I have, my friend. But I am never fatigued. I shall come to you again, in your regular order,' returned Mrs Pardiggle with demonstrative cheerfulness.

'So long as you goes now,' said he, folding his arms and shutting his eyes with an oath, 'you may do wot you like!'

Mrs Pardiggle accordingly rose, and made a little vortex[22] in the confined room from which the pipe itself very narrowly escaped. Taking one of her young family in each hand, and telling the others to follow closely, and expressing her hope that the brick-maker and all his house would be improved when she saw them next, she then proceeded to another cottage.

Further reading

Mrs Pardiggle is just one of Charles Dickens's formidable female characters. If you enjoyed her quirky personality, you might like to meet Mrs Joe and Miss Havisham in *Great Expectations*, Mercy and Charity Pecksniff in *Martin Chuzzlewit* and Miss Murdstone in *David Copperfield* (who is introduced in this anthology on page 71).

---

[21]**morosely**   sourly
[22]**vortex**   air swept around like a whirlwind

Activities

Children in the Coal Mines: The 1842 Report

Before you read

1   Look at the picture on page 125 and imagine you are a journalist for *The Illustrated London News* in 1839. This is what you have just seen. Describe your experience. Your article may shock some of your readers – but that is what you intend.

2   As a member of the Commission appointed to inquire into the employment of children in mines, what do you think you might discover? List some of your greatest concerns.

What's it about?

3   Call an 'overlooker' to trial. Get him to account for the deaths caused by one or more of the details given in section 20 of the Report and call some other witnesses to give evidence about what they have heard and seen. One of these witnesses should be a mine-owner.

4   Write the thoughts of a child at home at night after his or her first day's work down a mine.

5   Eleven of the findings are included in the extract you have read. Prepare a reading of one or two of them and present them to the class with full expression of your anger and astonishment.

Thinking about the text

6   Write a playscript in which a mine-owner is heard discussing saving money by cutting costs over safety issues, then act it out.

7   Sarah Gooder, Mary Davis and William Withers bring the Report to life. Their first-hand accounts are terrifying. Using their testimonies and any other aspects of the work you have already done on this text, prepare a presentation on the 1842 Report for another class.

The Cry of the Children

Before you read

1   The details in this poem are taken directly from the 1842 Report. Which of the details you've read in the Report would you expect to see in the poem?

What's it about?

2   What comparisons does the poet make between the lives of young animals and the lives of children? Draw two columns: list references to animals and nature in one column; in the second column, list references to children and the mines.

3   Notice in particular the verbs used: the birds 'chirp'; the iron wheels 'drone'. Underline the verbs in your columns.

4   These verses are full of references to light and dark. How does the poet use darkness to show us what the children's lives were like?

Thinking about the text

5   One of the intentions of the poem is to make not only the mine-owners but also the reader feel guilty. *The Cry of the Children* is an accusation. 'O cruel nation', the poet writes. Find how this line continues and discuss the powerful imagery.

6   Britain was busy developing as an industrial nation and the concept of 'childhood' was also quite different from the idea we have today. Some people wanted the mines, mills and factories to be profitable at any human cost. Others passionately disagreed. Write a letter to the poet as if:
    a   you are a mine-owner
    b   you are a campaigner for justice for the poor who has just read the poem.

How will the letters differ? Place them side by side in your file or book. Add a transcript of a bereaved parent's cry whose child has died in the mines. Imagine Elizabeth Barrett Browning reading them.

Narrative of a Pickpocket

Before you read

1   How do you imagine that children might have ended up living on the streets and picking pockets to earn enough to survive, despite the fact that the punishments for being caught were very severe?

What's it about?

2   How did the narrator of this passage end up on the streets? Do you think this was (is still) common?

3   How did he meet the pickpockets?

4   Describe one of the techniques they taught him.

5   The tone of this account is unemotional. The narrator describes things that have happened to him and things that he did as if they were 'just life'. Find some examples.

6   The narrator learns a new language. 'Fanned' is a word that he uses as part of his new vocabulary, learned on the streets. Find another one.

Thinking about the text

7   Imprisonment and transportation were two heavy punishments if pickpockets were caught. What impression do you get of how this boy – and possibly others like him – felt about these punishments? Discuss this in groups.

8   Henry Mayhew's vivid picture of the teeming underworld of 19th-century London was a gigantic survey of what he called 'the outcast class'. He wanted readers to understand how some people ended up as criminals, and not only to think about punishing them. Write a speech to give at a public meeting supporting his research and views.

Song of the Shirt

Before you read

1   Look at the picture on page 144 and talk about the issues it raises.

What's it about?

2   Look at verses 1, 2, 3 and 6, which tell us what is physically so hard about this work. Write down what the woman most hates and resents.

3   In verse 5 she says she hardly fears death. Why?

4   There are repeated words, 'Work – work – work', regular rhymes and rhythms. Write a sentence explaining how these aspects of the poem match the woman's life.

Thinking about the text

5   If a seamstress lived long enough to reach old age, what do you think she would look like, and why?

6   What is ironic (slightly sarcastic) about calling this poem *Song of the Shirt?*

7   Write an acrostic using the title of this poem to tell the life-story of a seamstress, highlighting its sadness and pains.

Mary Barton

Before you read

1   Feeling powerless can make people angry. Why didn't working men and women have the vote by 1839? How might it have helped their lives? Discuss this in groups and report back to the class. Find out when they *did* get the vote.

What's it about?

2   Why did thousands of people begin to starve? Re-read the first sentence. Then go on to find out what else became more and more terrible about their lives. Write a paragraph explaining the reasons for the start of the Chartist movement.

3   The neighbours all have a message for John Barton to take to the government. Give an example and explain why it is reasonable, but also why it is unlikely to have any effect.

4   How does the present of the shirt collar that Mrs Davenport gives to John Barton symbolise the hopelessness of his journey to London?

5   Many of the Chartists believed that the government would do something once they knew about the poverty of the working people. Find an example of this trust in the words spoken by John Barton.

Thinking about the text

6   Which of these words most sums up your feelings about the Chartists and their cause in this scene? Why?

   sad   hopeless   angry

7   The author gives us a picture of John Barton's poor but homely fireside. Imagine the comfort and grandeur and distance of parliament. If the members of parliament knew that the Chartists were marching, what might they say? Write a conversation between two or three of them that shows how difficult the challenge is to bring the two worlds together.

The Disturbances in the Manufacturing Districts

Before you read

1 Thomas Carlyle (1795–1881), writing *Signs of the Times*, called the Victorian age 'The Mechanical Age'. 'Nothing was done directly or by hand . . . and men are grown mechanical in head and heart as well as in hand.'

    Discuss what it must have been like to be a poor working man or woman or child in a mine, pit or factory when you had a grievance. What do you think you could do about it?

What's it about?

2 A reduction by a quarter of the wages of the working men in and around Manchester sparked the riots. These men became 'the half-starved thousands'. What slogan did they shout in the streets?

3 The riots were dangerous to lives and property. In the second paragraph, what did the marchers do?

4 Write some notes about what else they did. You will find this information under the heading 'Further particulars of the disturbances'.

Thinking about the text

5 The article states that *The Illustrated London News* will not support the Chartists if they say they will take the agonies of the poor and 'convert their rags into banners of rebellion and their hunger into the sign of blood'.

    Have a class debate. Are the marchers right to get violent, or is violence not the answer? What is the role of a newspaper in this situation?

1851; or the Adventures of Mr and Mrs Sandboys

Before you read

1   Look at the picture on page 157. Would it tempt you to have a day out there? Discuss what is on offer.

What's it about?

2   The Exhibition is flooded with visitors on the 'shilling days'. Who are they? What have they come to see?

3   Some of the people are described as having 'red coarse hands'. What other details of appearance does Mayhew give? In what ways do they support the general picture he is trying to give of the 'shilling people'?

4   What had the worries been about their behaviour? What does that tell us about the Victorian class system in Britain?

Thinking about the text

5   Mayhew's descriptions of working people sound patronising to readers today, but they reflect the opinions of many non-working-class people. Mayhew was also exceptionally determined to improve the lives of working people. Write a paragraph about how he thought the Great Exhibition could help to do this.

Bleak House

Before you read

1   You are going to meet Mrs Pardiggle. Here are some details about her:
    - formidable
    - loud voice
    - knocked down little chairs with her skirts
    - she seemed to come in like cold weather
    - 'I do not understand what it is to be tired; you cannot tire me if you try!'

    How do you imagine her? Write a short story: 'The Day Mrs Pardiggle Came to Our House'. See how close you can get to Dickens' version before reading the text.

What's it about?

2   In pairs, make a list of Mrs Pardiggle's 'Good Works'.

3   The author makes Mrs Pardiggle both scary and funny, although she does not mean to be either. Put examples of each in two columns.

4   What is the effect of their mother on the little Pardiggles? Draw a spidergram with Mrs Pardiggle in the middle and include things she has done in her chidren's lives and how they react.

5   The narrator, Miss Summerson, listens and watches Mrs Pardiggle at work. Draw a thought bubble and write in it three of her main reactions to what goes on in the brickmaker's cottage.

Thinking about the text

6   Mrs Pardiggle is being *benevolent* – she sets out to do acts of kindness for the poor. But there are unintended consequences.

    What do people like Mrs Pardiggle mean to do? What do you think it is like to be on the receiving end of her generosity? Write two paragraphs explaining the intentions and the effects of her charitable works.

Compare and contrast

1   Mrs Pardiggle in *Bleak House* and John Barton in *Mary Barton* are realistic and roundly drawn characters whom you could imagine meeting. They both want to help people but they do so in very different ways. Imagine that they tell you about themselves, explaining why and how they help the poor. Write down what they say, keeping to their 'voices' as carefully as you can.

2   'Poets are the unacknowledged legislators of the world,' said the famous poet Shelley (1792–1822) in his essay *A Defence of Poetry*. He meant that they may not make the laws but their thinking helps society to be more imaginative and full of purpose. People are 'startled with the electric life which burns within their words'.

    Which of the two poems, *Song of the Shirt* or *The Cry of the Children,* impresses you more as a call to the government for action? If you had been part of the government, what laws would you like to have created in response?

3   *Mary Barton* and the newspaper article *Disturbances in the Manufacturing Districts* cover the same ground: the reaction of the poor to terrible times. We can tell that John Barton is a peace-loving man; what would he do if he found himself in the middle of the Manchester riots? Write a chapter in which he gets caught up in violence in the streets. Describe what he does and how he feels.

4   The 1842 Report and the Great Exhibition of 1851 are examples of both ends of the scale of Victorian industrial achievement: the plight of thousands of Victorian working children; and the immense scientific and technological achievements made during the Victorian age. Less than a decade separated them. Imagine you are reading a newspaper on the morning of 2 May 1851, the day after the Great Exhibition opened. You remember serving on the Commission that produced the 1842 Report. What are your thoughts? Write them down.

5   Write an article for *The Illustrated London News* covering 'The scandal of child-pickpockets on the streets of London', or any other issue raised in the texts you have studied in this section.

4 Relationships

Isabella Bird disappearing off on her horse into the American West was a very different woman from the housewife of Mrs Beeton's *Book of Household Management*. The popular American monthly *Godey's Lady's Book and Magazine* urged its readers to see a woman's role like this:

The perfection of womanhood . . . is the wife and mother, the centre of the family, the magnet that draws man to the domestic altar that makes him a civilised being, a social Christian. The wife is truly the light of the home.

But Isabella Bird had other ideas, and she was not alone. Many girls longed for an education at school and university; many wanted to work; they wanted the vote; and they were exasperated by men's dominance, rights and freedom. Some women, like Mrs Poyser in George Eliot's novel *Adam Bede* (page 223), had a natural instinct for sorting things out and you might enjoy reading how she sees off the Squire who had come to sort *her* out. The author of this novel was really a woman called Mary Ann Evans, who had changed her name in order to get her books published. Perhaps she smiled as she wrote that chapter. Barbara Bodichon was her good friend (see page 207), and why not use the strong, free intelligence and imagination of such friends to give extra punch to a female character?

In this section you can read about boys and men who worried, dictated, blustered and betrayed, but also those who developed sensitive arguments about how to live with women and children and other men in an ever-more civilised society. Here too are women who shrieked, sorrowed, argued and – bravely – walked away. Many of their ideas and stories could be 21st-century ones. But these are excitingly and unmistakably Victorian voices.

Activities

1   Discuss in class:
    • Is marriage still important in modern society?
    • Victorians saw the man – the husband and father – as the head of the family. What do we think of that today?
    • Do girls and boys look for the same things in a marriage?

2   Mrs Beeton (see page 233) called women 'Household Generals'. She was referring to women who ran their homes on an income large enough to afford lots of servants, and those servants would need to be directed like a small army.

    Think about a house without hot running water, without electric light switches or irons, without washing machines or refrigeration; with lots of stairs, with huge empty grates for fires, and with a combined household of family members and servants in double figures.

    What instructions might a Household General have to give each morning? Write down that formidable list.

3   In 1842, Lord Shaftesbury said of working women: 'It is bad enough if you corrupt the man, but if you corrupt the woman, you poison the waters of life at the very fountain.'
    a   Discuss what you think he was saying about the importance of the woman's role in the home.
    b   Do you think views about the role of men and women in a partnership or family have changed since then?
    c   Think of questions for a class survey about this issue and include two columns: 'then' and 'now'.

The Pickwick Papers
by Charles Dickens

Mr Pickwick has formed a club with his friends Tracy Tupman, Augustus Snodgrass and Nathaniel Winkle, to share reports of journeys and adventures. He is staying at an inn famous for 'its enormous size. Never were there such labyrinths of uncarpeted passages, such clusters of mouldy, badly-lighted rooms, such huge numbers of small dens for eating or sleeping in, beneath any one roof, as are collected together between the four walls of the Great White Horse at Ipswich.'

Mr Pickwick hopes his room will be nice and comfortable, and he is certainly not anticipating the adventure he is about to have . . .

'This is your room, sir,' said the chambermaid.

'Very well,' replied Mr Pickwick, looking round him. It was a tolerably large double-bedded room, with a fire; upon the whole, a more comfortable-looking apartment than Mr Pickwick's short experience of the accommodations of the Great White Horse had led him to expect.

'Nobody sleeps in the other bed, of course,' said Mr Pickwick.

'Oh no, sir.'

'Very good. Tell my servant to bring me up some hot water at half-past eight in the morning, and that I shall not want him any more to-night.'

'Yes, sir.' And bidding Mr Pickwick good night, the chambermaid retired, and left him alone.

Mr Pickwick sat himself down in a chair before the fire, and fell into a train of rambling meditations. First he thought of his friends, and wondered when they would join him; then his mind reverted to Mrs Martha Bardell; and from that lady it wandered, by a natural process, to the dingy counting-house of Dodson and Fogg. From Dodson and Fogg's it flew off at a tangent to the very centre of the history of the queer client; and then it came back to the Great White Horse at Ipswich, with sufficient clearness to convince Mr Pickwick that he was falling asleep: so he roused himself, and began to undress, when he recollected he had left his watch on the table downstairs.

Now, this watch was a special favourite with Mr Pickwick, having been carried about, beneath the shadow of his waistcoat, for a greater number of years than we feel called upon to state at present. The possibility of going to sleep, unless it were ticking gently beneath his pillow, or in the watch-pocket over his head, had never entered Mr Pickwick's brain. So as it was pretty late now, and he was unwilling to ring his bell at that hour of the night, he slipped on his coat, of which he had just divested himself, and taking the japanned[1] candlestick in his hand, walked quietly downstairs.

---

[1]japanned   covered in a black lacquer, an oriental fashion

The more stairs Mr Pickwick went down, the more stairs there seemed to be to descend, and again and again, when Mr Pickwick got into some narrow passage, and began to congratulate himself on having gained the ground-floor, did another flight of stairs appear before his astonished eyes. At last he reached a stone hall, which he remembered to have seen when he entered the house. Passage after passage did he explore; room after room did he peep into; at length, just as he was on the point of giving up the search in despair, he opened the door of the identical room in which he had spent the evening, and beheld his missing property on the table.

Mr Pickwick seized the watch in triumph, and proceeded to retrace his steps to his bedchamber. If his progress downwards had been attended with difficulties and uncertainty, his journey back was infinitely more perplexing. Rows of doors, garnished with boots of every shape, make, and size, branched off in every possible direction. A dozen times did he softly turn the handle of some bedroom door, which resembled his own, when a gruff cry from within of 'Who the devil's that?' or 'What do you want here?' caused him to steal away, on tip-toe, with a perfectly marvellous celerity.[2] He was reduced to the verge of despair, when an open door attracted his attention. He peeped in – right at last! There were the two beds, whose situation he perfectly remembered, and the fire still burning. His candle, not a long one when he first received it, had flickered away in the draughts of air through which he had passed, and sunk into the socket, just as he closed the door after him. 'No matter,' said Mr Pickwick, 'I can undress myself just as well by the light of the fire.'

The bedsteads stood one on each side of the door; and on the inner side of each was a little path, terminating in a rush-bottomed chair, just wide enough to admit of a person's getting into, or out of bed, on that side, if he or she thought proper. Having carefully drawn the curtains of his bed on the outside,

---

[2]**celerity** speed

Mr Pickwick sat down on the rush-bottomed chair, and leisurely divested himself of his shoes and gaiters.[3] He then took off and folded up his coat, waistcoat, and neckcloth, and slowly drawing on his tasselled nightcap, secured it firmly on his head, by tying beneath his chin the strings which he always had attached to that article of dress. It was at this moment that the absurdity of his recent bewilderment struck upon his mind; and throwing himself back in the rush-bottomed chair, Mr Pickwick laughed to himself so heartily, that it would have been quite delightful to any man of well-constituted mind to have watched the smiles which expanded his amiable features as they shone forth from beneath the nightcap.

'It is the best idea,' said Mr Pickwick to himself, smiling till he almost cracked the nightcap strings – 'it is the best idea, my losing myself in this place, and wandering about those staircases, that I ever heard of. Droll,[4] droll, very droll.' Here Mr Pickwick smiled again, a broader smile than before, and was about to continue the process of undressing, in the best possible humour, when he was suddenly stopped by a most unexpected interruption; to wit, the entrance into the room of some person with a candle, who, after locking the door, advanced to the dressing-table, and set down the light upon it.

The smile that played on Mr Pickwick's features was instantaneously lost in a look of the most unbounded and wonder-stricken surprise. The person, whoever it was, had come in so suddenly and with so little noise, that Mr Pickwick had had no time to call out, or oppose their entrance. Who could it be? A robber? Some evil-minded person who had seen him come up-stairs with a handsome watch in his hand, perhaps. What was he to do?

The only way in which Mr Pickwick could catch a glimpse of his mysterious visitor, with the least danger of being seen

---

[3]**gaiter**   a cloth or leather covering your legs
[4]**droll**   amusing, especially in an unusual way

himself, was by creeping on to the bed, and peeping out from between the curtains on the opposite side. To this manoeuvre he accordingly resorted. Keeping the curtains carefully closed with his hand, so that nothing more of him could be seen than his face and nightcap, and putting on his spectacles, he mustered up courage, and looked out.

Mr Pickwick almost fainted with horror and dismay. Standing before the dressing-glass was a middle-aged lady in yellow curl-papers, busily engaged in brushing what ladies call their 'back hair'.

However the unconscious middle-aged lady came into that room, it was quite clear that she contemplated remaining there for the night; for she had brought a rushlight[5] and shade with her, which, with praiseworthy precaution against fire, she had stationed in a basin on the floor, where it was glimmering away, like a gigantic lighthouse, in a particularly small piece of water.

'Bless my soul,' thought Mr Pickwick, 'what a dreadful thing!'

'Hem!' said the lady; and in went Mr Pickwick's head with automaton-like rapidity.

'I never met with anything so awful as this,' thought poor Mr Pickwick, the cold perspiration starting in drops upon his nightcap. 'Never. This is fearful.'

It was quite impossible to resist the urgent desire to see what was going forward. So, out went Mr Pickwick's head again. The prospect was worse than before. The middle-aged lady had finished arranging her hair; had carefully enveloped it in a muslin nightcap with a small plaited border; and was gazing pensively on the fire.

'This matter is growing alarming,' reasoned Mr Pickwick with himself. 'I can't allow things to go on in this way. By the self-possession of that lady, it is clear to me that I must have

---

[5]**rushlight**   a narrow candle made out of rushes and dipped in tallow (animal fat)

come into the wrong room. If I call out, she'll alarm the house; but if I remain here, the consequences will be still more frightful.'

Mr Pickwick, it is quite unnecessary to say, was one of the most modest and delicate-minded of mortals. The very idea of exhibiting his nightcap to a lady overpowered him, but he had tied those confounded strings in a knot, and, do what he would, he couldn't get it off. The disclosure must be made. There was only one other way of doing it. He shrunk behind the curtains, and called out very loudly –

'Ha – hum!'

That the lady started at this unexpected sound was evident, by her falling up against the rushlight shade; that she persuaded herself it must have been the effect of imagination was equally clear, for when Mr Pickwick, under the impression that she had fainted away, stone-dead from fright, ventured to peep out again, she was gazing pensively on the fire as before.

'Most extraordinary female this,' thought Mr Pickwick, popping in again. 'Ha – hum!'

These last sounds, so like those in which, as legends inform us, the ferocious giant Blunderbore was in the habit of expressing his opinion that it was time to lay the cloth, were too distinctly audible to be again mistaken for the workings of fancy.

'Gracious Heaven!' said the middle-aged lady, 'what's that?'

'It's – it's – only a gentleman, ma'am,' said Mr Pickwick, from behind the curtains.

'A gentleman!' said the lady, with a terrific scream.

'It's all over,' thought Mr Pickwick.

'A strange man!' shrieked the lady. Another instant, and the house would be alarmed. Her garments rustled as she rushed towards the door.

'Ma'am,' said Mr Pickwick, thrusting out his head, in the extremity of his desperation. 'Ma'am.'

Now, although Mr Pickwick was not actuated by any definite object in putting out his head, it was instantaneously productive of a good effect. The lady, as we have already stated, was near the door. She must pass it, to reach the staircase, and she would most undoubtedly have done so, by this time, had not the sudden apparition of Mr Pickwick's nightcap driven her back into the remotest corner of the apartment, where she stood staring wildly at Mr Pickwick, while Mr Pickwick in his turn stared wildly at her.

'Wretch,' said the lady, covering her eyes with her hands, 'what do you want here?'

'Nothing, ma'am – nothing whatever, ma'am,' said Mr Pickwick earnestly.

'Nothing!' said the lady, looking up.

'Nothing, ma'am, upon my honour,' said Mr Pickwick, nodding his head so energetically, that the tassel of his nightcap danced again. 'I am almost ready to sink, ma'am, beneath the confusion of addressing a lady in my nightcap (here the lady hastily snatched off hers), but I can't get it off, ma'am (here Mr Pickwick gave it a tremendous tug, in proof of the statement). It is evident to me, ma'am, now, that I have mistaken this bedroom for my own. I had not been here five minutes, ma'am, when you suddenly entered it.'

'If this improbable story be really true, sir,' said the lady, sobbing violently, 'you will leave it instantly.'

'I will, ma'am, with the greatest pleasure,' replied Mr Pickwick.

'Instantly, sir,' said the lady.

'Certainly, ma'am,' interposed Mr Pickwick very quickly. 'Certainly, ma'am. I – I – am very sorry, ma'am,' said Mr Pickwick, making his appearance at the bottom of the bed, 'to have been the innocent occasion of this alarm and emotion; deeply sorry, ma'am.'

The lady pointed to the door. One excellent quality of Mr Pickwick's character was beautifully displayed at this moment, under the most trying circumstances. Although he had hastily put on his hat over his nightcap, after the manner of the old patrol; although he carried his shoes and gaiters in his hand, and his coat and waistcoat over his arm, nothing could subdue his native politeness.

'I am exceedingly sorry, ma'am,' said Mr Pickwick, bowing very low.

'If you are, sir, you will at once leave the room,' said the lady.

'Immediately, ma'am; this instant, ma'am,' said Mr Pickwick, opening the door, and dropping both his shoes with a loud crash in so doing.

'I trust, ma'am,' resumed Mr Pickwick, gathering up his shoes, and turning round to bow again, 'I trust, ma'am, that my unblemished character, and the devoted respect I entertain for your sex, will plead as some slight excuse for this – ' But before Mr Pickwick could conclude the sentence, the lady had thrust him into the passage, and locked and bolted the door behind him.

Whatever grounds of self-congratulation Mr Pickwick might have for having escaped so quietly from his late awkward situation, his present position was by no means enviable. He was alone, in an open passage, in a strange house, in the middle of the night, half dressed; it was not be supposed that he could find his way in perfect darkness to a room which he had been wholly unable to discover with a light, and if he made the slightest noise in his fruitless attempts to do so, he stood every chance of being shot at, and perhaps killed, by some wakeful traveller. He had no resource but to remain where he was until daylight appeared. So after groping his way a few paces down the passage, and, to his infinite alarm, stumbling over several pairs of boots in so doing, Mr Pickwick crouched into a little recess in the wall, to wait for morning as philosophically as he might.

He was not destined, however, to undergo this additional trial of patience: for he had not been long ensconced[6] in his

---

[6]**ensconced**   settled

present concealment when, to his unspeakable horror, a man, bearing a light, appeared at the end of the passage. His horror was suddenly converted into joy, however, when he recognised the form of his faithful attendant. It was indeed Mr Samuel Weller, who after sitting up thus late, in conversation with the Boots,[7] who was sitting up for the mail, was now about to retire to rest.

'Sam,' said Mr Pickwick, suddenly appearing before him, 'where's my bedroom?'

Mr Weller stared at his master with the most emphatic surprise; and it was not until the question had been repeated three several times, that he turned round, and led the way to the long-sought apartment.

'Sam,' said Mr Pickwick as he got into bed, 'I have made one of the most extraordinary mistakes to-night that ever were heard of.'

'Wery likely, sir,' replied Mr Weller drily.

'But of this I am determined, Sam,' said Mr Pickwick, 'that if I were to stop in this house for six months, I would never trust myself about it alone again.'

'That's the wery prudentest resolution as you could come to, sir,' replied Mr Weller. 'You rayther want somebody to look arter you, sir, wen your judgment goes out a wisitin'.'

'What do you mean by that, Sam?' said Mr Pickwick. He raised himself in bed, and extended his hand, as if he were about to say something more; but suddenly checking himself, turned round, and bade his valet[8] 'Good night.'

'Good night, sir,' replied Mr Weller. He paused when he got outside the door – shook his head – walked on – stopped – snuffed the candle – shook his head again – and finally proceeded slowly to his chamber, apparently buried in the profoundest meditation.

---

[7]**Boots**   a man or boy employed to shine the shoes and boots of customers
[8]**valet**   a manservant

Further reading

If you enjoyed meeting Mr Pickwick, you might like chapter 5, in which he learns how to drive. The vehicle is a horse-drawn carriage – a little green box on four wheels – from which the horse alternately stops short and shoots forward 'at a speed which it was wholly impossible to control'. Chapter 41 describes an episode when the poor Mr Pickwick goes to prison.

The Son's Veto

by Thomas Hardy

> A woman, no longer young and pretty but still striking, sits listening to a concert in a park. Who has come with her, and what is she thinking and feeling?

To the eyes of a man viewing it from behind, the nut-brown hair was a wonder and a mystery. Under the black beaver hat surmounted by its tuft of black feathers, the long locks, braided and twisted and coiled like the rushes of a basket, composed a rare, if somewhat barbaric, example of ingenious art. One could understand such weavings and coilings being wrought to last intact for a year, or even a calendar month; but that they should be all demolished regularly at bedtime, after a single day of permanence, seemed a reckless waste of successful fabrication.

And she had done it all herself, poor thing. She had no maid, and it was almost the only accomplishment she could boast of. Hence the unstinted pains.

She was a young invalid lady – not so very much of an invalid – sitting in a wheeled chair, which had been pulled up in the front part of a green enclosure, close to a bandstand where a concert was going on, during a warm June afternoon. It had place in one of the minor parks or private gardens that are to be found in the suburbs of London, and was the effort of a local association to raise money for some charity. There are worlds within worlds in the great city, and though nobody outside the immediate district had ever heard of the charity, or the band, or the garden, the enclosure was filled with an interested audience sufficiently informed on all these.

As the strains proceeded many of the listeners observed the chaired lady, whose back hair, by reason of her prominent position, so challenged inspection. Her face was not easily discernible, but the aforesaid cunning tress-weavings, the white ear and poll,[1] and the curve of a cheek which was neither flaccid nor sallow,[2] were signals that led to the expectation of good beauty in front. Such expectations are not infrequently disappointed as soon as the disclosure comes; and in the present case, when the lady, by a turn of the head, at length revealed herself, she was not so handsome as the people behind her had supposed, and even hoped – they did not know why.

For one thing (alas! the commonness of this complaint), she was less young than they had fancied her to be. Yet attractive her face unquestionably was, and not at all sickly. The revelation of its details came each time she turned to talk to a boy of twelve or thirteen who stood beside her, and the shape of whose hat and jacket implied that he belonged to a well-known public school. The immediate bystanders could hear that he called her 'Mother'.

When the end of the recital was reached, and the audience withdrew, many chose to find their way out by passing at her elbow. Almost all turned their heads to take a full and near look at the interesting woman, who remained stationary in the chair till the way should be clear enough for her to be wheeled out without obstruction. As if she expected their glances, and did not mind gratifying their curiosity, she met the eyes of several of her observers by lifting her own, showing these to be soft, brown, and affectionate orbs, a little plaintive[3] in their regard.

She was conducted out of the gardens, and passed along the pavement till she disappeared from view, the schoolboy walking beside her. To inquiries made by some persons who watched her away, the answer came that she was the second wife of the incumbent[4] of a neighbouring parish, and that she was lame. She was generally believed to be a woman with a story – an innocent one, but a story of some sort or other.

---

[1]**poll**   head
[2]**neither flaccid nor sallow**   not wrinkled nor unhealthily pale
[3]**plaintive**   mournful
[4]**incumbent**   holder of an office: in this case the clergyman

In conversing with her on their way home the boy who walked at her elbow said that he hoped his father had not missed them.

'He have been so comfortable these last few hours that I am sure he cannot have missed us,' she replied.

'*Has*, dear mother – not *have*!' exclaimed the public school-boy, with an impatient fastidiousness that was almost harsh. 'Surely you know that by this time!'

His mother hastily adopted the correction, and did not resent his making it, or retaliate, as she might well have done, by bidding him to wipe that crumby mouth of his, whose condition had been caused by surreptitious⁵ attempts to eat a piece of cake without taking it out of the pocket wherein it lay concealed. After this the pretty woman and the boy went onward in silence.

That question of grammar bore upon her history, and she fell into reverie,⁶ of a somewhat sad kind to all appearance. It might have been assumed that she was wondering if she had done wisely in shaping her life as she had shaped it, to bring out such a result as this.

In a remote nook in North Wessex, forty miles from London, near the thriving county-town of Aldbrickham, there stood a pretty village with its church and parsonage, which she knew well enough, but her son had never seen. It was her native village, Gaymead, and the first event bearing upon her present situation had occurred at that place when she was only a girl of nineteen.

How well she remembered it, that first act in her little tragi-comedy, the death of her reverend husband's first wife. It happened on a spring evening, and she who now and for many years had filled that first wife's place was then parlour-maid in the parson's house.

When everything had been done that could be done, and the death was announced, she had gone out in the dusk to visit

⁵**surreptitious**   undercover
⁶**reverie**   dreaming

her parents, who were living in the same village, to tell them the sad news. As she opened the white swing-gate and looked towards the trees which rose westward, shutting out the pale light of the evening sky, she discerned, without much surprise, the figure of a man standing in the hedge, though she roguishly exclaimed as a matter of form, 'O, Sam, how you frightened me!'

He was a young gardener of her acquaintance. She told him the particulars of the late event, and they stood silent, these two young people, in that elevated, calmly philosophic mind which is engendered when a tragedy has happened close at hand, and has not happened to the philosophers themselves. But it had its bearing upon their relations.

'And will you stay on now at the Vicarage, just the same?' asked he.

She had hardly thought of that. 'O yes – I suppose!' she said. 'Everything will be just as usual, I imagine?'

He walked beside her towards her mother's. Presently his arm stole round her waist. She gently removed it; but he placed it there again, and she yielded the point. 'You see, dear Sophy, you don't know that you'll stay on; you may want a home; and I shall be ready to offer one some day, though I may not be ready just yet.'

'Why, Sam, how can you be so fast! I've never even said I liked 'ee; and it is all your own doing, coming after me!'

'Still, it is nonsense to say I am not to have a try at you like the rest.' He stooped to kiss her a farewell, for they had reached her mother's door.

'No, Sam; you sha'n't!' she cried, putting her hand over his mouth. 'You ought to be more serious on such a night as this.' And she bade him adieu[7] without allowing him to kiss her or to come indoors.

The vicar just left a widower was at this time a man about forty years of age, of good family, and childless. He had led a

---

[7]**adieu**   goodbye

secluded existence in this college living, partly because there were no resident landowners; and his loss now intensified his habit of withdrawal from outward observation. He was seen still less than heretofore, kept himself still less in time with the rhythm and racket of the movements called progress in the world without. For many months after his wife's decease the economy of his household remained as before; the cook, the housemaid, the parlour-maid, and the man out-of-doors performed their duties or left them undone, just as Nature prompted them – the vicar knew not which. It was then represented to him that his servants seemed to have nothing to do in his small family of one. He was struck with the truth of this representation, and decided to cut down his establishment. But he was forestalled by Sophy, the parlour-maid, who said one evening that she wished to leave him.

'And why?' said the parson.

'Sam Hobson has asked me to marry him, sir.'

'Well – do you want to marry?'

'Not much. But it would be a home for me. And we have heard that one of us will have to leave.'

A day or two after she said: 'I don't want to leave just yet, sir, if you don't wish it. Sam and I have quarrelled.'

He looked up at her. He had hardly ever observed her before, though he had been frequently conscious of her soft presence in the room. What a kitten-like, flexuous,[8] tender creature she was! She was the only one of the servants with whom he came into immediate and continuous relation. What should he do if Sophy were gone?

Sophy did not go, but one of the others did, and things went on quietly again.

When Mr Twycott, the vicar, was ill, Sophy brought up his meals to him, and she had no sooner left the room one day than he heard a noise on the stairs. She had slipped down with the tray, and so twisted her foot that she could not

---

[8] **flexuous**   shapely

stand. The village surgeon was called in; the vicar got better, but Sophy was incapacitated for a long time; and she was informed that she must never again walk much or engage in any occupation which required her to stand long on her feet. As soon as she was comparatively well she spoke to him alone. Since she was forbidden to walk and bustle about, and, indeed, could not do so, it became her duty to leave. She could very well work at something sitting down, and she had an aunt a seamstress.

The parson had been very greatly moved by what she had suffered on his account, and he exclaimed, 'No, Sophy; lame or not lame, I cannot let you go. You must never leave me again!'

He came close to her, and, though she could never exactly tell how it happened, she became conscious of his lips upon her cheek. He then asked her to marry him. Sophy did not exactly love him, but she had a respect for him which almost amounted to veneration.[9] Even if she had wished to get away from him she hardly dared refuse a personage so reverend and august[10] in her eyes, and she assented forthwith to be his wife.

Thus it happened that one fine morning, when the doors of the church were naturally open for ventilation, and the singing birds fluttered in and alighted on the tie-beams of the roof, there was a marriage-service at the communion-rails, which hardly a soul knew of. The parson and a neighbouring curate had entered at one door, and Sophy at another, followed by two necessary persons, whereupon in a short time there emerged a newly-made husband and wife.

Mr Twycott knew perfectly well that he had committed social suicide by this step, despite Sophy's spotless character, and he had taken his measures accordingly. An exchange of livings had been arranged with an acquaintance who was incumbent of a church in the south of London, and as soon as possible the couple removed thither, abandoning their pretty home, with trees and shrubs and

---

[9]**veneration**   worship
[10]**august**   very dignified and imposing

glebe[11] for a narrow, dusty house in a long, straight street, and their fine peal of bells for the wretchedest one-tongued clangour that ever tortured mortal ears. It was all on her account. They were, however, away from every one who had known her former position; and also under less observation from without than they would have had to put up with in any country parish.

Sophy the woman was as charming a partner as a man could possess, though Sophy the lady had her deficiencies. She showed a natural aptitude for little domestic refinements, so far as related to things and manners; but in what is called culture she was less intuitive.[12] She had now been married more than fourteen years, and her husband had taken much trouble with her education; but she still held confused ideas on the use of 'was' and 'were', which did not beget a respect for her among the few acquaintances she made. Her great grief in this relation was that her only child, on whose education no expense had been and would be spared, was now old enough to perceive these deficiencies in his mother, and not only to see them but to feel irritated at their existence.

Thus she lived on in the city, and wasted hours in braiding her beautiful hair, till her once apple cheeks waned to pink of the very faintest. Her foot had never regained its natural strength after the accident, and she was mostly obliged to avoid walking altogether. Her husband had grown to like London for its freedom and its domestic privacy; but he was twenty years his Sophy's senior, and had latterly been seized with a serious illness. On this day, however, he had seemed to be well enough to justify her accompanying her son Randolph to the concert.

The next time we get a glimpse of her is when she appears in the mournful attire of a widow.

Mr Twycott had never rallied, and now lay in a well-packed cemetery to the south of the great city, where, if all

---

[11]**glebe**   the land belonging to a clergyman
[12]**intuitive**   instinctively aware, not working something out by thinking

the dead it contained had stood erect and alive, not one would have known him or recognized his name. The boy had dutifully followed him to the grave, and was now again at school.

Throughout these changes Sophy had been treated like the child she was in nature though not in years. She was left with no control over anything that had been her husband's beyond her modest personal income. In his anxiety lest her inexperience should be over-reached he had safeguarded with trustees all he possibly could. The completion of the boy's course at the public school, to be followed in due time by Oxford and ordination, had been all previsioned and arranged, and she really had nothing to occupy her in the world but to eat and drink, and make a business of indolence, and go on weaving and coiling the nut-brown hair, merely keeping a home open for the son whenever he came to her during vacations.

Foreseeing his probable decease long years before her, her husband in his lifetime had purchased for her use a semi-detached villa in the same long, straight road whereon the church and parsonage faced, which was to be hers as long as she chose to live in it. Here she now resided, looking out upon the fragment of lawn in front, and through the railings at the ever-flowing traffic; or, bending forward over the window-sill on the first floor, stretching her eyes far up and down the vista of sooty trees, hazy air, and drab house-facades, along which echoed the noises common to a suburban main thoroughfare.

Somehow, her boy, with his aristocratic school-knowledge, his grammars, and his aversions,[13] was losing those wide infantine sympathies, extending as far as to the sun and moon themselves, with which he, like other children, had been born, and which his mother, a child of nature herself, had loved in him; he was reducing their compass to a population of a few thousand wealthy and titled people, the mere veneer of a thousand million or so of others who did not interest him at all. He drifted

---

[13]**aversion**   a feeling of being repelled by something

further and further away from her. Sophy's *milieu*[14] being a sub-urb of minor tradesmen and under-clerks, and her almost only companions the two servants of her own house, it was not sur-prising that after her husband's death she soon lost the little artificial tastes she had acquired from him, and became – in her son's eyes – a mother whose mistakes and origin it was his painful lot as a gentleman to blush for. As yet he was far from being man enough – if he ever would be – to rate these sins of hers at their true infinitesimal value beside the yearning fond-ness that welled up and remained penned in her heart till it should be more fully accepted by him, or by some other person or thing. If he had lived at home with her he would have had all of it; but he seemed to require so very little in present circum-stances, and it remained stored.

Her life became insupportably dreary; she could not take walks, and had no interest in going for drives, or, indeed, in travelling anywhere. Nearly two years passed without an event, and still she looked on that suburban road, thinking of the vil-lage in which she had been born, and whither she would have gone back – O how gladly! – even to work in the fields.

Taking no exercise she often could not sleep, and would rise in the night or early morning to look out upon the then vacant thoroughfare, where the lamps stood like sentinels wait-ing for some procession to go by. An approximation to such a procession was indeed made early every morning about one o'clock, when the country vehicles passed up with loads of veg-etables for Covent Garden market. She often saw them creeping along at this silent and dusky hour – waggon after waggon, bearing green bastions[15] of cabbages nodding to their fall, yet never falling, walls of baskets enclosing masses of beans and peas, pyramids of snow-white turnips, swaying howdahs[16] of mixed produce – creeping along behind aged night-horses, who

---

[14]*milieu*   setting
[15]**bastion**   a wall or stronghold
[16]**howdah**   a seat or pavilion on an elephant's back

seemed ever patiently wondering between their hollow coughs why they had always to work at that still hour when all other sentient[17] creatures were privileged to rest. Wrapped in a cloak, it was soothing to watch and sympathize with them when depression and nervousness hindered sleep, and to see how the fresh green-stuff brightened to life as it came opposite the lamp, and how the sweating animals steamed and shone with their miles of travel.

They had an interest, almost a charm, for Sophy, these semirural people and vehicles moving in an urban atmosphere, leading a life quite distinct from that of the daytime toilers on the same road. One morning a man who accompanied a waggon-load of potatoes gazed rather hard at the house-fronts as he passed, and with a curious emotion she thought his form was familiar to her. She looked out for him again. His being an old-fashioned conveyance, with a yellow front, it was easily recognizable, and on the third night after she saw it a second time. The man alongside was, as she had fancied, Sam Hobson, formerly gardener at Gaymead, who would at one time have married her.

She had occasionally thought of him, and wondered if life in a cottage with him would not have been a happier lot than the life she had accepted. She had not thought of him passionately, but her now dismal situation lent an interest to his resurrection – a tender interest which it is impossible to exaggerate. She went back to bed, and began thinking. When did these market-gardeners, who travelled up to town so regularly at one or two in the morning, come back? She dimly recollected seeing their empty waggons, hardly noticeable amid the ordinary day-traffic, passing down at some hour before noon.

It was only April, but that morning, after breakfast, she had the window opened, and sat looking out, the feeble sun shining full upon her. She affected to sew, but her eyes never left the street. Between ten and eleven the desired waggon, now

---

[17]**sentient** living

unladen, reappeared on its return journey. But Sam was not looking round him then, and drove on in a reverie.

'Sam!' cried she.

Turning with a start, his face lighted up. He called to him a little boy to hold the horse, alighted, and came and stood under the window.

'I can't come down easily, Sam, or I would!' she said. 'Did you know I lived here?'

'Well, Mrs Twycott, I knew you lived along here somewhere. I have often looked out for 'ee.'

He briefly explained his own presence on the scene. He had long since given up his gardening in the village near Aldbrickham, and was now manager at a market-gardener's on the south side of London, it being part of his duty to go up to Covent Garden with waggon-loads of produce two or three times a week. In answer to her curious inquiry, he admitted that he had come to this particular district because he had seen in the Aldbrickham paper, a year or two before, the announcement of the death in South London of the aforetime vicar of Gaymead, which had revived an interest in her dwelling-place that he could not extinguish, leading him to hover about the locality till his present post had been secured.

They spoke of their native village in dear old North Wessex, the spots in which they had played together as children. She tried to feel that she was a dignified personage now, that she must not be too confidential with Sam. But she could not keep it up, and the tears hanging in her eyes were indicated in her voice.

'You are not happy, Mrs Twycott, I'm afraid?' he said.

'O, of course not! I lost my husband only the year before last.'

'Ah! I meant in another way. You'd like to be home again?'

'This is my home - for life. The house belongs to me. But I understand' - She let it out then. 'Yes, Sam, I long for home - *our* home! I *should* like to be there, and never leave it, and die there.' But she remembered herself. 'That's only a momentary feeling. I have a son, you know, a dear boy. He's at school now.'

'Somewhere handy, I suppose? I see there's lots on 'em along this road.'

'O no! Not in one of these wretched holes! At a public school – one of the most distinguished in England.'

'"Chok" it all! of course! I forget, ma'am, that you've been a lady for so many years.'

'No, I am not a lady,' she said sadly. 'I never shall be. But he's a gentleman, and that – makes it – O how difficult for me!'

The acquaintance thus oddly reopened proceeded apace. She often looked out to get a few words with him, by night or by day. Her sorrow was that she could not accompany her one old friend on foot a little way, and talk more freely than she could do while he paused before the house. One night, at the beginning of June, when she was again on the watch after an absence of some days from the window, he entered the gate and said softly, 'Now, wouldn't some air do you good? I've only half a load this morning. Why not ride up to Covent Garden with me? There's a nice seat on the cabbages, where I've spread a sack. You can be home again in a cab before anybody is up.'

She refused at first, and then, trembling with excitement, hastily finished her dressing, and wrapped herself up in cloak and veil, afterwards sidling downstairs by the aid of the handrail, in a way she could adopt on an emergency. When she had opened the door she found Sam on the step, and he lifted her bodily on his strong arm across the little forecourt into his vehicle. Not a soul was visible or audible in the infinite length of the straight, flat highway, with its ever-waiting lamps converging to points in each direction. The air was fresh as country air at this hour, and the stars shone, except to the north-eastward, where there was a whitish light – the dawn. Sam carefully placed her in the seat, and drove on.

They talked as they had talked in old days, Sam pulling himself up now and then, when he thought himself too familiar.

More than once she said with misgiving that she wondered if she ought to have indulged in the freak. 'But I am so lonely in my house,' she added, 'and this makes me so happy!'

'You must come again, dear Mrs Twycott. There is no time o' day for taking the air like this.'

It grew lighter and lighter. The sparrows became busy in the streets, and the city waxed denser around them. When they approached the river it was day, and on the bridge they beheld the full blaze of morning sunlight in the direction of St Paul's, the river glistening towards it, and not a craft stirring.

Near Covent Garden he put her into a cab, and they parted, looking into each other's faces like the very old friends they were. She reached home without adventure, limped to the door, and let herself in with her latch-key unseen.

The air and Sam's presence had revived her: her cheeks were quite pink – almost beautiful. She had something to live for in addition to her son. A woman of pure instincts, she knew there had been nothing really wrong in the journey, but supposed it conventionally to be very wrong indeed.

Soon, however, she gave way to the temptation of going with him again, and on this occasion their conversation was distinctly tender, and Sam said he never should forget her, notwithstanding that she had served him rather badly at one time. After much hesitation he told her of a plan it was in his power to carry out, and one he should like to take in hand, since he did not care for London work: it was to set up as a master greengrocer down at Aldbrickham, the county-town of their native place. He knew of an opening – a shop kept by aged people who wished to retire.

'And why don't you do it then, Sam?' she asked with a slight heartsinking.

'Because I'm not sure if – you'd join me. I know you wouldn't – couldn't! Such a lady as ye've been so long, you couldn't be a wife to a man like me.'

'I hardly suppose I could!' she assented, also frightened at the idea.

'If you could,' he said eagerly, 'you'd on'y have to sit in the back parlour and look through the glass partition when I was away sometimes – just to keep an eye on things. The lameness wouldn't hinder that . . . I'd keep you as genteel as ever I could, dear Sophy – if I might think of it!' he pleaded.

'Sam, I'll be frank,' she said, putting her hand on his. 'If it were only myself I would do it, and gladly, though everything I possess would be lost to me by marrying again.'

'I don't mind that! It's more independent.'

'That's good of you, dear, dear Sam. But there's something else. I have a son . . . I almost fancy when I am miserable sometimes that he is not really mine, but one I hold in trust for my late husband. He seems to belong so little to me personally, so entirely to his dead father. He is so much educated and I so little that I do not feel dignified enough to be his mother . . . Well, he would have to be told.'

'Yes. Unquestionably.' Sam saw her thought and her fear. 'Still, you can do as you like, Sophy – Mrs Twycott,' he added. 'It is not you who are the child, but he.'

'Ah, you don't know! Sam, if I could, I would marry you, some day. But you must wait a while, and let me think.'

It was enough for him, and he was blithe at their parting. Not so she. To tell Randolph seemed impossible. She could wait till he had gone up to Oxford, when what she did would affect his life but little. But would he ever tolerate the idea? And if not, could she defy him?

She had not told him a word when the yearly cricket match came on at Lord's between the public schools, though Sam had already gone back to Aldbrickham. Mrs Twycott felt stronger than usual: she went to the match with Randolph, and was able to leave her chair and walk about occasionally. The bright idea occurred to her that she could casually broach the subject while moving round among the spectators, when the boy's spirits were high with interest in the game, and he would weigh domestic matters as feathers in the scale beside the day's victory. They promenaded under the lurid July sun, this pair, so wide apart, yet so near, and Sophy saw the large proportion of boys like her own, in their broad white collars and dwarf hats, and all around the rows of great coaches under which was jumbled the *débris*[18] of luxurious luncheons; bones, pie-crusts, champagne-bottles, glasses, plates, napkins, and the family silver; while on the coaches sat the proud fathers and mothers; but never a poor mother like her. If Randolph had not appertained[19] to these, had not centred all his interests in them, had not cared exclusively for the class they belonged to, how happy would things have been! A great huzza[20] at some small per-formance with the bat burst from the multitude of relatives, and Randolph jumped wildly into the air to see what had happened. Sophy fetched up the sentence that had been already shaped; but she could not get it out. The occasion was, perhaps, an inopportune one. The contrast between her story and the display of fashion to which Randolph had grown to regard himself as akin would be fatal. She awaited a better time.

It was on an evening when they were alone in their plain suburban residence, where life was not blue but brown, that she ultimately broke silence, qualifying her announcement of a probable second marriage by assuring him that it would not take place for a long time to come, when he would be living quite independently of her.

The boy thought the idea a very reasonable one, and asked if she had chosen anybody? She hesitated; and he seemed to have a misgiving. He hoped his stepfather would be a gentle-man? he said.

'Not what you call a gentleman,' she answered timidly. 'He'll be much as I was before I knew your father;' and by degrees she acquainted him with the whole. The youth's face remained fixed for a moment; then he flushed, leant on the table, and burst into passionate tears.

---

[18]***débris***   litter
[19]**appertained**   belonged
[20]**huzza**   hurray, applause

His mother went up to him, kissed all of his face that she could get at, and patted his back as if he were still the baby he once had been, crying herself the while. When he had somewhat recovered from his paroxysm he went hastily to his own room and fastened the door.

Parleyings were attempted through the keyhole, outside which she waited and listened. It was long before he would reply, and when he did it was to say sternly at her from within: 'I am ashamed of you! It will ruin me! A miserable boor! a churl! a clown! It will degrade me in the eyes of all the gentlemen of England!'

'Say no more – perhaps I am wrong! I will struggle against it!' she cried miserably.

Before Randolph left her that summer a letter arrived from Sam to inform her that he had been unexpectedly fortunate in obtaining the shop. He was in possession; it was the largest in the town, combining fruit with vegetables, and he thought it would form a home worthy even of her some day. Might he not run up to town to see her?

She met him by stealth, and said he must still wait for her final answer. The autumn dragged on, and when Randolph was home at Christmas for the holidays she broached the matter again. But the young gentleman was inexorable.[21]

It was dropped for months; renewed again; abandoned under his repugnance; again attempted; and thus the gentle creature reasoned and pleaded till four or five long years had passed. Then the faithful Sam revived his suit with some peremptoriness.[22] Sophy's son, now an undergraduate, was down from Oxford one Easter, when she again opened the subject. As soon as he was ordained, she argued, he would have a home of his own, wherein she, with her bad grammar and her ignorance, would be an encumbrance[23] to him. Better obliterate[24] her as much as possible.

---

[21]**inexorable**   unrelenting, can't be moved or persuaded
[22]**peremptoriness**   an urgent, commanding manner
[23]**encumbrance**   hindrance
[24]**obliterate**   wipe out

He showed a more manly anger now, but would not agree. She on her side was more persistent, and he had doubts whether she could be trusted in his absence. But by indignation and contempt for her taste he completely maintained his ascendancy; and finally taking her before a little cross and altar that he had erected in his bedroom for his private devotions, there bade her kneel, and swear that she would not wed Samuel Hobson without his consent. 'I owe this to my father!' he said.

The poor woman swore, thinking he would soften as soon as he was ordained and in full swing of clerical work. But he did not. His education had by this time sufficiently ousted his humanity to keep him quite firm; though his mother might have led an idyllic[25] life with her faithful fruiterer and greengrocer, and nobody have been anything the worse in the world.

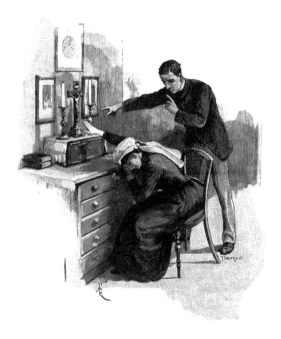

---

[25]**idyllic**   extremely pleasant, beautiful or peaceful

Her lameness became more confirmed as time went on, and she seldom or never left the house in the long southern thoroughfare, where she seemed to be pining her heart away. 'Why mayn't I say to Sam that I'll marry him? Why mayn't I?' she would murmur plaintively to herself when nobody was near.

Some four years after this date a middle-aged man was standing at the door of the largest fruiterer's shop in Aldbrickham. He was the proprietor, but to-day, instead of his usual business attire, he wore a neat suit of black; and his window was partly shuttered. From the railway-station a funeral procession was seen approaching: it passed his door and went out of the town towards the village of Gaymead. The man, whose eyes were wet, held his hat in his hand as the vehicle moved by; while from the mourning coach a young smooth-shaven priest in a high waistcoat looked black as a cloud at the shop-keeper standing there.

Further reading

Thomas Hardy often wrote about women in immensely difficult circumstances. For futher reading you could try the opening chapter of *The Mayor of Casterbridge*, in which a man sells his wife. He also gave some of his women characters great power and charisma; Bathsheba Everdene in *Far from the Madding Crowd* is an independently minded farmer, and in chapter 4 you can read about how she turns down an offer of marriage. For another of Hardy's short stories, try *To Please His Wife*.

Laws Concerning Women
by Barbara Bodichon

You could imagine Barbara Bodichon speaking heatedly on a stage, determined to make her opinions known to a hall full of people. *These laws concerning women are unfair*, she thinks, *and everyone needs to realise it.*

A woman of twenty-one becomes an independent human creature, capable of holding and administering property to any amount; or, if she can earn money, she may appropriate her earnings freely to any purpose she thinks good. Her father has no power over her or her property. But if she unites herself to a man, the law immediately steps in, and she finds herself legislated for, and her condition of life suddenly and entirely changed.' Whatever age she may be of, she is again considered as an infant, – she is again under '*reasonable restraint*,' – she loses her separate existence, and is merged in that of her husband . . .

Truly . . . she has no legal right to any property; not even her clothes, books, and household goods are her own, and any money which she earns can be robbed from her legally by her husband, nay, even after the commencement of a treaty of marriage she cannot dispose of her own property without the knowledge of her betrothed. If she should do so, it is deemed a fraud in law and can be set aside after marriage as an injury to her husband.

It is always said, even by those who support the existing law, that it is in fact never acted upon by men of good feeling. That is true; but the very admission condemns the law, and it is not right that the good feeling of men should be all that a woman can look to for simple justice.

There is now a large and increasing class of women who gain their own livelihood, and the abolition of the laws which give husbands this unjust power is most urgently needed.

Rich men and fathers might still make what settlements they pleased, and appoint trustees for the protection of minors and such women as needed protection; but we imagine it well proved that the principle of protection is wrong, and that the education of freedom and responsibility will enable women to take better care of themselves and others too than can be insured to them by any legal precautions.

Upon women of the labouring classes the difficulty of keeping and using their own earnings presses most hardly. In that rank of life where the support of the family depends often on the joint earnings of husband and wife, it is indeed cruel that the earnings of both should be in the hands of one, and not even in the hands of that one who has naturally the strongest desire to promote the welfare of the children.

All who are familiar with the working classes know how much suffering and privation[1] is caused by the exercise of this *right* by drunken and bad men. It is true that men are legally bound to support their wives and children, but this does not compensate women for the loss of their moral right to their own property and earnings, nor for the loss of the mental development and independence of character gained by the possession and thoughtful appropriation of money; nor, it must be remembered, can the claim to support be enforced on the part of the wife unless she appeals to a court of law. Alas, how much will not a woman endure before she will publicly plead for a maintenance!

Why, we ask, should there be this difference between the married and unmarried condition of women? And why does marriage make so little legal difference to men, and such a mighty legal difference to women?

Further reading

The 19th-century history textbooks in your school will have chapters that tell you more about laws governing women's rights in marriage and their struggle for the vote. Two such textbooks are *Presenting the Past 3* by Grey and Little, published by Collins (2002), and *Revolution, Radicalism and Reform* by Richard Brown, pubished by Cambridge University Press in

---

[1]**privation** lacking all the things you need in life

1998. (Cambridge University Press also published *The Victorians* by Joan Evans in 1966: a large illustrated collection of quotations from the age, with an excellent chapter on women. It's always worth looking in second-hand bookshops for books about the Victorians.)

Little Women is a novel that explores the tussle between ambitions and life at the hearth in a family of four sisters in America at the time Ambrose Bierce was writing his short stories (see page 102). It has to be said that life at the hearth wins! Louisa M. Alcott, who wrote this famous book in 1868, intended it as a hymn to women's domestic life.

MOUNTAINEERING IN THE TYROL: TURNING A CORNER.

In the fierce debate about women's capabilities and rights, some women – like this one – were just getting on with activities like mountaineering in the Tyrol

The Small House at Allington
by Anthony Trollope

Adolphus Crosbie has done a dreadful thing. He has become engaged to two girls – and both within a month. First, he had fallen in love with Lily Dale; now he has fatally promised himself to Lady Alexandrina de Courcy, thrilled with the thought of leaping into a titled family. The world will find out, and he is doomed whatever the outcome.

He had said to himself that it would be much to have a countess for a mother-in-law; but now, even already, although the passion to which he had looked was not yet garnered,[1] he was beginning to tell himself that the thing was not worth possessing.

As he sat in the train, with a newspaper in his hand, he went on acknowledging to himself that he was a villain. Lady Julia had spoken the truth to him on the stairs at Courcy, and so he confessed over and over again. But he was chiefly angry with himself for this, – that he had been a villain without gaining anything by his villainy; that he had been a villain, and was to lose so much by his villainy. He made comparison between Lily and Alexandrina, and owned to himself, over and over again, that Lily would make the best wife that a man could take to his bosom. As to Alexandrina, he knew the thinness of her character. She would stick by him, no doubt; and in a circuitous, discontented, unhappy way, would probably be true to her duties as a wife and mother. She would be nearly such another as Lady Amelia Gazebee. But was that a prize sufficiently rich to make him contented with his own prowess and skill in winning it? And was that a prize sufficiently rich to justify him to himself for his terrible villainy? Lily Dale he had loved; and he now declared to himself that he could have continued to love her through his whole

---

[1] **garnered**   gathered in

life. But what was there for any man to love in Alexandrina de Courcy? While resolving, during his first four or five days at the castle, that he would throw Lily Dale overboard, he had contrived to quiet his conscience by inward allusions to sundry heroes of romance. He had thought of Lothario,[2] Don Juan,[3] and of Lovelace;[4] and had told himself that the world had ever been full of such heroes. And the world, too, had treated such heroes well; not punishing then at all as villains, but caressing them rather, and calling them curled darlings. Why should not he be a curled darling as well as another? Ladies had ever been fond of the Don Juan character, and Don Juan had generally been popular with men also. And then he named to himself a dozen modern Lotharios – men who were holding their heads well above water, although it was known that they had played this lady false, and brought that other one to death's door, or perhaps even to death itself. War and love were alike, and the world was prepared to forgive any guile[5] to militants in either camp.

But now that he had done the deed he found himself forced to look at it from quite another point of view. Suddenly that character of Lothario showed itself to him in a different light, and one in which it did not please him to look at it as belonging to himself. He began to feel that it would be almost impossible for him to write that letter to Lily, which it was absolutely necessary that he should write. He was in a position in which his mind would almost turn to thoughts of self-destruction as the only means of escape. A fortnight ago he was a happy man, having everything before him that a man ought to want; and now – now that he was the accepted son-in-law of an earl, and the confident expectant of high promotion – he was the most miserable, degraded wretch in the world!

---

[2]**Lothario**   a seducer of women (from an 18th-century play, *The Fair Penitent* by Nicholas Rowe)
[3]**Don Juan**   a Spanish nobleman who seduced women, the subject of a 17th-century play by Molière
[4]**Lovelace**   a 17th-century poet who wrote 'To Althea, from Prison'
[5]**guile**   a cunning deception

He changed his clothes at his lodgings in Mount Street and went down to his club to dinner. He could, at any rate, do nothing that night. His letter to Allington must, no doubt, be written at once; but, as he could not send it before the next night's post, he was not forced to set to work upon it that evening. As he walked along Piccadilly on his way to St James's Square, it occurred to him that it might be well to write a short line to Lily, telling her nothing of the truth, – a note written as though his engagement with her was still unbroken, but yet written with care, saying nothing about that engagement, so as to give him a little time. Then he thought that he would telegraph to Bernard and tell everything to him. Bernard would, of course, be prepared to avenge his cousin in some way, but for such vengeance Crosbie felt that he should care little. Lady Julia had told him that Lily was without father or brother, thereby accusing him of the basest cowardice. 'I wish she had a dozen brothers,' he said to himself. But he hardly knew why he expressed such a wish.

He returned to London on the last day of October, and he found the streets at the West End nearly deserted. He thought, therefore, that he should be quite alone at his club, but as he entered the dinner-room he saw one of his oldest and most intimate friends standing before the fire. Fowler Pratt was the man who had first brought him into Sebright's, and had given him almost his earliest start on his successful career in life. Since that time he and his friend Fowler Pratt had lived in close communion, though Pratt had always held a certain ascendancy in their friendship. He was in age a few years senior to Crosbie, and was in truth a man of better parts. But he was less ambitious, less desirous of shining in the world, and much less popular with men in general. He was possessed of a moderate private fortune on which he lived in a quiet, modest manner, and was unmarried, not likely to marry, inoffensive, useless, and prudent. For the first few years of Crosbie's life in London he had lived very much with his friend Pratt, and had been accustomed to depend much on his friend's counsel; but latterly, since he had himself become somewhat noticeable, he had found more pleasure in the society of such men as Dale, who were not his superiors either in age or wisdom. But there had been no coolness between him and Pratt, and now they met with perfect cordiality.

'I thought you were down in Barsetshire,' said Pratt.

'And I thought you were in Switzerland.'

'I have been in Switzerland,' said Pratt.

'And I have been in Barsetshire,' said Crosbie. Then they ordered their dinner together.

'And so you're going to be married?' said Pratt, when the waiter had carried away the cheese.

'Who told you that?'

'Well, but you are? Never mind who told me, if I was told the truth.'

'But if it be not true?'

'I have heard it for the last month,' said Pratt, 'and it has been spoken of as a thing certain; and it is true; is it not?'

'I believe it is,' said Crosbie, slowly.

'Why, what on earth is the matter with you, that you speak of it in that way? Am I to congratulate you, or am I not? The lady, I'm told, is a cousin of Dale's.'

Crosbie had turned his chair from the table round to the fire, and said nothing in answer to this. He sat with his glass of sherry in his hand, looking at the coals, and thinking whether it would not be well that he should tell the whole story to Pratt. No one could give him better advice; and no one, as far as he knew his friend, would be less shocked at the telling of such a story. Pratt had no romance about women, and had never pretended to very high sentiments.

'Come up into the smoking-room and I'll tell you all about it,' said Crosbie. So they went off together, and, as the smoking-room was untenanted, Crosbie was able to tell his story.

He found it very hard to tell; – much harder than he had beforehand fancied. 'I have got into terrible trouble,' he began by saying. Then he told how he had fallen suddenly in love with

Crosbie at his club – an original illustration for *The Small House at Allington* by
John Everett Millais

Lily, how he had been rash and imprudent, how nice she was –
'infinitely too good for such a man as I am,' he said; – how she
had accepted him, and then how he had repented. 'I should
have told you beforehand,' he then said, 'that I was already half
engaged to Lady Alexandrina de Courcy.' The reader, however,
will understand that this half-engagement was a fiction.

'And now you mean that you are altogether engaged to her?'

'Exactly so.'

'And that Miss Dale must be told that, on second thoughts,
your have changed your mind?'

'I know that I have behaved very badly,' said Crosbie.

'Indeed you have,' said his friend.

'It is one of these troubles in which a man finds himself
involved almost before he knows where he is.'

'Well; I can't look at it exactly in that light. A man may amuse himself with a girl, and I can understand his disappointing her and not offering to marry her, – though even that sort of thing isn't much to my taste. But, by George, to make an offer of marriage to such a girl as that in September, to live for a month in her family as her affianced husband, and then coolly go away to another house in October, and make an offer to another girl of higher rank – '

'You know very well that that has had nothing to do with it.'

'It looks very like it. And how are you going to communicate these tidings to Miss Dale?'

'I don't know,' said Crosbie, who was beginning to be very sore.

'And you have quite made up your mind that you'll stick to the earl's daughter?'

The idea of jilting[6] Alexandrina instead of Lily had never as yet presented itself to Crosbie, and now, as he thought of it, he could not perceive that it was feasible.

'Yes,' he said, 'I shall marry Lady Alexandrina; – that is, if I do not cut the whole concern, and my own throat into the bargain.'

'If I were in your shoes I think I should cut the whole concern. I could not stand it. What do you mean to say to Miss Dale's uncle?'

'I don't care a —— for Miss Dale's uncle,' said Crosbie. 'If he were to walk in at that door this moment, I would tell him the whole story, without – '

As he was yet speaking, one of the club servants opened the door of the smoking-room, and seeing Crosbie seated in a lounging-chair near the fire, went up to him with a gentleman's card.[7] Crosbie took the card and read the name. 'Mr Dale, Allington.'

'The gentleman is in the waiting-room,' said the servant.

Crosbie for the moment was struck dumb. He had declared that very moment that he should feel no personal disinclination

---

[6]**jilting**   leaving, rejecting
[7]**gentleman's card**   a small card on which is printed personal details such as name and address

to meet Mr Dale, and now that gentleman was within the walls of the club, waiting to see him!

'Who's that?' asked Pratt. And then Crosbie handed him the card. 'Whew-w-w-hew,' whistled Pratt.

'Did you tell the gentleman I was here?' asked Crosbie.

'I said I thought you were upstairs, sir.'

'That will do,' said Pratt. 'The gentleman will no doubt wait for a minute.' And then the servant went out of the room. 'Now, Crosbie, you must make up your mind. By one of these women and all her friends you will ever be regarded as a rascal, and they of course will look out to punish you with such punishment as may come to their hands. You must now choose which shall be the sufferer.'

The man was a coward at heart. The reflection that he might, even now, at this moment, meet the old squire on pleasant terms, – or at any rate not on terms of defiance, pleaded more strongly in Lily's favour than had any other argument since Crosbie had first made up his mind to abandon her. He did not fear personal ill-usage; – he was not afraid lest he should be kicked or beaten; but he did not dare to face the just anger of the angry man.

'If I were you,' said Pratt, 'I would not go down to that man at the present moment for a trifle.'

'But what can I do?'

'Shirk away out of the club. Only if you do that it seems to me that you'll have to go on shirking for the rest of your life.'

'Pratt, I must say that I expected something more like friendship from you.'

'What can I do for you? There are positions in which it is impossible to help a man. I tell you plainly that you have behaved very badly. I do not see that I can help you.'

'Would you see him?'

'Certainly not, if I am to be expected to take your part.'

'Take any part you like, – only tell him the truth.'

'And what is the truth?'

'I was part engaged to that other girl before; and then, when I came to think of it, I knew that I was not fit to marry

Miss Dale. I know I have behaved badly; but, Pratt, thousands have done the same thing before.'

'I can only say that I have not been so unfortunate as to reckon any of those thousands among my friends.'

'You mean to tell me, then, that you are going to turn your back on me?' said Crosbie.

'I haven't said anything of the kind. I certainly won't undertake to defend you, for I don't see that your conduct admits of defence. I will see this gentleman if you wish it, and tell him anything that you desire me to tell him.'

At this moment the servant returned with a note for Crosbie. Mr Dale had called for paper and envelope, and sent up to him the following missive: – 'Do you intend to come down to me? I know that you are in the house.'

'For heaven's sake go to him,' said Crosbie. 'He is well aware that I was deceived about his niece, – that I thought he was to give her some fortune. He knows all about that, and that when I learned from him that she was to have nothing – '

'Upon my word, Crosbie, I wish you could find another messenger.'

'Ah! you do not understand,' said Crosbie in his agony: 'You think that I am inventing this plea about her fortune now. It isn't so. He will understand. We have talked all this over before, and he knew how terribly I was disappointed. Shall I wait for you here, or will you come to my lodgings? Or I will go down to the Beaufort, and will wait for you there.' And it was finally arranged that he should get himself out of this club and wait at the other for Pratt's report of the interview.

'Do you go down first?' said Crosbie.

'Yes: I had better,' said Pratt. 'Otherwise you may be seen. Mr Dale would have his eye upon you, and there would be a row in the house.' There was a smile of sarcasm on Pratt's face as he spoke which angered Crosbie even in his misery, and made him long to tell his friend that he would not trouble him with this mission, – that he would manage his own affairs himself; but he was weakened and mentally humiliated by the sense of his own rascality, and had already lost the power of asserting himself, and of maintaining his ascendancy. He was beginning to recognise the fact that he had done that for which he must endure to be kicked, to be kicked morally if not materially; and that it was no longer possible for him to hold his head up without shame.

Pratt took Mr Dale's note in his hand and went down into the strangers' room. There he found the squire standing, so that he could see through the open door of the room to the foot of the stairs down which Crosbie must descend before he could leave the club. As a measure of first precaution the ambassador closed the door; then he bowed to Mr Dale, and asked him if he would take a chair.

'I wanted to see Mr Crosbie,' said the squire.

'I have your note to that gentleman in my hand,' said he. 'He has thought it better that you should have this interview with me; – and under all the circumstances perhaps it is better.'

'Is he such a coward that he dare not see me?'

'There are some actions, Mr Dale, that will make a coward of any man. My friend Crosbie is, I take it, brave enough in the ordinary sense of the word, but he has injured you.'

'It is all true, then?'

'Yes, Mr Dale; I fear it is all true.'

'And you call that man your friend! Mr – ; I don't know what your name is.'

'Pratt; – Fowler Pratt. I have known Crosbie for fourteen years, – ever since he was a boy; and it is not my way, Mr Dale, to throw over an old friend under any circumstances.'

'Not if he committed a murder?'

'No; not though he committed a murder.'

'If what I hear is true, this man is worse than a murderer!'

'Of course, Mr Dale, I cannot know what you have heard. I believe that Mr Crosbie has behaved very badly to your niece, Miss Dale; I believe that he was engaged to marry her, or, at any rate, that some such proposition had been made.'

'Proposition! Why, sir, it was a thing so completely understood that everybody knew it in the county. It was so positively fixed that there was no secret about it. Upon my honour, Mr Pratt, I can't as yet understand it. If I remember right, it's not a fortnight since he left my house at Allington, – not a fortnight. And that poor girl was with him on the morning of his going as his betrothed beside. Not a fortnight since! And now I've had a letter from an old family friend telling me that he is going to marry one of Lord de Courcy's daughters! I went instantly off to Courcy, and found that he had started for London. Now, I have followed him here; and you tell me it's all true.'

'I am afraid it is, Mr Dale; too true.'

'I don't understand it; I don't, indeed. I cannot bring myself to believe that the man who was sitting the other day at my table should be so great a scoundrel. Did he mean it all the time that he was there?'

'No; certainly not. Lady Alexandrina de Courcy was, I believe, an old friend of his; – with whom, perhaps, he had had some lover's quarrel. On his going to Courcy they made it up; and this is the result.'

'And that is to be sufficient for my poor girl?'

'You will, of course, understand that I am not defending Mr Crosbie. The whole affair is very sad, – very sad, indeed. I can only say, in his excuse, that he is not the first man who has behaved badly to a lady.'

'And that is his message to me, is it? And that is what I am to tell my niece? You have been deceived by a scoundrel. But what then? You are not the first! Mr Pratt, I give you my word as a gentleman, I do not understand it. I have lived a good deal out of the world, and am, therefore, perhaps, more astonished than I ought to be.'

'Mr Dale, I feel for you – '

'Feel for me! What is to become of my girl? And do you suppose that I will let this other marriage go on; that I will not tell the de Courcys, and all the world at large, what sort of a man this is; – that I will not get at him to punish him? Does he think that I will put up with this?'

'I do not know what he thinks; I must only beg that you will not mix me up in the matter – as though I were a participator in his offence.'

'Will you tell him from me that I desire to see him?'

'I do not think that that would do any good.'

'Never mind, sir; you have brought me his message; will you have the goodness now to take back mine to him?'

'Do you mean at once – this evening, – now?'

'Yes, at once – this evening, – now; – this minute.'

'Ah; he has left the club; he is not here now; he went when I came to you.'

'Then he is a coward as well as a scoundrel.' In answer to which assertion, Mr Fowler Pratt merely shrugged his shoulders.

'He is a coward as well as a scoundrel. Will you have the kindness to tell your friend from me that he is a coward and a scoundrel, – and a liar, sir.'

'If it be so, Miss Dale is well quit of her engagement.'

'That is your consolation, is it? That may be all very well nowadays; but when I was a young man, I would sooner have burnt out my tongue than have spoken in such a way on such a subject. I would, indeed. Good-night, Mr Pratt. Pray make your friend understand that he has not yet seen the last of the Dales; although, as you hint, the ladies of that family will no doubt have learned that he is not fit to associate with them.' Then, taking up his hat, the squire made his way out of the club.

'I would not have done it,' said Pratt to himself, 'for all the beauty, and all the wealth, and all the rank that ever were owned by a woman.'

Further reading

You could pick up the threads of Crosbie's story in chapter 30, although many readers think of this book more as the story of Lily Dale, as clearly Trollope's own sympathies were with his heroine. After what he does to Lily, Crosbie's fine future turns to dust.

For another 'reversal of fortune' story, try Guy de Maupassant's *The Necklace*, a short story first published in France in 1885.

Definition of a Gentleman

by John Henry Newman

The opening lines of *Definition of a Gentleman* are famous: a gentleman 'is one who never inflicts pain'. Read on, and see if you agree with the rest of Cardinal Newman's thoughts.

Hence it is, that it is almost a definition of a gentleman, to say he is one who never inflicts pain. This description is both refined and, as far as it goes, accurate. He is mainly occupied in merely removing the obstacles which hinder the free and unembarrassed action of those about him; and he concurs with their movements rather than takes the initiative himself. His benefits may be considered as parallel to what are called comforts or conveniences in arrangements of a personal nature: like an easy chair or a good fire, which do their part in dispelling cold and fatigue, though nature provides both means of rest and animal heat without them. The true gentleman in like manner carefully avoids whatever may cause a jar or a jolt in the minds of those with whom he is cast all clashing of opinion, or collision of feeling, all restraint, or suspicion, or gloom, or resentment; his great concern being to make every one at their ease and at home. He has his eyes on all his company; he is tender towards the bashful, gentle towards the distant, and merciful towards the absurd; he can recollect to whom he is speaking; he guards against unseasonable allusions, or topics which may irritate; he is seldom prominent in conversation, and never wearisome. He makes light of favours while he does them, and seems to be receiving when he is conferring. He never speaks of himself except when compelled, never defends himself by a mere retort, he has no ears for slander or gossip, is scrupulous in imputing motives to those who interfere with him, and interprets everything for the best. He is never mean or little in his disputes, never takes unfair advantage, never mistakes personalities or sharp sayings for arguments, or insinuates evil which he dare not say out. From a long-sighted prudence, he observes the maxim of the ancient sage, that we should ever conduct ourselves towards our enemy as if he were one day to be our friend. He has too much good sense to be affronted at insults, he is too well employed to remember injuries, and too indolent to bear malice. He is patient, forbearing, and resigned, on philosophical principles; he submits to pain, because it is inevitable, to bereavement, because it is irreparable, and to death, because it is his destiny. If he engages in controversy of any kind, his disciplined intellect preserves him from the blundering discourtesy of better, though less educated, minds; who, like blunt weapons, tear and hack instead of cutting clean, who mistake the point in argument, waste their strength on trifles, misconceive their adversary, and leave the question more involved than they find it. He may be right or wrong in his opinion, but he is too clear-headed to be unjust; he is as simple as he is forcible, and as brief as he is decisive.

Further reading

Cardinal Newman's writing about this is illuminated by reading the great novels of the Victorian age. How men behaved in those stories dictates much of the progress of the plot and many of the novels' messages. Crosbie in *The Small House at Allington* (see page 210) is just one of the Victorian 'gentlemen' whose actions reveal him to be the opposite. As a result, according to the thinking of the day, Trollope has to exile him from the society he loves. Dr Lydgate in *Middlemarch* by George Eliot is a perfect example of a gentleman (and an exciting character; his good behaviour doesn't make him dreary).

You might find it interesting to read William Cobbett's *Advice to a Father*, which he wrote just before the Victorian era began, to see how 'gentlemanly behaviour' extends to a man in his home.

Adam Bede

by George Eliot

This extract is taken from *Adam Bede*, a book about the lives of a small rural community of people. In class-ridden Victorian England, some people had considerably more power than others not only over their own lives but also over the lives of those around them.

Mrs Poyser lives at Hall Farm. She and her husband work hard and always have done. She is not pleased to get a visit from the old Squire, Mr Donnithorne, the owner of both Hall Farm and another farm nearby. She suspects he is bringing bad news, and she's right. He wants a rearrangement of the old way in which the land is shared between the two farms. But he has reckoned without Mrs Poyser.

It was probably owing to the conversation she had had with her husband on their way home from church, concerning this problematic stranger, that Mrs Poyser's thoughts immediately reverted to him when, a day or two afterwards, as she was standing at the house-door with her knitting, in that eager leisure which came to her when the afternoon cleaning was done, she saw the old Squire enter the yard on his black pony, followed by John the groom. She always cited it afterwards as a case of prevision,[1] which really had something more in it than her own remarkable penetration, that the moment she set eyes on the Squire, she said to herself, 'I shouldna wonder if he's come about that man as is a-going to take the Chase Farm, wanting Poyser to do something for him without pay. But Poyser's a fool if he does.'

Something unwonted[2] must clearly be in the wind, for the old Squire's visits to his tenantry were rare; and though Mrs Poyser had during the last twelvemonth recited many imaginary speeches, meaning even more than met the ear, which she was quite determined to make to him the next time

---

[1] **prevision**   imagining or thinking about something before it happens
[2] **unwonted**   unusual

he appeared within the gates of the Hall Farm, the speeches had always remained imaginary.

'Good-day, Mrs Poyser,' said the old Squire, peering at her with his short-sighted eyes – a mode of looking at her which, as Mrs Poyser observed, 'allays aggravated her: it was as if you was a insect, and he was going to dab his finger-nail on you.'

However, she said, 'Your servant, sir,' and curtsied with an air of perfect deference³ as she advanced towards him: she was not the woman to misbehave towards her betters, and fly in the face of the catechism,⁴ without severe provocation.

'Is your husband at home, Mrs Poyser?'

'Yes, sir; he's only i' the rick-yard. I'll send for him in a minute, if you'll please to get down and step in.'

'Thank you; I will do so. I want to consult him about a little matter; but you are quite as much concerned in it, if not more. I must have your opinion too.'

'Hetty, run and tell your uncle to come in,' said Mrs Poyser, as they entered the house, and the old gentleman bowed low in answer to Hetty's curtsy; while Totty, conscious of a pinafore stained with gooseberry jam, stood hiding her face against the clock, and peeping round furtively.

'What a fine old kitchen this is!' said Mr Donnithorne, looking round admiringly. He always spoke in the same deliberate, well-chiselled, polite way, whether his words were sugary or venomous. 'And you keep it so exquisitely clean, Mrs Poyser. I like these premises, do you know, beyond any on the estate.'

'Well, sir, since you're fond of 'em, I should be glad if you'd let a bit o' repairs be done to 'em, for the boarding's i' that state, as we're like to be eaten up wi' rats and mice; and the cellar, you may stan' up to your knees i' water in't, if you like to go down; but perhaps you'd rather believe my words. Won't you please to sit down, sir?'

---

³**deference**   respect, deferring to
⁴**catechism**   a book of questions and answers to teach people about
    Christianity

'Not yet; I must see your dairy. I have not seen it for years, and I hear on all hands about your fine cheese and butter,' said the Squire, looking politely unconscious that there could be any question on which he and Mrs Poyser might happen to disagree. 'I think I see the door open, there: you must not be surprised if I cast a covetous[5] eye on your cream and butter. I don't expect that Mrs Satchell's cream and butter will bear comparison with yours.'

'I can't say, sir, I'm sure. It's seldom I see other folks's butter, though there's some on it as one's no need to see – the smell's enough.'

'Ah, now this I like,' said Mr Donnithorne, looking round at the damp temple of cleanliness, but keeping near the door. 'I'm sure I should like my breakfast better if I knew the butter and cream came from this dairy. Thank you, that really is a pleasant sight. Unfortunately, my slight tendency to rheumatism makes me afraid of damp: I'll sit down in your comfortable kitchen. Ah, Poyser, how do you do? In the midst of business, I see, as usual. I've been looking at your wife's beautiful dairy – the best manager in the parish, is she not?'

Mr Poyser had just entered in shirt-sleeves and open waistcoat, with a face a shade redder than usual, from the exertion of 'pitching'.[6] As he stood, red, rotund, and radiant, before the small, wiry, cool, old gentleman, he looked like a prize apple by the side of a withered crab.

'Will you please to take this chair, sir?' he said, lifting his father's arm-chair forward a little: 'you'll find it easy.'

'No, thank you, I never sit in easy-chairs,' said the old gentleman, seating himself on a small chair near the door. 'Do you know, Mrs Poyser – sit down, pray, both of you – I've been far from contented, for some time, with Mrs Satchell's dairy management. I think she has not a good method, as you have.'

---

[5]**covetous**   desiring something too much, especially something which belongs to someone else
[6]**pitching**   tossing hay using a pitchfork

'Indeed, sir, I can't speak to that,' said Mrs Poyser, in a hard voice, rolling and unrolling her knitting, and looking icily out of the window, as she continued to stand opposite the Squire. Poyser might sit down if he liked, she thought: *she* wasn't going to sit down, as if she'd give in to any such smooth-tongued palaver. Mr Poyser, who looked and felt the reverse of icy, did sit down in his three-cornered chair.

'And now, Poyser, as Satchell is laid up, I am intending to let the Chase Farm to a respectable tenant. I'm tired of having a farm on my own hands – nothing is made the best of in such cases, as you know. A satisfactory bailiff[7] is hard to find; and I think you and I, Poyser, and your excellent wife here, can enter into a little arrangement in consequence, which will be to our mutual advantage.'

'Oh,' said Mr Poyser, with a good-natured blankness of imagination as to the nature of the arrangement.

'If I'm called upon to speak, sir,' said Mrs Poyser, after glancing at her husband with pity at his softness, 'you know better than me; but I don't see what the Chase Farm is t' us – we've cumber enough wi' our own farm. Not but what I'm glad to hear o' anybody respectable coming into the parish: there's some as ha' been brought in as hasn't been looked on i' that character.'

'You're likely to find Mr Thurle an excellent neighbour, I assure you: such a one as you will feel glad to have accommodated by the little plan I'm going to mention; especially as I hope you will find it as much to your own advantage as his.'

'Indeed, sir, if it's anything to our advantage, it'll be the first offer o' that sort I've heared on. It's them as take advantage that get advantage i' this world, *I* think: folks have to wait long enough afore it's brought to 'em.'

'The fact is, Poyser,' said the Squire, ignoring Mrs Poyser's theory of worldly prosperity, 'there is too much dairy land, and too little plough land, on the Chase Farm, to suit Thurle's

---

[7]**bailiff**   agent or steward working for a landlord

purpose – indeed, he will only take the farm on condition of some change in it: his wife, it appears, is not a clever dairy-woman, like yours. Now, the plan I'm thinking of is to effect a little exchange. If you were to have the Hollow Pastures, you might increase your dairy, which must be so profitable under your wife's management; and I should request you, Mrs Poyser, to supply my house with milk, cream, and butter, at the market prices. On the other hand, Poyser, you might let Thurle have the Lower and Upper Ridges, which really, with our wet seasons, would be a good riddance for you. There is much less risk in dairy land than corn land.'

Mr Poyser was leaning forward, with his elbows on his knees, his head on one side, and his mouth screwed up – apparently absorbed in making the tips of his fingers meet so as to represent with perfect accuracy the ribs of a ship. He was much too acute a man not to see through the whole business, and to foresee perfectly what would be his wife's view of the subject; but he disliked giving unpleasant answers: unless it was on a point of farming practice, he would rather give up than have a quarrel, any day; and, after all, it mattered more to his wife than to him. So, after a few moments' silence, he looked up at her and said mildly, 'What dost say?'

Mrs Poyser had had her eyes fixed on her husband with cold severity during his silence, but now she turned away her head with a toss, looked icily at the opposite roof of the cow-shed, and spearing her knitting together with the loose pin, held it firmly between her clasped hands.

'Say? Why, I say you may do as you like about giving up any o' your corn land afore your lease is up, which it won't be for a year come next Michaelmas, but I'll not consent to take more dairy work into my hands, either for love or money; and there's nayther love nor money here as I can see, on'y other folks' love o' theirselves, and the money as is to go into other folks' pockets. I know there's them as is born t' own the land, and them as is born to sweat on't – here Mrs Poyser paused to gasp a little – 'and I know it's christened folks' duty to submit to their betters as fur as flesh and blood 'ull bear it: but I'll not make a martyr o' myself, and wear myself to skin and bone, and worret myself as if I was a churn wi' butter a-coming in't, for no landlord in England, not if he was King George himself.'

'No, no, my dear Mrs Poyser, certainly not,' said the Squire, still confident in his own powers of persuasion, 'you must not overwork yourself; but don't you think your work will rather be lessened than increased in this way? There is so much milk required at the Abbey, that you will have little increase of cheese and butter making from the addition to your dairy; and I believe selling the milk is the most profitable way of disposing of dairy produce, is it not?'

'Ay, that's true,' said Mr Poyser, unable to repress an opinion on a question of farming profits, and forgetting that it was not in this case a purely abstract question.

'I dare say,' said Mrs Poyser bitterly, turning her head half-way towards her husband, and looking at the vacant arm-chair – 'I dare say it's true for men as sit i' the chimney-corner and make believe as everything's cut wi' ins an' outs to fit int' everything else. If you could make a pudding wi' thinking o' the batter, it 'ud be easy getting dinner. How do I know whether the milk 'ull be wanted constant? What's to make me sure as the house won't be put o' board wage afore we're many months older, and then I may have to lie awake o' nights wi' twenty gallons o' milk on my mind – and Dingall 'ull take no more butter, let alone paying for it; and we must fat pigs till we're obliged to beg the butcher on our knees to buy 'em, and lose half of 'em wi' the measles. And there's the fetching and carrying, as 'ud be welly half a day's work for a man an' hoss – *that*'s to be took out o' the profits, I reckon? But there's folks 'ud hold a sieve under the pump and expect to carry away the water.'

'That difficulty – about the fetching and carrying – you will not have, Mrs Poyser,' said the Squire, who thought that this entrance into particulars indicated a distant inclination to compromise on Mrs Poyser's part – 'Bethell will do that regularly with the cart and pony.'

'Oh, sir, begging your pardon, I've never been used t' having gentlefolks's servants coming about my back places, a-making love to both gells at once, and keeping 'em with their hands on their hips listening to all manner o' gossip when they should be down on their knees a'scouring. If we're to go to ruin, it shanna be wi' having our back-kitchen turned into a public.'[8]

'Well, Poyser,' said the Squire, shifting his tactics, and looking as if he thought Mrs Poyser had suddenly withdrawn from the proceedings and left the room, 'you can turn the Hollows into feeding-land. I can easily make another arrangement about supplying my house. And I shall not forget your readiness to accommodate your landlord as well as a neighbour. I know you will be glad to have your lease renewed for three years when the present one expires; otherwise, I dare say Thurle, who is a man of some capital, would be glad to take both the farms, as they could be worked so well together. But I don't want to part with an old tenant like you.'

To be thrust out of the discussion in this way would have been enough to complete Mrs Poyser's exasperation, even without the final threat. Her husband, really alarmed at the possibility of their leaving the old place where he had been bred and born – for he beleved the old Squire had small spite enough for anything – was beginning a mild remonstrance explanatory of the inconvenience he should find in having to buy and sell more stock, with – 'Well, sir, I think as it's rether hard . . . ' when Mrs Poyser burst in with the desperate determination to have her say out this once, though it were to rain notices to quit, and the only shelter were the workhouse.[9]

'Then, sir, if I may speak – as, for all I'm a woman, and there's folks as thinks a woman's fool enough to stan by an' look on while the men sign her soul away, I've a right to speak, for I make one quarter o' the rent, and save another quarter – I

---

[8] **a public**   an inn
[9] **the workhouse**   an institution maintained by the state for able-bodied poor people to do unpaid work in return for food and lodging; these places were feared and families were often separated

Dinnertime at St Pancras Workhouse

say, if Mr Thurle's so ready to take farms under you, it's a pity but what he should take this, and see if he likes to live in a house wi' all the plagues o' Egypt in't – wi' the cellar full o' water, and frogs and toads hoppin' up the steps by dozens – and the floors rotten, and the rats and mice gnawing every bit o' cheese, and runnin' over our heads as we lie i' bed till we expect 'em to eat us up alive – as it's a mercy they hanna eat the children long ago. I should like to see if there's another tenant besides Poyser as 'ud put up wi' never having a bit o' repairs done till a place tumbles down – and not then, on'y wi' begging and praying, and having to pay half – and being strung up wi' the rent as it's much if he gets enough out o' the land to pay, for all he's put his own money into the ground beforehand. See if you'll get a stranger to lead such a life here as that: a maggot must be born i' the rotten cheese to like it, I reckon. You may run away from my words, sir,' continued Mrs Poyser, following the old Squire beyond the door – for after the first moments of stunned surprise he had got up, and, waving his hand towards her with a smile, had walked out towards his pony. But it was impossible for him to get away immediately, for John was walking the pony up and down the yard, and was some distance from the causeway when his master beckoned.

'You may run away from my words, sir, and you may go spinnin' underhand ways o' doing us a mischief, for you've got old Harry to your friend, though nobody else is, but I tell you for once as we're not dumb creatures to be abused and made money on by them as ha' got the lash i' their hands, for want o' knowin' how t' undo the tackle. An' if I'm the only one as speaks my mind, there's plenty o' the same way o' thinking i' this parish and the next to't, for your name's no better than a brimstone match in everybody's nose – if it isna two-three old folks as you think o' saving your soul by giving 'em a bit o' flannel and a drop o' porridge. An' you may be right i' thinking it'll take but little to save your soul, for it'll be the smallest savin' y' iver made, wi' all your scrapin'.'

There are occasions on which two servant-girls and a waggoner may be a formidable audience, and as the Squire rode away on his black pony, even the gift of short-sightedness did not prevent him from being aware that Molly and Nancy and Tim were grinning not far from him. Perhaps he suspected that sour old John was grinning behind him – which was also the fact. Meanwhile the bull-dog, the black-and-tan terrier, Alick's sheepdog, and the gander hissing at a safe distance from the pony's heels, carried out the idea of Mrs Poyser's solo in an impressive quartet.

Mrs Poyser, however, had no sooner seen the pony move off than she turned round, gave the two hilarious damsels[10] a look which drove them into the back kitchen, and, unspearing her knitting, began to knit again with her usual rapidity, as she re-entered the house.

'Thee'st done it now,' said Mr Poyser; a little alarmed and uneasy, but not without some triumphant amusement at his wife's outbreak.

---

[10]**damsels** girls

'Yes, I know I've done it,' said Mrs Poyser; 'ut I've had my say out, and I shall be th' easier for't all my life. There's no pleasure i' living, if you're to be corked up for ever, and only dribble your mind out by the sly, like a leaky barrel. I shan't repent saying what I think, if I live to be as old as th' old Squire; and there's little likelihoods – for it seems as if them as aren't wanted here are th' only folks as aren't wanted i' th' other world.'

'But thee wutna like moving from th' old place this Michaelmas twelvemonth,' said Mr Poyser, 'and going into a strange parish, where thee know'st nobody. It'll be hard upon us both, and upo' father too.'

'Eh, it's no use worreting; there's plenty o' things may happen between this and Michaelmas twelvemonth. The Captain may be master afore then, for what we know,' said Mrs Poyser, inclined to take an unusually hopeful view of an embarrassment which had been brought about by her own merit, and not by other people's fault.'

'*I'm* none for worreting,' said Mr Poyser, rising from his three-cornered chair, and walking slowly towards the door; 'but I should be loath to leave the old place, and the parish where I was bred and born, and father afore me. We should leave our roots behind us, I doubt, and niver thrive[11] again.'

Further reading

Writing about ordinary people living ordinary lives was a completely new feature of Victorian novelists. When George Eliot wrote *Adam Bede*, she created Mrs Poyser as a poor working woman who was a lively representative of the class that had always been downtrodden by the upper classes. Suddenly you could see that those days were going to be over; perhaps not yet, but one day. Read on in the book to see what happens next.

If you'd like to read about another character who trounces his 'betters', read chapter 18 of Trollope's *The Last Chronicle of Barset*, where a poor curate, Mr Crawley, makes a horrible bishop's wife squirm.

---

[11]**thrive**   flourish

The Book of Household Management
by Mrs Isabella Beeton

The Book of Household Management was written to include information for the following: the mistress, housekeeper, cook, kitchen-maid, butler, footman, coachman, valet, upper and under house-maids, lady's-maid, maid-of-all-work, laundry-maid, nurse and nurse-maid, monthly wet and sick nurses . . . Perhaps not surprisingly the book is 1,112 pages long.

Strength and honour are her clothing; and she shall rejoice in time to come. She openeth her mouth with wisdom; and in her tongue is the law of kindness. She looketh well to the ways of her household, and eateth not the bread of idleness. Her children arise up, and call her blessed; her husband also, and he praiseth her   Proverbs, 31: 25–28

As with the Commander of an Army, or the leader of an enterprise, so is it with the mistress of a house. Her spirit will be seen through the whole establishment; and just in proportion as she performs her duties intelligently and thoroughly, so will her domestics follow in her path. Of all those acquirements, which more particularly belong to the feminine character, there are none which take a higher rank, in our estimation, than such as enter into a knowledge of household duties; for on these are perpetually dependent the happiness, comfort and well-being of a family. In this opinion we are borne out by the author of 'The Vicar of Wakefield,'[1] who says: 'The modest virgin, the prudent wife, and the careful matron, are much more serviceable in life than petticoated philosophers, blustering heroines, or virago[2] queans.[3] She who makes her husband and her children happy, who reclaims the one from vice and trains up the other to virtue, is a much greater character than ladies described in

---

[1] **the author of 'The Vicar of Wakefield'** the 18th-century Anglo-Irish writer Oliver Goldsmith
[2] **virago** loud, ill-tempered
[3] **quean** a woman with a bad reputation

romances, whose whole occupation is to murder mankind with shafts from their quiver, or their eyes.'

Pursuing this Picture, we may add, that to be a good housewife does not necessarily imply an abandonment of proper pleasures or amusing recreation; and we think it the more necessary to express this, as the performance of the duties of a mistress may, to some minds, perhaps seem to be incompatible with the enjoyment of life. Let us, however, proceed to describe some of those home qualities and virtues which are necessary to the proper management of a household, and then point out the plan which may be the most profitably pursued for the daily regulation of its affairs.

Further reading

You can take a look at the whole of Mrs Beeton's *Book of Household Management* in an Oxford World's Classics edition. Two recent books, *Provisions: A Reader from 19th-Century Women* by Judith Fetterley and *Children at the Hearth: 19th-Century Cooking, Manners and Games* by Barbara Sewell are American explorations of life at the time Mrs Beeton was alive and writing in England.

If you can get hold of an old copy of *Household Words* you'll see domestic life as Charles Dickens saw it. He edited these weekly magazines, which were bound together every few months and which contained recipes, adverts, gardening tips and short stories. They are a true first-hand glimpse of Victorian life.

My Rights

by Susan Coolidge

> Very few women at the start of Queen Victoria's reign would have
> worried about how different their lives were from the lives of their
> fathers, brothers, husbands and sons. The first three verses of this
> poem seem like a hymn to the kind of unchanging and protected
> domestic contentment which, for women who were not poor, pro-
> vided a safe and comfortable setting. But *My Rights* goes on slightly
> unexpectedly. See what you think.

Yes, God has made me a woman,
  And I am content to be
Just what He meant, not reaching out
  For other things, since He
Who knows me best and loves me most has ordered this
            for me.

A woman, to live my life out
  In quite womanly ways,
Hearing the far-off battle,
  Seeing as through a haze
The crowding, struggling world of men fight through their
            busy days.

I am not strong or valiant,
  I would not join the fight
Or jostle with crowds in the highways
  To sully my garments white;
But I have rights as a woman, and here I claim my right.

The right of a rose to bloom
  In its own sweet, separate way,
With none to utter a nay
  If it reaches a root
Or points a thorn, as even a rose-tree may.

The right of a lady-birch to grow,
　　To grow as the Lord shall please,
By never a sturdy oak rebuked,
　　Denied nor sun nor breeze,
For all its pliant[1] slenderness, kin to the stronger trees.

The right to a life of my own, –
　　Not merely a casual bit
Of somebody else's life, flung out
　　That, taking hold of it,
I may stand as a cipher[2] does after a numeral writ.

The right to gather and glean
　　What food I need and can
From the garnered store of knowledge
　　Which man has heaped for man,
Taking with free hands freely and after an ordered plan.

The right – ah, best and sweetest! –
　　To stand all undismayed
Whenever sorrow or want or sin
　　Call for a woman's aid,
With none to cavil[3] or question, by never a look gainsaid.

I did not ask for a ballot;
　　Though very life were at stake,
　　I would beg for the nobler justice
That men for manhood's sake
　　Should give ungrudgingly,
　　Nor withhold till I must fight and take.

---

[1]**pliant**　supple, can easily bend
[2]**cipher**　code
[3]**cavil**　raise annoying, petty objections

The fleet foot and the feeble foot
    Both seek the self-same goal,
The weakest soldier's name is writ,
    On the great army-roll,
And God, who made man's body strong, made too the
                         woman's soul.

Further reading

Sarah Chauncey Woolsey, under her pen-name Susan Coolidge, wrote the famous children's novel *What Katy Did*, in which the energetic Katy Carr has an accident and learns to be a 'better' girl once she is an invalid. *What Katy Did* and the sequels *What Katy Did at School* and *What Katy Did Next* were extremely popular among schoolgirls and still sell well.

A Doll's House

by Henrik Ibsen

> Nora forged her father's name on a cheque and used it to borrow money from a man called Krogstad. This makes her sound like a criminal, but she wanted the money to take her sick husband, Torvald Helmer, abroad where he might get better. She saved up all her 'pin' money – little amounts of money for her own use – in order to pay it all back.
>
> But Krogstad turned up and threatened to tell Helmer – and when the news did come out, Helmer was furious and said Nora was not fit to be a wife and mother and must leave the house. But what if no one else found out? Nora could stay, then, if they could hush it up. How kind, how gracious of him, he thinks. But in this scene, the last of the play, Nora's heartache turns into something else . . . and Helmer is utterly amazed.

HELMER: You will remain here in my house – that goes without saying – but I shall not allow you to bring up the children . . . I shouldn't dare trust you with them. Oh, to think that I should have to say this to someone I've loved so much – someone I still . . . Well, that's all over – it must be; from now on, there'll be no question of happiness, but only of saving the ruin of it – the fragments – the mere façade . . .

[*There is a ring at the front door.*]

HELMER [*collecting himself*]: What's that – at this hour? Can the worst have – Could he . . .? Keep out of sight, Nora – say that you're ill.

[NORA *remains motionless.* HELMER *goes and opens the hall door.*]

MAID [*at the door, half-dressed*]: There's a letter for the Mistress.

HELMER: Give it to me. [*He takes the letter and shuts the door.*] Yes, it's from him. You're not to have it – I shall read it myself.

NORA: Yes, read it.

HELMER [*by the lamp*]: I hardly dare – it may mean ruin for both of
us. No, I *must* know! [*Tearing open the letter, he runs his eye over a few
lines, looks at a paper that is enclosed, then gives a shout of joy.*] Nora!
[*She looks at him inquiringly.*]

Nora! Wait, I must just read it again. . . . Yes, it's true; I'm
saved! Nora, I'm saved!

NORA: And I?

HELMER: You too, of course. We're both saved – both you
and I. Look, he's sent you back your bond. He says that he
regrets . . . and apologizes . . . a fortunate change in his
life . . . Oh, never mind what he says – we're saved, Nora, no
one can touch you now. Oh Nora, Nora – Wait, first let me
destroy the whole detestable business. [*Casting his eye over the
bond*] No, I won't even look at it – I shall treat the whole
thing as nothing but a bad dream. [*Tearing the bond and the
two letters in pieces, he throws them on the stove, and watches them
burn.*] There! Now it's all gone. He said in his letter than
since Christmas Eve you'd . . . Oh, Nora, these three days
must have been terrible for you.

NORA: They've been a hard struggle, these three days.

HELMER: How you must have suffered – seeing no way out except
. . . No, we'll put all those hateful things out of our minds.
Now we can shout for joy, again and again: 'It's all over – it's
all over!' Listen, Nora – you don't seem to realize – it's all over.
What's the matter? Such a grim face? Poor little Nora, I see
what it is: you simply can't believe that I've forgiven you. But I
have, Nora, I swear it – I've forgiven you everything. I know
now that what you did was all for love of me.

NORA: That is true.

HELMER: You loved me as a wife *should* love her husband. It was
just that you hadn't the experience to realize what you were

doing. But do you imagine that you're any less dear to me for not knowing how to act on your own? No, no, you must simply rely on me – I shall advise you and guide you. I shouldn't be a proper man if your feminine helplessness didn't make you twice as attractive to me. You must forget all the hard things that I said to you in that first dreadful moment when it seemed as if the whole world was falling about my ears. I've forgiven you, Nora, I swear it – I've forgiven you.

NORA: Thank you for your forgiveness. [*She goes out through the door to the right.*]

HELMER: No, don't go. [*He looks in.*] What are you doing out there?

NORA [*off*]: Taking off my fancy-dress.

HELMER [*at the open door*]: Yes, do. Try to calm down and set your mind at peace, my frightened little songbird. You can rest safely, and my great wings will protect you. [*He paces up and down by the door.*] Oh, Nora, how warm and cosy our home is; it's your refuge, where I shall protect you like a hunted dove that I've saved from the talons of a hawk. Little by little, I shall calm your poor fluttering heart, Nora, take my word for it. In the morning you'll look on all this quite differently, and soon everything will be just as it used to be. There'll be no more need for me to tell you that I've forgiven you – you'll feel in your heart that I have. How can you imagine that I could ever think of rejecting – or even reproaching – you? Ah, you don't know what a real man's heart is like, Nora. There's something indescribably sweet and satisfying for a man to know deep down that he has forgiven his wife – completely forgiven her, with all his heart. It's as if that made her doubly his – as if he had brought her into the world afresh! In a sense, she has become both his wife and his child. So from now on, that's what you shall be to me, you poor, frightened, helpless, little darling. You mustn't worry about anything, Nora – only be absolutely frank with me, and I'll be both your will and your conscience . . . Why, what's this? Not in bed? You've changed your clothes!

NORA [*in her everyday things*]: Yes, Torvald, I've changed my clothes.

HELMER: But why? At *this* hour!

NORA: I shan't sleep tonight.

HELMER: But, my dear Nora –

NORA [*looking at her watch*]: It's not so very late. Sit down here; Torvald – you and I have a lot to talk over. [She *sits down at one side of the table.*]

HELMER: Nora – what is all this? Why do you look so stern?

NORA: Sit down – this'll take some time. I have a lot to talk to you about.

HELMER [*sitting across the table from her*]: Nora, you frighten me – I don't understand you.

NORA: No, that's just it – you don't understand me. And I've never understood you – until tonight. No, you mustn't interrupt – just listen to what I have to say. Torvald, this is a reckoning.

HELMER: What do you mean by that?

NORA [*after a short pause*]: Doesn't it strike you that there's something strange about the way we're sitting here?

HELMER: No . . . what?

NORA: We've been married for eight years now. Don't you realize that this is the first time that we two – you and I, man and wife – have had a serious talk together?

HELMER: Serious? What do you mean by that?

NORA: For eight whole years – no, longer than that – ever since we first met, we've never exchanged a serious word on any serious subject.

HELMER: Was I to keep forever involving you in worries that you couldn't possibly help me with?

NORA: I'm not talking about worries; what I'm saying is that we've never sat down in earnest together to get to the bottom of a single thing.

HELMER: But, Nora dearest, what good would that have been to you?

NORA: That's just the point – you've never understood me. I've been dreadfully wronged, Torvald – first by Papa, and then by you.

HELMER: What? By your father and me? The two people who love you more than anyone else in the world?

NORA [*shaking her head*]: You've never loved me, you've only found it pleasant to be in love with me.

HELMER: Nora – what are you saying?

NORA: It's true, Torvald. When I lived at home with Papa, he used to tell me his opinion about everything, and so I had the same opinion. If I thought differently, I had to hide it from him, or he wouldn't have liked it. He called me his little doll, and he used to play with me just as I played with my dolls. Then I came to live in your house –

HELMER: That's no way to talk about our marriage!

NORA [*undisturbed*]: I mean when I passed out of Papa's hands into yours. You arranged everything to suit your own tastes, and so I came to have the same tastes as yours . . . or I pretended to. I'm not quite sure which . . . perhaps it was a bit of both – sometimes one and sometimes the other. Now that I come to look at it, I've lived here like a pauper[1] – simply from hand to mouth. I've lived by performing tricks for you, Torvald. That was how you wanted it. You and Papa have

---

[1] **pauper**   a poor person supported by charity

committed a grievous sin against me: it's your fault that I've made nothing of my life.

HELMER: That's unreasonable, Nora – and ungrateful. Haven't you been happy here?

NORA: No, that's something I've never been. I thought I had, but really I've never been happy.

HELMER: Never . . . happy?

NORA: No, only gay. And you've always been so kind to me. But our home has been nothing but a play-room. I've been your doll-wife here, just as at home I was Papa's doll-child. And the children have been my dolls in their turn. I liked it when you came and played with me, just as they liked it when I came and played with them. That's what our marriage has been, Torvald.

HELMER: There is some truth in what you say, though you've exaggerated and overstated it. But from now on, things will be different. Play-time's over, now comes lesson-time.

NORA: Whose lessons? Mine or the children's?

HELMER: Both yours and the children's, Nora darling.

NORA: Ah, Torvald, you're not the man to teach me to be a real wife to you –

HELMER: How can you say that?

NORA: – and how am I fitted to bring up the children?

HELMER: Nora!

NORA: Didn't you say yourself, a little while ago, that you daren't trust them to me?

HELMER: That was in a moment of anger – you mustn't pay any attention to that.

NORA: But you were perfectly right – I'm not fit for it. There's another task that I must finish first – I must try to educate myself. And you're not the man to help me with that; I must do it alone. That's why I'm leaving you.

HELMER [*leaping to his feet*]: What's that you say?

NORA: I must stand on my own feet if I'm to get to know myself and the world outside. That's why I can't stay here with you any longer.

HELMER: Nora – Nora . . . !

NORA: I want to go at once. I'm sure Kristina will take me in for the night.

HELMER: You're out of your mind. I won't let you – I forbid it.

NORA: It's no good your forbidding me anything any longer. I shall take the things that belong to me, but I'll take nothing from you – now or later.

HELMER: But this is madness . . .

NORA: Tomorrow I shall go home – to my old home, I mean – it'll be easier for me to find something to do there.

HELMER: Oh, you blind, inexperienced creature . . . !

NORA: I must try to *get* some experience, Torvald.

HELMER: But to leave your home – your husband and your children. . . . You haven't thought of what people will say.

NORA: I can't consider that. All I know is that this is necessary for me.

HELMER: But this is disgraceful. Is this the way you neglect your most sacred duties?

NORA: What do you consider is my most sacred duty?

HELMER: Do I have to tell you that? Isn't it your duty to your husband and children?

NORA: I have another duty, just as sacred.

HELMER: You can't have. What duty do you mean?

NORA: My duty to myself.

HELMER: Before everything else, you're a wife and a mother.

NORA: I don't believe that any longer. I believe that before everything else I'm a human being – just as much as you are . . . or at any rate I shall try to become one. I know quite well that most people would agree with you, Torvald, and that you have warrant for it in books; but I can't be satisfied any longer with what most people say, and with what's in books. I must think things out for myself and try to understand them.

HELMER: Shouldn't you first understand your place in your own home? Haven't you an infallible[2] guide in such matters – your religion?

NORA: Ah, Torvald, I don't really know what religion is.

HELMER: What's that you say?

NORA: I only know what Pastor Hansen taught me when I was confirmed. He told me that religion was this, that, and the other. When I get away from all this, and am on my own, I want to look into that too. I want to see if what Pastor Hansen told me was right – or at least, if it is right for me.

HELMER: This is unheard-of from a young girl like you. But if religion can't guide you, then let me rouse your conscience. You must have *some* moral sense. Or am I wrong? Perhaps you haven't.

NORA: Well, Torvald, it's hard to say; I don't really know – I'm so bewildered about it all. All I know is that I think quite differently from you about things; and now I find that the law is quite different from what I thought, and I simply can't convince myself that the law is right. That a woman shouldn't have the right to spare her old father on his deathbed, or to save her husband's life! I can't believe things like that.

HELMER: You're talking like a child; you don't understand the world you live in.

NORA: No, I don't. But now I mean to go into that, too. I must find out which is right – the world or I.

---

[2]**infallible**   never wrong, incapable of making a mistake

HELMER: You're ill, Nora – you're feverish. I almost believe you're out of your senses.

NORA: I've never seen things so clearly and certainly as I do tonight.

HELMER: Clearly and certainly enough to forsake your husband and your children?

NORA: Yes.

HELMER: Then there's only one possible explanation . . .

NORA: What?

HELMER: You don't love me any more.

NORA: No, that's just it.

HELMER: Nora! How can you say that?

NORA: I can hardly bear to, Torvald, because you've always been so kind to me – but I can't help it. I don't love you any more.

HELMER [*with forced self-control*]: And are you clear and certain about that, too?

NORA: Yes, absolutely clear and certain. That's why I won't stay here any longer.

HELMER: And will you also be able to explain how I've forfeited your love?

NORA: Yes, I can indeed. It was this evening, when the miracle didn't happen – because then I saw that you weren't the man I'd always thought you.

HELMER: I don't understand that. Explain it.

NORA: For eight years I'd waited so patiently – for, goodness knows, I realized that miracles don't happen every day. Then this disaster overtook me, and I was completely certain that now the miracle would happen. When Krogstad's letter was lying out there, I never imagined for a moment that you would submit to his conditions. I was completely certain that you would say to him 'Go and publish it to the whole world!' And when that was done . . .

HELMER: Well, what then? When I'd exposed my own wife to shame and disgrace?

NORA: When that was done, I thought – I was completely certain – that you would come forward and take all the blame – that you'd say 'I'm the guilty one.'

HELMER: Nora!

NORA: You think that I should never have accepted a sacrifice like that from you? No, of course I shouldn't. But who would have taken my word against yours? That was the miracle I hoped for . . . and dreaded. It was to prevent *that* that I was ready to kill myself.

HELMER: Nora, I'd gladly work night and day for you, and endure poverty and sorrow for your sake. But no man would sacrifice his *honour* for the one he loves.

NORA: Thousands of women have.

HELMER: Oh, you're talking and thinking like a stupid child.

NORA: Perhaps . . . But you don't talk or think like the man I could bind myself to. When your first panic was over – not about what threatened me, but about what might happen to *you* – and when there was no more danger, then, as far as you were concerned, it was just as if nothing had happened at all. I was simply your little songbird, your doll, and from now on you would handle it more gently than ever because it was so delicate and fragile. [*Rising*] At that moment, Torvald, I realized that for eight years I'd been living here with a strange man, and that I'd borne him three children. Oh, I can't bear to think of it – I could tear myself to little pieces!

HELMER: [*sadly*]: Yes. I see – I see. There truly is a gulf between us. . . . Oh but Nora, couldn't we somehow bridge it?

NORA: As I am now, I'm not the wife for you.

HELMER: I could change . . .

NORA: Perhaps – if your doll is taken away from you.

HELMER: But to lose you – to lose you, Nora! No, no, I can't even imagine it . . .

NORA [*going out to the right*]: That's just why it must happen. [*She returns with her outdoor clothes, and a little bag which she puts on a chair by the table.*]

HELMER: Nora! Not now, Nora – wait till morning.

NORA [*putting on her coat*]: I couldn't spend the night in a strange man's house.

HELMER: But couldn't we live here as brother and sister?

NORA [*putting her hat on*]: You know quite well that that wouldn't last. [*She pulls her shawl round her.*] Good-bye, Torvald. I won't see my children – I'm sure they're in better hands than mine. As I am now, I'm no good to them.

HELMER: But some day, Nora – some day . . . ?

NORA: How can I say? I've no idea what will become of me.

HELMER: But you're my wife – now, and whatever becomes of you.

NORA: Listen, Torvald: I've heard that when a wife leaves her husband's house as I'm doing now, he's legally freed from all his obligations to her. Anyhow, *I* set you free from them. You're not to feel yourself bound in any way, and nor shall I. We must both be perfectly free. Look, here's your ring back – give me mine.

HELMER: Even that?

NORA: Even that.

HELMER: Here it is.

NORA: There. Now it's all over. Here are your keys. The servants know all about running the house – better than I did. Tomorrow, when I've gone, Kristina will come and pack my things that I brought from home; I'll have them sent after me.

HELMER: Over! All over! Nora, won't you ever think of me again?

NORA: I know I shall often think of you – and the children, and this house.

HELMER: May I write to you, Nora?

NORA: No . . . you must never do that.

HELMER: But surely I can send you –

NORA: Nothing – nothing.

HELMER: – or help you, if ever you need it?

NORA: No, I tell you, I couldn't take anything from a stranger.

HELMER: Nora – can't I ever be anything more than a stranger to you?

NORA [*picking up her bag*]: Oh, Torvald – there would have to be the greatest miracle of all . . .

HELMER: What would that be – the greatest miracle of all?

NORA: Both of us would have to be so changed that – Oh, Torvald, I don't believe in miracles any longer.

HELMER: But I'll believe. Tell me: 'so changed that . . . '?

NORA: That our life together could be a real marriage. Good-bye.

[*She goes out through the hall.*]

HELMER [*sinking down on a chair by the door and burying his face in his hands*]: Nora! Nora! [*He rises and looks round.*] Empty! She's not here any more! [*With a glimmer of hope*] 'The greatest miracle of all . . . '?

[*From below comes the noise of a door slamming.*]

Further reading

If you found the end of A Doll's House thought-provoking, read the whole play. It won't take long and you'll see how Nora and Helmer arrived at their quarrel.

Hedda Gabler is another of Ibsen's plays that explores a woman's emotions when she feels repressed by marriage and society.

Activities

Pickwick Papers

Before you read

1   Look at the picture of Mr Pickwick on page 179 and brainstorm in your class words that could describe him. Then think of words that could not describe him. From the lists compiled by everyone, write your own sentences beginning:

Mr Pickwick seems to be . . . He is most definitely not . . .

What's it about?

2   Mr Pickwick's character is revealed in little ways throughout this extract. How? Make a table like this one and fill in the spaces with quotes from the text.

Mr Pickwick is:	We know this because it says:
considerate to servants	
forgetful	
able to laugh at himself	

3   Why does Mr Pickwick get in a muddle about where his room is?

4   We can tell that Mr Pickwick is not a threat to a lady by how Dickens makes gentle fun of his nightclothes, his going-to-bed routine and by the speed with which he spins behind the bed-curtains when the lady comes in. Choose five or six short phrases from this scene and use them to draw a cartoon strip.

5   One of his problems is to do with his nightcap. What other problems does he have or make for himself throughout this extract? Draw a spidergram entitled 'Pickwick's Problems'.

Thinking about the text

6   Mr Weller puts in an appearance at the end of the chapter. He clearly knows Mr Pickwick extremely well. Imagine you are Sam Weller in the servants' bar in the inn that night. What do you say to anyone who may have seen Mr Pickwick stranded in the corridor that makes it quite clear that your master is innocent and a gentleman? In pairs, improvise some dialogue.

The Son's Veto

Before you read

1   Imagine two characters in an unusual situation. A mother wants to do something and her son will not let her. What might the issue be? How is it that the son has more power? Write a short playscript in which their argument takes place.

What's it about?

2   Draw a timeline showing when the main events in this story take place.

3   The first tension between Sophy and Randolph is over language – how Sophy speaks. What two things could be said to be unexpected about this? Do you think the author wants us to feel curious, shocked or angry? Explain your own reaction.

4   Mr Twycott 'knew perfectly well he had committed social suicide' by marrying Sophy. Explain what he means by this, and also how Sophy suffers much more than he does by the end of the first section of the story.

5   Write character descriptions of Sam Hobson and Mr Twycott using all the evidence you can find in the story.

6   Why does the priest look 'black as a cloud' at the shopkeeper in the final lines?

Thinking about the text

7   If Sam had voiced his thoughts as the funeral procession went past, what might he have said? If Randolph had spoken at Sophy's funeral, what might *he* have said?
    Write these two views of Sophy's life.

8   Do you think the author wants us to feel sorry for Sophy or angry with her? Debate this in class.

Laws Concerning Women

Before you read

1   What do you know about modern laws concerning married women and their ownership of property and how they can spend the money that they inherit or earn? Do you think they have more, fewer or the same rights as unmarried women or as men? What do you think their rights *should* be? Talk about this in class.

  You could check some of the facts before the next lesson.

What's it about?

2   Write two sentences using your own words to summarise
   a   the rights of unmarried women at the age of 21
   b   the rights of married women over 21.

3   Some phrases used by the author have an emotional weight to them. Why does she say a woman is 'again considered as an infant' when she marries, and that her money 'can be robbed from her legally' by her husband? Describe the images that these two statements conjure up in the reader's mind.

4   Why is the law even harder on women of the labouring classes?

Thinking about the text

5   Have a class debate about the issue raised in the final sentence.

6   Design a poster encouraging people to attend a meeting in 1854 about women's rights to property and earnings.

7   Imagine that you are the editor of a magazine that calls for support for women's rights. In your next issue, you will be including the illustration on page 209. You would like to feature five other images and/or articles showing women involved in unexpected and potentially dangerous activities. What will these be?

The Small House at Allington

Before you read

1 Think of a time when you did something you knew to be wrong, or knew someone else who did this. Which of the following caused you or this other person the most pain or embarrassment or difficulty?
   ● doing something wrong in the first place
   ● being found out
   ● trying to explain

Talk about this in pairs.

What's it about?

2 Explain Crosbie's situation at the start of this passage by answering these questions:
   a What had he promised Lily Dale?
   b What then attracted him about Alexandrina de Courcy and what has he promised her?
   c How does he feel now about Lily and Alexandrina?

3 Mr Dale struggles to stay calm but his language gives him away. Look at each of the sentences below, draw your own table like this one and say what they show about how he is feeling.

What he says	The emotion he is feeling
What is to become of my girl?	
Is he such a coward that he dare not see me?	
I would sooner have burnt out my tongue than have spoken in such way on such a subject.	

Thinking about the text

4 Pratt does not offer Crosbie much comfort and he doesn't defend him to Mr Dale, but is he still a good friend? In groups, discuss Pratt's thoughts and values and what you would have done in his place.

5 Do you think the author is 'siding' with any of these characters? What do you think happens next? Write the next chapter.

Definition of a Gentleman

Before you read

1   Do we still have 'gentlemen' in the 21st century? As a class, brainstorm words associated with this concept before you decide.

What's it about?

2   In pairs, re-read this passage and write down all the things you can find that the writer believes a true gentleman thinks, says and does. Number your list as you go.

3   Now get into groups and compare your lists, reading them aloud and 'ticking them off' as your own list is covered. Then decide between you if any of them are strictly 19th-century definitions and if any are still important today. You might wish to think about whether or not any of these apply to women as well as men in a modern world.

Thinking about the text

4   Think back to the brainstorming session you had before reading the text and discuss as a class any ways in which you've now changed your mind.

5   Write your own 'Definition of a Gentleman in the 21st Century'.

Adam Bede

Before you read

1 The author says of Mrs Poyser, 'she was not the woman to misbehave towards her betters . . . without severe provocation'.
   a What impression does this give you of her?
   b What would be your advice to anyone attempting to discuss something with her?

What's it about?

2 At the heart of the matter are these two questions: write down the answers.
   - What does the Squire hope to get out of this meeting?
   - What does Mrs Poyser feel about her home?

3 Mrs Poyser draws on the images of her own life on the farm to get her points across. Explain what she means when she says the following:
   a 'I'll not . . . worret myself as if I was a churn wi' butter a-coming in't' for no landlord in England, not if he was King George himself.'
   b 'If you could make a pudding wi' thinking o' the batter, it 'ud be easy getting dinner.'
   c ' . . . a maggot must be born i' the rotten cheese to like it . . . '
   Find two more examples.

4 Are the Poysers right to feel threatened? A clue can be found here: ' . . . though it were to rain notices to quit, and the only shelter were the workhouse'. What does this mean?

5 Act out Mrs Poyser's impassioned speech beginning 'You may run away from my words, sir'.

6 Describe or draw the look on the Squire's face as he turns to leave.

Thinking about the text

7 Re-read what the Poysers say to each other when the Squire has gone, then sum up what each thinks about what has happened.

8 The Squire has the authority to go ahead with his plan. Do you think he will? Exchange views and then hot-seat the Squire.

The Book of Household Management

Before you read

1 In pairs, think about your home. Discuss the jobs that need to be done to make it 'run' properly. Write a few notes.

2 Housewives in Mrs Beeton's day had none of our modern appliances. For example, even an iron had to be heated in front of a fire before you could use it. What extra work would this have entailed for women and their servants?

What's it about?

3 Two kinds of women are described in the first section: the virtuous commander of an army and one 'whose whole occupation is to murder mankind with shafts from their quiver, or their eyes'. Discuss what Mrs Beeton means. Then draw these two women on a poster with a title such as 'The Fight for Domestic Virtue'.

4 Mrs Beeton's language has a ring of authority about it. She wants her book to govern the lives of wives and mothers. Choose a sentence that particularly strikes you for its weight and vision and copy it out; then rewrite it in your own words. Compare the two, check with a partner, and see if the message has kept the authority of the original.

5 The serious message of this beginning perhaps sounds lofty and sexist to us now, but it carries a serious message. What is it? Sum it up for a modern age.

Thinking about the text

6 When Mrs Beeton compares the 'mistress of the house' to a commander of an army, she is perfectly serious. It was a very 19th-century view of a well-run house. Imagine you are a child living in a family household in the 21st century where your mother or guardian sees herself like this. Write an account of what life is like for you – it can be funny or frightening.

My Rights

Before you read

1   Do men and women have the same rights nowadays? Or are they different? Discuss this in class.

What's it about?

2   Look at the five verses that begin 'The right of . . . ' (e.g. 'The right of a rose to bloom . . . ') and write down five sentences that sum up each of those rights.

3   What does she *not* want the right to do?

4   Who does the poet believe has given her those rights? How can this add weight to her argument?

Thinking about the text

5   This poem has the steady rhythms of a hymn. Its regular pattern of beats and rhymes underpin the poet's certainties. Write a verse in reply which expresses your own views. (You don't have to use the same structure if you prefer not to.)

A Doll's House

Before you read

1   What clues does the title give you for what this play may be about? Brainstorm your suggestions in class and make notes.

2   Your families see you as sons or daughters, brothers or sisters. At school you are pupils/students. When you grow up you'll have a professional role and/or be someone's partner or parent. How do you see yourself?

   In pairs, discuss how possible or impossible it is to untangle yourself from your roles and relationships. Share your conclusions with the class.

What's it about?

3   Look at Helmer's speech beginning 'You loved me as a wife *should* love her husband . . . '. If you could ask him to explain his view of marriage in one sentence, what would he reply? Write it down.

4   Helmer's affectionate names for Nora reveal how he sees her. One is 'my frightened little songbird'. Find another name. What do the names he chooses tell us about *him*?

5   Nora finds the strength to tell Helmer some dreadful truths. One is that they have never had a serious talk together in the whole of their marriage. Write down some others that strike you as important and describe Helmer's reactions to them.

6   Look back at the notes you made in answer to question 1. Were your original ideas about the play correct?

Thinking about the text

7   Do you think Nora will ever come back? Do you think Helmer can change? Hot-seat these two.

8   In pairs, read the parts of Nora and Helmer. Then choose some lines to memorise or act out in front of the class.

Compare and contrast

1   Compare the views held by Mrs Beeton and Sarah Coolidge on a woman's role.

2   Imagine a three-way conversation between those two women and Barbara Bodichon. How would the sparks fly? Write it as a playscript and dramatise it. You could add a male character, making sure that he supports one side or the other to make it even more argumentative.

3   Sophy, whose son rules her life in *The Son's Veto*, and Nora at the beginning of *A Doll's House* have something in common. They share a typical female Victorian approach to male superiority/authority/threat to virtue. Imagine that Sophy reads in the newspaper about Nora leaving her husband. What would her reaction be? Write down her thoughts.

4   Helmer wanted to rule Nora in their marriage and Crosbie wanted to have status in society by marrying Alexandrina de Courcy. Both men thought about their positions more than they thought about love and friendship, and they lost Nora and Lily as a result. To what extent do you think they were victims of the age (encouraged to be like this because that's how men generally thought) as well as of the shortcomings of their characters? Have a debate in class.

5   Look at the various men in this section and see who comes closest to the *Definition of a Gentleman*.

6   Mrs Poyser is a tremendous character. The Squire completely underestimates her. Why is she so enjoyable to read about?

7   Isabella Bird was intrepid, resourceful and independent: a truly extraordinary Victorian woman. Perhaps there are other real and literary characters you have enjoyed meeting in this section. If you could time-travel and meet two or three, who would they be?

Notes on authors

Elizabeth Barrett Browning (1806–61) was the eldest of 12 children and educated at home. Her published poetry and great success caught the attention of Robert Browning, a very famous poet of the times. Her father did not approve of the relationship that grew up between them and in 1846 they eloped to Italy, where they lived happily together for the remaining 15 years of her life.

Mrs Beeton (1836–65) was born Isabella Mayson and married Samuel Orchard Beeton in 1856. She also wrote *A History of the Origins, Properties and Uses of All Things Connected with Home Life and Comfort*, and the format of displaying recipes and pictures is still one that is common today. As well as recipes, she was concerned with etiquette (how to behave) and the employment of servants. She died of puerperal fever when only 28.

Ambrose Bierce (1842–1914?) enlisted in the Union Army at the outbreak of the American Civil War and served with distinction until he was invalided out in 1865. His end is a mystery. All his short stories have a fascinating twist to them.

Isabella Bird (1831–1904) was the daughter of a clergyman and grew up in Cheshire. Early in life she suffered from a spinal complaint and was sent by her doctor to America and Canada to improve her health. This started a life-long love of travel and adventure. She wrote several books, among which two of the most famous are *A Lady's Life in the Rocky Mountains* and *Among the Tibetans*.

Barbara Bodichon (1827–91) came from a family that was committed to making changes in society. Her grandfather had worked closely with William Wilberforce in his great campaign against the slave trade. Her father was a supporter of the rights of women and gave her £300 a year despite it being unusual to do this for a daughter. At first she didn't marry because she felt the marriage laws 'enslaved' women; later she married Eugène Bodichon, a Frenchman, who shared her political views. When she died she left money to Girton College, a women's college at Cambridge University.

Samuel Butler (1835-1902) was the son of a clergyman and the grandson of a bishop. He didn't share his family's faith and went to New Zealand to be a sheep farmer for a while. Then he came back to England and became a painter and writer. He wrote many books, but *The Way of All Flesh* is his most famous.

Susan Coolidge (1835-1905) was the name taken by Sarah Woolsey when she wrote and successfully had published her famous children's novel *What Katy Did* in 1872. She was encouraged by the editor who had helped Louisa M. Alcott to fame with *Little Women* in 1868.

Charles Dickens (1812-70) is probably the most loved writer of Victorian times. His books not only told great stories, depicting the life of the times, but they changed society. He was determined to show the depths of poverty and misery that so many people endured and was even asked to become a member of parliament. He refused because he was sure his books were a more successful pathway to reform. When he died, his grave was left open in Poet's Corner in Westminster Abbey and filled by the flowers that were thrown in until they overflowed.

George Eliot (1819-80) was born Mary Ann (or Marian) Evans. She changed her name to a man's in order to be published more easily. She lived openly with a married man, George Lewes, and shocked Victorian society with her free thinking. Her greatest novel is considered to be *Middlemarch*, but it was the success of *Adam Bede* that made her reveal her real name.

Mrs Gaskell (1810-65) wrote several novels including *Cranford*, which was based on Knutsford where she was born. *Wives and Daughters* and *North South* are two others that are particularly famous. She was especially keen to explore the needs of the poor and to help create greater understanding between employers and workers. She was a great friend of Charlotte Brontë (author of *Jane Eyre*), though not of Charles Dickens, who once exclaimed, 'If I were Mr Gaskell, Oh Heaven how I would beat her!'

Thomas Hardy (1840-1928) was born near Dorchester in Dorset. He studied architecture but always wanted to write, and among his most famous novels are *Jude the Obscure, The Mayor of Casterbridge* and *Tess of the D'Urbervilles*. The theme of all his novels is the struggle men and women have with difficulties in their lives. He was hugely admired in his lifetime and friends with all the major novelists. Among the pall-bearers of his coffin were J. M. Barrie and Rudyard Kipling.

Thomas Hood (1799–1845) was born in London, the son of a book-seller. He edited various journals with his literary friends and wrote a great deal of verse, the most famous of which is *Song of the Shirt*.

M. V. Hughes (1866–1956) wrote in the preface to her autobiogra-phy, 'We were just an ordinary, suburban, Victorian family, undistin-guished ourselves and unacquainted with distinguished people.' She thought few people would be interested in her life (which she wrote in the 1930s, then an old lady) but her book was read by many and has recently been reprinted by Persephone Books. It is a moving account of everyday life for a London girl in the 1870s.

Henrik Ibsen (1828–1906) was a major Norwegian playwright who has been called the Father of Modern Drama. He was considered scan-dalous by many people, who thought drama in Victorian times should be deeply moral and that it should show a simple link between being good and being happy. His plays, of which *A Doll's House* is the most famous, wrestle with ideas of how to be true to yourself when the soci-ety you live in holds very different ideas and values.

The Illustrated London News was started by Herbert Ingram and first published on 14 May 1842. It cost sixpence and had 16 pages and 32 woodcuts – pictures printed from engraved wood. Ingram thought that a newspaper with pictures would sell – and he was right. He used its popularity to campaign for 'the English poor'.

Charles Kingsley (1819–75) was Chaplain to Queen Victoria, Canon of Westminster and Cambridge Professor of History. He was also a Christian Socialist, who campaigned for better conditions for working people. He was concerned about the little boys who swept chimneys by climbing up inside them, as they were often burned and sometimes died. He wrote *The Water Babies* in 1862 to startle people into taking notice and it was loved straightaway. Queen Victoria read it to her children, with the result that even more people read it.

The first aim of **Guglielmo Marconi** (1874–1937) in perfecting communication without wires was to break the isolation of people at sea. Those who survived the sinking of the *Titanic* owed their lives to the distress calls from the Marconi wireless equipment on board. When he died, wireless stations across the world were silent for two minutes.

Henry Mayhew (1812–87) ran away from Westminster School and later became a dramatist and journalist. In 1841 he was co-founder and briefly editor of *Punch* magazine. He is chiefly remembered for his passionate and detailed investigations into the lives of the London poor. Readers of his work helped to put pressure on parliament to make changes.

The Venerable John Henry, Cardinal Newman (1801–90) was a convert from the Church of England to Roman Catholicism. With his magnetic personality and love of words, he rose to be one of the most famous holders of high church office and also one of the most respected writers and speakers of his day.

Leo Tolstoy (1828–1910), one of Russia's most famous writers, studied law as a young man and later fought in the Crimean War. He then managed his vast estates in the Volga Steppes with his wife, Sophia Andreyevna, and their 13 children. Teaching and caring for the peasants on his land marked him out as a very unusual man for his times. His beliefs about how society should be run (without interference from the powerful established Russian Church) made him many followers and many enemies. *War and Peace* is his greatest work. He died in a dramatic run away from home at the small railway station of Astapovo.

Anthony Trollope (1815–82) held a senior position in the Post Office and it was his suggestion that led to the introduction of the pillar box for letters. He was a much-loved and successful novelist of many books such as those in the *Barchester Chronicles*, which detailed the lives of a fictional community in an imaginary county in the West Country. He was a close friend of George Eliot.

Mark Twain (1835–1910) was born in America, and the adventures of Tom Sawyer and Huckleberry Finn are his two most famous stories. Huck Finn was especially enjoyed at the time for showing a young boy's belief in 'doing the right thing' even when the whole of society seems to be against him. Twain has been called the Father of American Literature and many schools are named after him.

Jules Verne (1828–1905) was born in France and as a child ran off to be a cabin boy on a merchant ship. He was caught and sent back to his parents but never lost the spirit of adventure. He wrote many fantastical stories such as *Journey to the Centre of the Earth* and *Around the World in Eighty Days*.

H. G. Wells (1866–1946) first worked in a draper's shop (selling cloth and clothes), then became a teacher, writing all the time. His book *The Time Machine*, published in 1895, was hugely successful and when *The War of the Worlds* was published three years later his reputation was made.